Socialism, Social Welfare
and the Soviet Union

Radical Social Policy

GENERAL EDITOR:

Vic George

*Professor of Social Policy and
Administration and Social Work
University of Kent*

Socialism, Social Welfare and the Soviet Union

Vic George and Nick Manning

Routledge & Kegan Paul
London, Boston and Henley

First published in 1980
by Routledge & Kegan Paul Ltd
39 Store Street London WC1E 7DD
9 Park Street Boston, Mass. 02108, USA
and Broadway House, Newtown Road,
Henley-on-Thames, Oxon RG9 1EN
Set in Press Roman 10pt by Columns
and printed in Great Britain by
Billing & Sons Limited
Guildford, London and Worcester

British Library Cataloguing in Publication Data

George, Victor

Socialism, social welfare and the Soviet Union. –
(Radical social policy).
1. Russia – Social policy
2. Public welfare – Russia
3. Communism and social policy
I. Title   II. Manning, Nick   III. Series
361.6'2'0947   HN525   80-40733

ISBN 0 7100 0608 X

CONTENTS

Introduction

The primary aims of this book are, first, to explore the Marxist view of what constitutes socialist policy in the areas of income, social security, education, health and housing. This is done by looking at the works of Marx, Engels and Lenin and it forms the first section of each chapter other than the final. Second, to review the development of economic and social policy since the October Revolution of 1917 and to show the inter-relationship between the two. Most of chapter 1 is devoted to this as well as the second section of chapters 2-5. Third, to describe and to discuss the ways in which each of the four social services functions to-day and the extent to which each operation matches the Marxist ideal. This is done in the third and fourth sections of chapters 2-5.

Fourth, to examine in general terms the relationship between social-ist social policy as conceived by contemporary Marxist writers and the political economy of the Soviet Union in order to highlight and summarise the extent to which the two are related and how this differs from the corresponding situation in advanced capitalist societies.

Both of us visited the Soviet Union in the course of writing this book and our visits helped to give some reality to our reading of secondary sources on which this book is largely based. There are many gaps in the available literature, both Russian and English, on Soviet social policy and this has inevitably limited our understanding of Soviet social policy in several ways. Nevertheless, the literature proved fairly adequate for our purposes. We were interested in painting a broad picture of the main issues raised above rather than a detailed examination of very specific or specialised concerns of Soviet social policy.

In the postscript of the second edition of their book *Soviet*

Communism in 1937, Beatrice and Sidney Webb concluded their views
of the Soviet Union as follows:

> In 1933, when settling the title of the book-to-be, we chose 'Soviet
> Communism' to express our purpose of describing the actual organisa-
> tion of the USSR. Before publication in 1935, we added the query 'A
> New Civilisation?' What we have learnt of the developments during
> 1936-1937 has persuaded us to withdraw the interrogation mark (B.
> and S. Webb, *Soviet Communism: A New Civilisation*, Gollancz,
> 1937, vol. II, pp. 1213-14).

These changes, in their views, are characteristic of the experiences of
many who try to understand what has happened in the Soviet Union. It
is not possible to look at the Soviet Union in a totally unbiased way.
One's values, attitudes and feelings colour one's views and conclusions in
varying ways and degrees.

We started with a bias against the Soviet Union, largely because of the
curtailment of civil and political liberties in the country. As our work
progressed, however, we came to realise that if the political system represents the negative aspects of Soviet society, the economic and the
welfare systems are its positive aspects. We concur with Lindblom's
comments about eastern European societies, that 'in history many of
man's greatest excesses are the other side of some great altruistic effort'
(C. Lindblom, *Politics and Markets,* Basic Books, 1977, p.5). Our book
is concerned with the acceptable face of Soviet society, its economic
and social welfare system which compares very favourably with that of
welfare capitalist societies. Others have written at length about the unacceptable face of the Soviet Union and no doubt our readers will have
come across some of these writings.

We would like to thank A. McAuley, L. Holmes, D. Smith and G.
Andrusz who made valuable comments on different chapters. We owe
particular thanks to Margaret Joyce and Susan Stobbs for typing several
drafts of the manuscript. Parts of the book have been tried on an undergraduate course and we benefited from the discussion in seminars. We,
of course, accept the final responsibility for the views expressed in the
book.

Vic George
Nick Manning
University of Kent at Canterbury

1

Economic development and social policy

Even the most cursory reading of the literature on the Soviet Union reveals a clear relationship between the development of economic and of social policy. Social policies have been expanded, contracted or modified to suit the goals of economic policy. Economic policy has always held the upper hand, though there have been periods when social policy was less subservient. Broadly speaking, three periods can be discerned in this developing relationship. During the first decade of the Soviet Union, social policy aims were infused with egalitarianism even though in practice they were difficult to implement because of the absence of adequate resources. The Stalinist period witnessed a change in the sense that social policy aims were aligned closely to the aims of economic policy. The tremendous emphasis on rapid economic growth dictated the shape and the scope of social policies. The post-Stalinist period, with its expanded economic base, has treated social policy on a more equal footing with economic policy. The government's aim has been to allow an increasing proportion of the country's wealth to be consumed by the public both in terms of consumer goods and in social services provided free or almost free at the point of consumption.

The unfolding of economic and social policy over the years can best be understood within the context of the development of the country's economic and political system and the dominant ideology. This inter-relationship between the various parts of society has also to be seen in relation to the personalities of the country's political leaders. The Soviet Union has been governed by such strong men — Lenin, Stalin, Khrushchev and Brezhnev — that their personalities must have exercised some influence over government policies. Their influence, however, has

1

to be seen within the objective societal conditions which set severe limits to their contribution.

Marx expressed this role of great men in history as follows:

> Men make their own history, but they do not make it just as they please; they do not make it under circumstances chosen by themselves but under circumstances directly encountered, given and transmitted from the past.[1]

Subsequent discussion in this chapter should provide enough evidence to substantiate this thesis.

It is commonplace to state that economic, political, ideological and social factors interact to decide government policies. The discussion in this chapter, however, suggests that economic factors have dominated the other factors most of the time. By economic factors we mean the state of the country's economy, the methods of production and the relationships into which Soviet workers entered at their places of employment and elsewhere. It is a loose, materialistic interpretation of history which allows non-material factors an important role and sometimes a determining one. Engels expressed this loose inter-relationship between economic and other factors well:

> According to the materialist conception of history, the determining element in history is *ultimately* the production and reproduction in real life . . . If therefore somebody twists this into the statement that the economic element is the *only* determining one, he transforms it into a meaningless, abstract, and absurd phrase.[2]

A loose, materialistic interpretation of the development of economic and social policy allows us not only to collect facts without undue constraints but also to present such facts as much as possible in relation to each other. In such broad areas of human life, a stringent theoretical framework can distort reality by excluding facts that do not fit into the theoretical framework. Collection of facts, however, without any adherence to theory can result in nothing more than a meaningless, descriptive account of events over the years. Thus a flexible theoretical approach avoids the pitfalls of both blind empiricism and rigid theorising.

Apart from examining the inter-relationship between economic and social policy, this chapter has another aim — to discuss the extent to which Soviet society is becoming socialist in character over the years. Any selection of criteria of a socialist society is somewhat arbitrary for at least two reasons. First, there are substantial differences of opinion between Marx and Engels on the one hand and Lenin on the other. The views of Marx and Engels were interpreted by Lenin to suit the particular conditions of the Soviet Union. Second, there are equally important differences of opinion among Soviet leaders themselves as to what constitutes a socialist society. Though Lenin's views have remained supreme in the official pronouncements since the Revolution, they have been interpreted and stressed differently by Stalin, Khrushchev and Brezhnev to suit their particular policies. Bearing these difficulties in mind, we have based our discussion on only the main criteria which Lenin used and which received substantial support from the other Soviet leaders at the outset of the Revolution. We have selected three main criteria which are the very basic ones and which featured prominently in the discussions among Soviet leaders prior to and during the Revolution.

First, the means of production and distribution would be transferred from private hands to the government. Such a transfer would abolish social classes in the Soviet society and hence political and economic domination and exploitation of one population group by another. It would also make government macro-planning easier and in this way facilitate both balanced and rapid economic growth. Second, though people would be paid according to their work during the transitional stage of socialism, economic policy would reduce income differentials substantially. Economic incentives would be gradually replaced by ideological incentives for work. In the distant future, when the Soviet society was transformed from socialist to communist, economic rewards would be distributed according to need, the differences in esteem between manual and mental labour would vanish and people would work unselfishly for the benefit of themselves and their fellow citizens. Third, after the brief period of the dictatorship of the proletariat, full freedom in the domain of politics, literature and ideology would blossom to match the achievements of economic freedom. Participation would be a central feature of decision-making in all the aspects of economic and social institutions. Again, in the distant future of the communist society, this process of participation and self-government would reach its zenith with the abolition of the state as an oppressive apparatus.

All three aims presupposed the existence of an advanced industrial capitalist society prior to the Revolution. Lenin and the other revolutionary leaders were well aware that Czarist Russia was anything but an advanced industrial society. They hoped, however, that the Soviet Revolution would spark off a series of successful socialist revolutions in the advanced capitalist countries of Europe, with the result that material and technical aid would be provided to the Soviet Union to build its economy. When such revolutions did not materialise, Lenin and his colleagues acknowledged that the Soviet road to socialism and communism would be more difficult and more lengthy than they at first envisaged. We need, therefore, to examine not whether the above three

3

basic criteria of a socialist society have been achieved but rather whether steady progress has been made towards their fulfilment.

For the sake of convenience we divide the historical discussion in this chapter into seven periods, acknowledging that they merge into each other and they overlap in many ways.

The first eight months – 1917-18

The October Revolution of 1917 was an almost bloodless affair. The coalition government that had tried to rule the country since the February Revolution of that year caved in under the workers' pressure guided by the Bolshevik party under Lenin. The ease with which the Bolsheviks came to power is partly a tribute to their disciplined and intelligent political campaigning. Primarily, however, it was indicative of the utter bankruptcy of the Czarist regime. As Carr has put it: 'The old order collapsed, not because new claimants for power were pushing it aside, but through its own inherent rottenness.'[3]

The same rotten state of Czarist society, however, is also indicative of the daunting task that faced the small Bolshevik party that came to power amidst the hostility of all the European governments. Marx's brilliant analysis of how capitalist systems functioned was not of much help as to how to set up and run a socialist society. Both Marx and Engels refrained from any detailed discussion on how a socialist society would be organised and administered on the very good grounds that this was the task of the leaders of actual socialist governments in different countries. This meant, however, that the Bolsheviks had no blueprint for the creation of a socialist Soviet Union. They had to experiment, to improvise and to learn from their mistakes.

It was partly for this reason that the first eight months of the Bolshevik government saw gradual and cautious changes only. Lenin, in particular, was anxious to retain what was useful from the existing capitalist system and to proceed in a gradual and slow way towards the new social order. He saw the transition period as containing an economic system with elements from both socialism and capitalism. Nationalisation of banks and factories proceeded slowly and in many cases the reason for the nationalisation was the fact that the owners had either closed down the enterprise or had acted openly against the new government in such ways as refusing to obey government decrees or dismissing their workers and closing down temporarily. In such cases, the government was acting in a defensive way rather than in an aggressive utopian manner, as has often been suggested.

Similarly in the policy of workers' control, Lenin's government moved very cautiously at first. The decree of 14 November 1917 authorised local workers' committees to participate in the running of their industries but it reserved the right of the owners and managers to give orders on how the industry should be run and made it illegal for workers' committees to disobey such orders. The government was anxious to maintain industrial production and was well aware of the problems involved in atomised planning by individual enterprises under the inexperienced guidance of workers' committees.

The same cautious approach was shown in the case of land reform. The land decree of 8 November 1917 nationalised all land and conferred the right to cultivate the land to the peasants. This process had begun anyhow before the decree was issued and many peasants had taken over land belonging to the aristocracy. The decree encouraged but did not even attempt to compel peasants to cultivate their land collectively. Local committees were to be set up to supervise the distribution of land but, in practice, the distribution of land was not done in any organised way. In spite of its caution and the haphazard way it was implemented the decree resulted in the abolition of the landed aristocracy and the creation of a landed peasantry. Lenin's hopes were that the peasants would gradually join co-operatives on a voluntary basis for both economic and ideological reasons. Co-operative farming would be more productive than individual peasant farming and it would also be more in line with the collective ideology of a socialist society. As we shall see later, the policy soon ran into severe difficulties.

It was, however, the gradual policy in the industrial field that ran into difficulties first from two quarters, as Dobb notes: 'the zeal of factory workers' committees and the outbreak of the Civil War in the Summer of 1918.'[4] Workers' committees established control over production in some large factories even before the Revolution. The Bolshevik party supported this practice because it furthered its revolutionary aims. It was not, therefore, unexpected that factory committees would be anxious to take control of factories after the Revolution. In many cases committees took control of factories against the express orders of the government; and in other cases committees ran their factories in isolation from the rest of the economy with disastrous economic results. Thus during the first few months, the Soviet government found itself in the difficult position of having to control and guide the very movement which it encouraged before the Revolution. It was, however, the invasion of the Soviet Union by the German, the British and other foreign armies in support of the White Armies that changed the situation dramatically. The ensuing Civil War hardened attitudes on all sides and the Soviet government found itself fighting for its survival. Dobb writes:

In these circumstances, not only did the attitude of the bourgeoisie to the new regime harden, and any willingness to co-operate that they had shown previously evaporated overnight, but for the Soviet government military necessities immediately took precedence over all other considerations.[5]

The result of this new situation was the decree of 28 June 1918, which nationalised all large companies without exception.

The same cautious approach of the first eight months can be found in the field of social policy. In spite of the long and protracted involvement of the Bolshevik party in social security issues before the Revolution, the new government moved gradually. In December 1917, provisions were made for unemployment, sickness, maternity and death benefit for wage-earners only, thus excluding the majority of the population who were self-employed peasants. Medical care was made free of charge to all wage-earners, again leaving out the peasantry. In housing, a government decree in November 1917 requisitioned all housing belonging to the rich to be distributed among the working class. This was no wild measure, for it involved the new government in very little expense and at the same time rectified to some degree the anomalous maldistribution of urban housing. Expectations were running high prior to and during the Revolution and the government very rightly tried to satisfy those expectations which were not contrary to its own programme.

War communism period

Briefly, then, in both economic and social policy the new Bolshevik government moved with caution, realising the difficulties involved in rapid change under the very low socio-economic conditions that were prevailing in the country. Lenin's government was not given to wild and utopian schemes and ventures as it has often been suggested by various authors. This caution and gradualism, however, was swept aside by the whirlwind of the Civil War. War communism is the phrase used to describe the economic and social policies during the Civil War period, i.e. June 1918 to December 1920. We have already seen that the outbreak of the Civil War forced the Soviet government to nationalise all large enterprises. During the Civil War medium-sized enterprises were brought under government ownership while in November 1920 even small enterprises were nationalised. The demands, devastations and fears aroused by the war made it impossible for the Soviet government to continue its gradual policies of nationalisation and its policies of the mixed economy.

Nowhere does the influence of war conditions become clearer on government policy than in the issue of wages and prices. During the early part of the Civil War, the Soviet government lost some of the richest parts of the country in terms of agricultural produce, minerals and power to the combined forces of the White Armies and of the invading foreign powers. In addition, the massive destruction of railways and other forms of transport made it that much more difficult to bring food and raw materials to the cities. Starvation was a real threat in the cities and many people migrated to the rural areas where they could find food. The price of all goods rose substantially as they became in short supply. To cope with the situation the government printed more money but this added more fuel to the inflationary situation. Anxious to supply some food to industrial workers, the government paid higher and higher prices for foodstuffs to the peasants. Since money had lost its value, however, peasants became increasingly reluctant to sell food to the government. This left the government with no option but to requisition compulsorily foodstuffs from the peasants in order to feed the army and the workers. Both peasants and workers were paid in kind and municipal services, such as the post office and transport, were provided free. Money was being largely replaced as the medium for exchange of goods not because of ideological reasons but out of sheer necessity. There was no other way open to the government for dealing with the desperate economic and military situation. It is true that many 'Leftist' communists welcomed the abolition of money but this was not the view of the government. Lenin was quite clear that the economic policies of war communism were forced on his government. 'War communism was thrust upon us by war and ruin. It was not, nor could it be, a policy that corresponded to the economic tasks of the proletariat. It was a temporary measure.'[6]

The same war destructions, inflation and semi-starvation of the urban population brought about a sharp collapse in labour discipline with strikes, demonstrations, protests and absenteeism running very high. Again, in the chaotic and desperate situation, the government had no option but to impose strict sanctions against labour indiscipline and to use the trade unions as an instrument for implementing government measures. There is no doubt that the Soviet government lost control of the situation, was blown off course, and either introduced measures or allowed situations to develop which in normal circumstances would not have been approved of. Social policy shows signs of a turn to utopianism during this period. The decree of 31 October 1918 extended social security protection both in terms of risks to include old age and in terms of pensions to cover the peasants. The only logical explanation of such a measure at a time of national economic chaos was the government's anxiety to win peasants to its side at a time of civil war and at a time when peasants were being alienated by the requisitioning of foodstuffs by the government. In education, the decrees of August and October 1918 made primary education free and compulsory and made secondary and higher education free to all without any requirements for academic

7

entrance qualifications. A very vigorous liberalising campaign in education was inaugurated that aimed at changing the content of what was taught in schools in favour of the liberal subjects; teaching methods were altered to be in line with the ideas of progressive education writers; and the relationships between pupils and teachers were democratised to the extreme. In the field of family policy the same trend towards utopianism was evident. Divorce was made very easy, legal responsibilities of family members to each othere were eroded and parental responsibility for the maintenance of their children was reduced. Legal distinctions between legitimate and illegitimate children were abolished, abortion was legalised, and acts of bigamy, incest, adultery and homosexuality ceased to be criminal offences. In all these spheres of social policy the Soviet government either intentionally or unintentionally, willingly or unwillingly, lent support to a movement that was utopian and ahistorical. One cannot build socialism in conditions of mass poverty, illiteracy and general backwardness. Nor can one change customs, beliefs and attitudes in such sensitive areas as family relationships, sexual issues, child-rearing and discipline overnight. The effectiveness of these social policy measures was either minimal or detrimental to social and economic stability, as the following chapters will show.

The New Economic Policy – 1921-8

The defeat of the White Russian armies and the foreign invading armies made a return to normality possible. The experience of the country during those two-and-a-half years, however, inevitably meant that the government could not easily return to its earlier policy of the gradual but steady transformation of capitalism to socialism. Many writers have seen the New Economic Policy enunciated by Lenin as a general retreat or a tactical retreat from the heady ideological policies of the war communism period. As was argued above, many of the war communism policies were undesirable and had been forced on the Soviet government by the abnormal war conditions. Therefore the New Economic Policy was not an ideological retreat of any kind but a return to the ideological and theoretical framework that guided the policies of the government during its first eight months in office. Lenin's discussion of the New Economic Policy was in the same framework of state capitalism that he had used prior to the war communism: a steady advance towards socialism with elements of socialism and capitalism during the transition stage but with socialist measures and features increasingly dominating over the capitalist, until the elimination of the latter was reached.

The New Economic Policy involved the de-nationalisation of small-scale enterprise, but the retention of medium-sized and large enterprise in government hands. Private trade was made legal again though foreign trade and banking remained a government responsibility. Confiscation of food from the peasants was abandoned in favour of a tax, first in kind and later in cash. After payment of the tax, peasants could do as they pleased with their produce by selling it in the private market. Money was again made the medium of exchange and payment in kind was abolished. In all these ways the New Economic Policy abandoned the policies forced on the government by the Civil War and returned to the earlier forms of government planning. The commanding heights of the economy were retained in the hands of the government and general guidelines for the economy were laid down also by the government, but within that framework small private enterprise and private initiative in industry and in agriculture were accepted for the time being and encouraged.

In spite of strong opposition from the left of the Communist party, the New Economic Policy was accepted and proved a success. Industrial output increased so that by 1926 it reached its pre-war level, compared with 1921 when it had dropped to one-fifth of the pre-war level. Agriculture also benefited in both production and the extent of planted area. By 1921 the total agricultural output had dropped by more than one-half of its pre-war level and the area planted with crops had declined by more than one-third; but by 1925 agriculture had reached its pre-war levels, both in terms of sown area and output. This improvement in agricultural output, however, was not matched by a corresponding improvement in the amount of food the peasants marketed. In the words of Nove, 'the peasants were eating better, selling less'.[7] This was partly due to the fact that the number of landed peasants increased. Before the Revolution it was mainly the large estates and the Kulak farms that provided the overwhelming proportion of marketed food. The disappearance of the large estates and the reduction in the number of Kulaks meant that land was distributed more equally among a large number of farmers. What had happened then was that the more egalitarian distribution of land meant a greater consumption of food. Another reason may also have been the low price of foodstuffs in comparison with the price of industrial goods. Lowering the price of industrial goods could have acted as an incentive to greater agricultural production for those peasants who wanted to buy them, but such a policy ran the risk of not only reducing the accumulation of capital for industry if demand was not stimulated, but also of encouraging the growth of consumer industry if demand was over-stimulated. The general body of opinion in the government was in favour of the growth of heavy industry rather than consumer industry. Clearly the New Economic Policy was a transitional measure and its relative success raised more sharply the question of what kind of industrial, and hence agricultural, policy was to succeed it.

Three major inter-related economic issues dominated political discussion from just before Lenin's death in 1924 to the inauguration of the first Five Year Plan in 1928: the nature of industrialisation, the pace of the industrialisation process and the relationship between industry and agriculture. This is the classical problem of all developing societies. Whereas, however, many developing societies attempt to solve it by trying to attract foreign capital, the Soviet government was unable to resort to this solution. The capital for industrialisation had to be found from the savings, voluntary and compulsory, of the Soviet people. This inevitably meant that the peasants, who formed the majority of the population and who provided the food for workers, had to bear the main brunt of the government's policy to raise capital for industrialisation.

There was general agreement that the country should concentrate its efforts, at the beginning anyhow, on heavy industrialisation. This would provide a secure base for industrial growth in the future in all directions including consumer goods. What divided the left from the right in the Communist party was the pace of industrialisation. The right wing of the party argued that the New Economic Policy had to be continued for a very long time and hence industrialisation would take place at a slow pace. This was necessary in order not to alienate the peasants who would provide the food and the savings for industrial expansion. The phrase 'riding into socialism on a peasant nag' sums up well the gradualist policy. The left of the party argued that such a slow pace posed serious problems. In the first place, there was no guarantee that the peasant nag would march in the right direction. The longer the NEP lasted, the more attached the peasants were likely to become to such capitalist values as individualism and profits. The longer the stalemate lasted, the greater the likelihood that workers, too, might lose their enthusiasm for socialism. Finally, there was always the fear of outside military intervention and the sooner the country was industrialised the better it would be able to cope with such a situation.

Both sides were in agreement, however, that collectivisation of farms was necessary for the growth of productivity. Yet as late as 1927, state farms and collective farms accounted for only 1 per cent of the cultivated land and 2 per cent of the total grain produce. Both sides hoped that individual farmers would see the advantages of collective farming and would voluntarily collectivise their farms. No such progress, however, had been made during the NEP and it is difficult to see why farmers would voluntarily give up their traditional independence for the sake of an untested form of farming that guaranteed them little natural improvement. The unwillingness of farmers to collectivise was an added argument against slow industrialisation, for the productivity of individual farming was very low and was likely to remain so in the future because of the lack of mechanisation. It was Stalin who cut the Gordian knot at the end of the 1920s, but before we examine how he did it we need to examine the growth of social policy during the period of the NEP.

Generally speaking, social policy was modified or was beginning to be modified towards more realistic goals away from the ultra-radical or utopian goals of the war communism period. In social security the coverage of the scheme was confined to working-class people, leaving out, again, the majority of the population consisting of peasants. In addition, payment of benefits was made conditional to the satisfaction of certain employment conditions. In other words, the scheme was made similar to the one that existed during the first eight months after the Revolution. In the area of health, too, the return to reality was clear. The country did not possess the financial, personnel or physical re-sources for a national health service and health priorities had therefore to be established. According to Hyde, three priorities were established: 'Firstly, to workers because they were insured, and especially to those in key sectors; secondly, to the rising generation; and thirdly, to agricul-ture.'[8] In education the progressive teaching methods and the free school regime continued in the cities, but opposition to these practices was mounting as more people realised the educational ill-effects. In the area of family relationships and sexual relationships the same trend was evident during the NEP period. Gradually it was becoming clear that sexual freedom was not the same as sexual licence. Lenin's insistence that sexual promiscuity was not a personal affair only, but a matter of concern for society as well provided the theoretical framework for a change in policy. In the field of family relationships, the family code of 1926 strengthened and widened filial responsibility i.e. the responsibility of individuals to support needy relatives. Parental responsibility for children also began to be strengthened as the number of children roam-ing the streets reached unacceptable proportions. But if social policy during this period was modified to more realistic goals, it began to be able to deliver some of the things it promised, unlike the war commun-ism period when social policy promised far more than it could possibly deliver. Moreover, though social policy was confined to more realistic goals, it was not changed into a mere appendage of economic policy as turned out to be the case during the subsequent period of Stalin's rule.

The industrialisation period – 1928-40

The rise of Stalin to power and his enormous influence in political events tend to dominate many discussions of Soviet history of this period. Yet the scene for Stalin's performance was set by the dilemmas of economic policy that were discussed in the previous section. The decision of the Communist party at its fourteenth congress in 1925 to

11

go ahead with heavy industrialisation at a fast pace inevitably meant that peasants had to produce enough raw materials for industry and enough food for the industrial workers and that they had to make these raw materials and foodstuffs available at low prices so that the maximum possible of the nation's savings could be invested in the building of heavy industry. Workers, too, would have to pay a price in the sense that heavy industrialisation would not produce enough consumer goods and in the sense that their wages would not be so high as to take up too much of the savings capacity of the country. Sacrifices, in other words, had to be made by everyone, but above all by the agrarian population. 'Between seed-time and harvest,' writes Dobb, 'Soviet economy had an unusually long time to wait before the fruit of its labours were ripe to be enjoyed'.[9] Socialism in an underdeveloped country with no possibilities of outside financial assistance could only be built through the immediate hard work and hardships of its people. The benefits would be reaped in the years to come.

It is within these objective conditions that Stalin's role must be seen. Though not in complete command of the party at this stage, Stalin broke away from the political consensus regarding the undesirability of the use of violence to coerce peasants towards industrialisation. Accompanied by army units he went to Siberia in 1928, closed down private agricultural markets, ordered peasants to deliver grain and punished those who failed to comply. Though he was censured by the Politbureau of the party, the 'Urals-Siberian method', as Stalin's campaign was euphemistically known, marked a turning point. Violence could produce immediate results with the peasants. By the end of 1928 most of Stalin's notable critics were expelled from the party and his position as leader became secure. The decision of the party in 1928 to embark on the first Five Year Plan (1928-33) with ambitious industrial and agrarian targets made forced collectivisation almost inevitable. First the Kulaks and then the other peasants were forced, where necessary at gun point, to join collective farms. Those who refused were imprisoned, exiled or shot. An estimated 4-5 million people suffered in these ways. The ferocity of the government's drive towards collectivisation was bound to have immediate results. In 1928 only 2.7 per cent of all sown area was in state or collective farms, whereas the corresponding proportions for 1930 and 1935 were 33.6 per cent and 94.1 per cent respectively. But the peasants did not give in without retaliating. They slaughtered their livestock — cattle, sheep, goats, pigs, horses, etc. — in large numbers, causing not only a famine of meat, dairy produce and hides, but also a reduction in animal power for the cultivation of land and for transportation that could be ill-afforded at this stage.

These were serious setbacks but they were of a temporary nature. As Campbell points out, collectivisation meant that 'the decisions about the division of agricultural output into consumption and transfers to the urban economy would no longer rest with the individual peasant but would instead be under the control of representatives of the regime'.[10] Thus, in spite of the decline in harvests in the early 1930s, government procurements of agricultural produce were stepped up. The peasants were producing less but they were allowed to consume even less. Hardship and famine were common in the countryside but even then rationing of foodstuffs was necessary in the urban areas during the early 1930s. It was not until the end of the 1930s that collective farms managed to reach the position that prevailed in 1928 as regards the number of livestock and the volume of production. Productivity per person in agriculture, however, increased during this period due to increased mechanisation. If the total volume of agricultural produce did not increase, it was because the total number working in agriculture declined owing to mass emigration to the towns. The rural population declined from 82 per cent of the total Soviet population in 1926 to 67 per cent in 1939.[11]

On the industrial field, there is no doubt that both the first and the second Five Year Plans were tremendously successful. By the end of this period, the Soviet Union compared very favourably with the rest of the industrial world in terms of heavy industrial production. Such heavy industries as iron and steel, coal, electricity, mineral mining, chemicals, tractors, railways and so on increased their output by three to five times between 1928 and 1938. The growth in consumer goods was inevitably less impressive because most of the nation's resources were put initially into heavy industry. Moreover, when initial targets in heavy industry were in danger of not being realised, consumer goods' targets were cut down to facilitate the achievement of heavy goods' targets. Nevertheless, by the end of the 1930s consumer goods were more plentiful than in 1928, even though demand had also increased and the quality had not always improved. Thus, though the Soviet Union had become one of the world's leaders in heavy industrial production, it was still extremely backward as far as consumer goods were concerned. Referring to the situation in the late 1930s, Sorlin comments that

> there was still an absence of anything approaching luxury articles. Enormous patience was required to find a table or a chair, kitchen equipment, toilet articles, or bicycles. Goods obtained after hours of waiting in line at the shops were of the poorest quality.[12]

This tremendous drive towards the growth of heavy industry inevitably had serious implications for social policy as well as other related aspects of economic policy. In the first place, private enterprise in industry and in trade was at first indirectly and later directly forced to disappear. This was done not only for ideological reasons but also

13

because of the government's policy to restrict the growth of consumer goods where private enterprise dominated. Thus, by the end of the 1930s, one of the three basic aims of the Revolution — the socialisation of the means of production and distribution — had been achieved. Whether the cost in human lives to achieve this goal was necessary will remain an unanswered question on economic considerations. On moral grounds the answer must be in the negative and yet so few important changes in history are achieved peacefully.

The emphasis on rapid industrialisation meant a sharp demand for labour which was satisfied by the flow of women and peasants. Such inexperienced, untrained and undisciplined labour had to be moulded to industrial production in one way or another. In the words of Bauman, the state faced the necessity of imposing 'the "spirit" of employeeship on the listless mass of peasants and former peasants, a task which was in essence contrary to the liberating spirit of socialism'.[13] If the policy of workers' participation had been neglected so far, it was now repudiated both in theory and in practice. Industrial discipline replaced workers' participation and thus the third of the three main aims of the Revolution had been abandoned, at least in its original formulation. Trade unions until the 1930s had been attempting to perform two slightly contradictory functions: to protect their members' interests and to assist management in fulfilling and raising production targets. Now they were forced to give more emphasis to the second function. By the end of the decade, however, complaints were mounting that they neglected their members' interests and though an attempt was made to rectify the situation, it never came to much. Industrial discipline had its positive as well as its negative sides from the socialist point of view. On the positive side, a great deal of emphasis was placed on the training of the rural migrants and of women. Emphasis was placed on increasing places in technical schools and factory schools to produce skilled workers. Similarly, the scientific and technical departments of universities were expanded to produce the highly qualified personnel that industry so badly needed. Industrial safety was stepped up and occupational health services were improved. According to Hyde, the new principle for the health service during this period was 'On from the struggle against epidemics to the fight for more healthy working conditions'.[14] Thus a separate occupational health service was developed and child-care facilities for women at work were expanded.

Labour indiscipline was accompanied by high rates of labour turnover — over 100 per cent in 1930. Positive measures would take a long time to have any effect and they were, therefore, strengthened by negative measures. Stalin's famous 'Six Point Speech' in 1931 set the scene for such measures. In the first place the policy of the later years of the NEP of reducing wage inequalities was strongly repudiated.

The consequence of wage equalisation is that the unskilled worker
lacks the incentive to become a skilled worker and is thus deprived of
the prospect of advancement; as a result, he feels himself a 'sojourner'
in the factory, working only temporarily so as to earn a little and
then going off to 'seek his fortune' elsewhere . . . Hence the heavy
turnover of labour power.[15]

Dobb quotes a report from the Central Council of Trade Unions in 1928
which claimed 'that the ratio of wages in the most skilled category to
those in the lowest was 3:1; that only 8.5 per cent of workers earned less
than half the average wage and 48 per cent between a half and the
average wage'.[16] If these figures are correct, then wage equalisation
had advanced a great deal. Stalin's reaction was not only in relation to
the then existing situation but to the whole notion of equality under
socialism: 'The kind of socialism under which everybody would get the
same pay . . . is unknown to Marxism', he declared.[17] Wage differentials
between skilled and unskilled workers were increased, basic wages were
set at a low level and could be increased by increased productivity, payments by piecework were to be used where possible, wages in essential
industries were to be higher than in non-essential industries, and special
benefits in kind such as housing, dining-rooms, etc. were provided for
the technical staff in industry. All these measures could be, and were,
justified in Marxist terms; after all, Marx had said that during socialism
people would be paid according to their work. Stalin's economic policies,
dictated by the drive towards industrialisation, are still partially pursued
today and they are justified by a similar harsh economic doctrine, as we
shall see later.

The new mood for speedy industrialisation meant changes in family
relations too. In addition to government campaigns to reinstate the
family as the basic social unit of Soviet society, a series of laws were
passed that were designed to have the same effect. Divorce was made
more difficult and parents could be prosecuted for neglecting their
children. To help increase the birth rate, abortion was made illegal and
new allowances were granted to expectant mothers and to the heads of
large families.

Social security experienced important changes designed to help
increase productivity and strengthen labour discipline. First and foremost, unemployment benefit was abolished on the grounds that there
were enough jobs for all who wanted to work. Absenteeism could lead to
loss of temporary benefits. The entitlement to benefit as well as the
amount of benefit became subject to a satisfactory length of employment. Social security benefits for those employed in essential industries
were made preferable in a variety of ways to benefits in other industries.
Retired workers were encouraged to return to work. Finally, the whole

administrative machinery was changed to be more receptive to the
government's wider economic policies.

In the field of education, the early policies of experimentation,
liberalisation, and open discussion were sharply ended in favour of more
traditional and orthodox methods. The basic subjects were emphasised
again at the expense of other subjects. The importance of examinations
and the authority of the teacher were restored with a vengeance. Labour
discipline and hard work in industry were reflected in the school system
too.

In all these ways, education, social security, health, housing and
family policy became mere appendages to economic policy. Some of the
changes were necessary to facilitate economic growth but others were
not. What was so debasing for the idea of socialism was the obsession
with rapid economic growth at all costs and the tendency to use
'common sense' arguments to justify every traditional approach to
policy-making. The ideology of capitalist industrialisation provided the
guiding principles for economic growth in a society where the means of
production and distribution were nationalised.

The administrative machinery of the government and of the
Communist party were not only expanded and strengthened but they
were made more authoritarian, capricious, secretive and almost un-
accountable to the public. The party came to dominate the government
and Stalin became the undisputed leader of the party. The Great Purge
of 1936-8 with the trials, executions, murders and arrests of about eight
million real and imaginary opponents of the regime weakened the
vitality of the party and debased the idea of socialism at home and
abroad.

The war period and its aftermath — 1940-53

Economic planning embodied in the third Five Year Plan was influenced
by the fears of the impending war with Hitler. Defence expenditures
were raised at the expense of other expenditures but particularly of
those on consumer goods. Thus no sooner had the Soviet people recon-
structed their heavy industry to reach the stage at which consumer industries could be expanded than they had to forego once again any improvement in their standard of living. The invasion of the Soviet Union
by Germany inevitably meant a substantial deterioration in the
country's economic performance. The swift advance of German troops
into Soviet territory meant that the most industrialised and the most
fertile parts of the country were occupied by the Germans. The destruction of factories, of farms and of houses, and the death toll, were
heavier than those experienced by other European countries. To some

extent this was the result of the dogged resistance of the Russians after the initial set-backs. It was also due, however, to the systematic devastations by the retreating German armies during the last phases of the war.

War conditions meant that labour discipline had to be strengthened even more. Workers for certain industries were mobilised, change of jobs was illegal, holidays were abolished, and so on. Standards of living suffered and rationing had to be introduced for food and other consumer goods with preferential treatment being given to those employed in key industries. The Soviet Union emerged out of the war exhausted but with its national feeling strengthened and its international status and influence greatly enhanced.

The fourth Five Year Plan in 1946 indicated what everyone was expecting: investment priority was given to heavy industry. With the reconstruction of heavy industry went some modernisation, with the result that the country's pre-war industrial strength was restored by 1948 and was substantially surpassed after that. Progress was slower in the consumer goods' industries not only because less priority was given to them but also because they had been more neglected during the war. Nevertheless, by 1950 the pre-war level of production in consumer goods was generally reached and was surpassed in some cases. Real wages of industrial workers also rose but in the absence of abundant consumer goods they were of little real benefit.

The improvements in agricultural production were far more modest. This period witnessed a marked tendency towards amalgamation of small collective farms into larger units. Thus by 1952 the number of collective farms was reduced by almost three times. It was hoped that larger farm units would be more productive as they would be more amenable to mechanisation; they would help to reduce the population drift to the towns since they would be in a better position to provide better social and cultural activities. Laudable though these intentions were, the rise in agricultural production remained slow because the prices of agricultural produce paid by the government to farmers were not raised in spite of general price inflation during this period. The collective farmers were once again being required to bear a disproportionate burden of the economic reconstruction.

The magnitude of the task for economic recovery limited the scope for any wide-ranging changes in social policy at the end of the war. In the field of social security, expenditure was of necessity high because of the benefits that had to be paid to war victims. New allowances were introduced for mothers of many children because of obvious demographic factors. Mothers with ten or more children were also awarded the honorary title of 'mother heroines'. In education, means-tested fees were introduced in 1940 for the top classes of secondary education and for all higher education for political and economic reasons. These fees continued until after Stalin's death. Education was also used to increase the technically qualified labour force on a compulsory basis. Thus in 1940 the State Labour Reserve Scheme was introduced under which young people aged 14-17 years were given industrial training, after which they could be assigned to particular jobs. Housing had always been a problem in the towns but the war obviously worsened the situation both in towns and villages. The re-building of housing after the war was slow as emphasis had to be given to the rebuilding of factories, railways, and other industrial plants. Nevertheless, the gradual rebuilding of devastated towns and villages brought about improvements in the standards of housing, even though shortage of housing in towns remained as serious a problem as ever. The striking economic fact of this period is that the vast investment in defence requirements and in industry left few resources for any major expansion in social policy.

The Khrushchev period — 1956-64

Many of the changes introduced during this period had their beginnings in the Malenkov/Molotov interregnum of 1953-6. Khrushchev's speech to the twentieth party congress in 1956 denouncing Stalinism symbolised the end of an era and the beginning of a new one. Khrushchev's reforms were wide-ranging and attempted to achieve the following broad objectives: (a) The end of capricious Stalinist dictatorship and its replacement by the Leninist free type of 'democratic centralism' form of government. This was a return as far as possible to the forms of political debate and the forms of political decision-making prevalent during most of the NEP period. (b) The re-establishment of legal rights protecting ordinary people from arbitrary arrest and secret trials. (c) The promotion of a more balanced form of economic growth and (d) the reduction of inequalities in incomes, education and life chances. We shall be concerned only with the last two objectives in this section.

As has been mentioned several times so far, a more balanced form of economic growth meant a relative reduction of investment in heavy industry and a corresponding rise of investment in light industry for consumer goods. An emphasis on consumer goods in turn meant an increased allocation of resources to agriculture, partly because food is a primary consumer commodity, partly because many other consumer goods are based on agricultural raw materials and partly because the rural population still formed the largest population section. The Khrushchev reforms were, in other words, intended to revitalise agriculture. Thus prices of foodstuffs procured by government were raised, and tax concessions to collective farms were introduced — but most important of all, compulsory delivery quotas of agricultural produce which had existed from the early years of Stalinism were abolished in 1958. Instead of compulsory delivery quotas, government agencies entered into agreements with collective farms about the volume of produce and the price to be paid in any one year. These changes resulted in a substantial rise in the incomes of collective farmers, not only because prices were higher but also because incentives were introduced for higher productivity and because they made easier regional specialisation in farm production. The process of amalgamating small collective farms into larger units was continued and it was coupled with greater delegation of responsibility including, for the first time, the right of collective farms to own their own agricultural machinery. All these changes had the desired effect of increasing production and productivity, as well as increasing the incomes of collective farmers during most of this period.

In industry the new balanced growth policy meant that more emphasis was placed on consumer goods even though most of the investment was still allocated to heavy industry. Nevertheless, statistics of consumer goods tell a clear story of growth of consumer goods. Furniture production increased in price terms fivefold between 1953 and 1964; washing machines from 3.5 thousand units to 2.86 million units; refrigerators from 49 thousand units to 1.13 million units; vacuum cleaners from 45.5 thousand units to 764.5 thousand units; television sets from 84 thousand to 2.93 million sets; motor-cycles from 143 thousand to 687 thousand; private cars from 77 thousand to 385 thousand between the same two years; and so on.[18]

Policies towards the reduction of income inequalities started with wages. A minimum wage was introduced, taxes on low incomes were reduced and some of the higher salaries were cut down. Working conditions were improved, mobility of labour was made easier by repealing the legislation which made absenteeism and unauthorised job changes illegal, and the length of the working week was reduced while holidays with pay were increased.

The same broad policy of reducing inequality was extended to various aspects of social policy. The social security legislation of 1956 and 1964 modernised the social security system and made it one of the best in the world. In 1956 the existing benefits were increased, they were made less directly connected to people's employment status and safeguards were introduced for the low paid. In 1964 the scheme was extended to cover collective farmers who, until then, had had to rely on inadequate mutual benefit schemes. Apart from egalitarian principles there were good demographic reasons for extending the scheme to collective farmers — to reduce the depopulation of the countryside. In the field of education the reforms of 1958 were extremely important in creating even for a brief period of time a greater degree of equality of

19

opportunity. These reforms abolished fees for secondary and higher education and they extended compulsory education to eight years. Those who wanted to proceed to higher education had to spend two years in full-time employment. Preferential treatment was given to those who had worked for many years prior to applying for university education. In this way it was hoped that the proportion of people from working-class backgrounds who reached higher education would be increased. In housing, too, substantial progress was made. The number of new dwellings was increased substantially so that in 1961-2, the number of new dwellings per thousand inhabitants was the highest in Europe.[19] These reforms were long overdue. The Soviet people had made heavy sacrifices over long periods of time in order to build a secure industrial base for their economy. By the mid-1950s it was clear that this had been substantially achieved and though the Soviet Union had begun to direct its resources on a large scale towards space exploration, it could no longer justifiably ignore the welfare of its citizens. Economic conditions were thus ripe for these reforms. The death of Stalin and the rise of Khrushchev also provided the right political situation for such changes. It was this congruence between economic and political factors that enabled Khrushchev's reforming zeal to come to fruition.

The changed economic situation necessitated some very important changes in government economic planning and the running of industries. So long as the number of enterprises was small and so long as their main objective was to produce heavy goods or consumer goods of a basic standard, it was possible for the central government agencies to lay down production targets and then ensure that enterprises fulfilled these targets. Moreover, as long as labour was plentiful, enterprises could expand production by increasing their labour force. By the mid-1950s all these features of the economy were changing. Labour was in short supply as a result of the war losses, the number and size of the enterprises had grown substantially and the decision had been taken by the party to expand both the quantity and the quality of consumer goods. For all these reasons the established forms of economic planning were not functioning well. What the new economic situation demanded was more say to the consumers, greater freedom of enterprises to run their affairs, and greater productivity per worker. These were the central ideas proposed by Professor E. Liberman in his well-known article in *Pravda* on 9 September 1962, which were introduced on an experimental basis in a few consumer goods industries and were gradually extended to most industries. According to Professor Liberman, what was radically new about these reforms 'was that they recognised the decisive role of profits as a yardstick of efficiency and a source of incentive to the producer'.[20] Enterprises were allowed to decide for themselves how to meet government targets: the more they fulfilled such targets, the more profitable they became; and the more profitable they became, the more they could pay to their workers in terms of dividends over and above their basic wages. It is generally acknowledged that these reforms have helped to increase productivity. Implicitly, however, they are also an acknowledgment that Soviet people are still motivated as much by self-interest as by socialist ideology. A centrally-planned economy has to find the best possible ways and means of ensuring that decisions taken at the centre allow enough initiative and provide adequate incentives at the local level, because without these possibilities economic growth is bound to stagnate. This is not only a difficult task at any one time but a changing one too, according to the level of technological development, the nature of the particular enterprise, the standard of living in the country, and so on. The day when people will be motivated in their work by altruism and by the interests of the general community is far too distant. It is in the light of these circumstances that the claim made by the programme of the Communist party that 'the present generation of Soviet people shall live in Communism' was grossly over-optimistic.[21]

The Brezhnev period – 1964-

The downfall of Khrushchev was the result of a number of interacting factors: the problems and difficulties of agriculture in his last years of office, his lapse into authoritarian rule without having the Stalinist power to back such behaviour, and his extravagant promises to the Russian people. Other reasons were his 'hare-brained' schemes at home, his hazardous policy ventures abroad and, above all, the growing fear in conservative circles that his de-Stalinisation policies were going too far and were threatening the stability of the country. He was replaced by the partnership of Kosygin and Brezhnev, out of which the latter emerged as the real leader.

The Brezhnev period is one of gradual economic growth, even if the pace of growth has slackened. The Soviet Union has today become the second most powerful industrial and military power in the world after the United States – no mean achievement in a space of sixty years. Its heavy industry continues to expand at a rate faster than that of most advanced capitalist societies, though whether the pace can be maintained once the emphasis is switched to consumer goods remains to be seen. An official Soviet publication claims that during the twenty-year period (1951-75) 'the annual growth rate of industrial production averaged to 4.6 per cent in the advanced capitalist countries and 9.6 per cent in the U.S.S.R'.[22] Brezhnev's period has witnessed as great an emphasis on consumer goods as the preceding period and this is likely to continue for, in spite of its immense industrial power, the Soviet Union is still a

21

long way behind the advanced capitalist countries in this field. According to Medvedev, 'in 1970 only 32 families out of 100 had refrigerators, 51 out of 100 had television sets and 52 out of 100 had washing machines. Not more than 2 per cent of Soviet families possessed automobiles'.[23] These figures are clearly well below those of all advanced capitalist societies.

In agriculture a greater emphasis has been placed on mechanisation at the expense of the state budget rather than the budget of individual farms. Emphasis is also increasingly being placed on the improvement of roads and transport in the countryside and the increase in storage and processing facilities in the farms to reduce wastage of farm produce. Lavigne goes as far as to claim that the 'cities are short of milk, eggs and poultry, not because production is inadequate but because there is no effective marketing mechanism'.[24] Guaranteed wages for collective farm workers have been introduced. Previously wages were paid out of the funds of the collective farm after government quotas had been met. The result was that wages were low, they fluctuated a great deal and varied equally as much between farms for reasons beyond the control of farm workers. The result of these changes has been that the gap between collective farm workers' wages and state farm workers' wages has narrowed from 20 per cent in 1965 to 14 per cent in 1970.[25] In spite of all these improvements, it is generally acknowledged that agriculture is still the Achilles' heel of the Soviet economy. An official government publication recognises that 'the speedy creation of a modern industrial basis for agriculture is the most urgent problem of the moment'.[26]

The reforms of the 1960s in the decentralisation of decision-making in industrial enterprises, coupled with collective and individual incentive schemes, have been generally applied and they have led to a general improvement in both the quality and the quantity of industrial production. These reforms were followed by the reform of the Labour Code in 1970 and 1971 which provided workers with greater security against arbitrary dismissals, improved benefits for redundant workers and increased the workers' freedom to change jobs. If, however, the obligation of the state to provide employment in a secure way has been stressed, the obligation of the citizen to work has not been forgotten. Thus, according to one Soviet economist, ' "He who does not work, neither shall he eat" is the most important and fundamental watchword of socialist society'.[27] This attitude towards employment has implications for social security benefits which will be discussed in chapter 2.

If Khrushchev's period exhibits major social reforms and some radical measures, Brezhnev's is best seen as the period of consolidation and useful piecemeal social engineering. Thus the major reforms of 1956 and 1964 for social security have been consolidated and improved upon during this period. Social security benefits have been increased in relation to wages and benefits for collective farmers have been improved substantially to make them very similar, though still inferior, to those of the rest of the population. In education, Khrushchev's reforms have been removed because of opposition from parents, employers and university authorities who complained that the emphasis on work experience prior to university education undermined academic ability and achievement. Thus, for the second time in its history, the Soviet Union experimented briefly in polytechnical education and abandoned it in a hurry. In the field of health, one discerns over the years a gradual expansion of services and a gradual improvement in the quality of services. The result has been that the Soviet Union can boast one of the best health services in the world in terms of universality of service, accessibility to service, etc. In terms of personnel it shows an equally good record, so that today it has, according to World Health Organisation estimates, the highest number of doctors per thousand population. More conservative estimates by Ryan give the Soviet Union fractionally second place in the world after Israel.[28] Housing is still the most inadequate of the four social services. In spite of substantial resources invested in housing during this period, it is acknowledged that the 'provision of people with better housing will remain a serious problem for a number of years to come.'[29] Demographic trends such as marriage and divorce rates and population mobility make the solution of the 'housing problem' that much more complicated. Whereas as late as 1959 only 48 per cent of the population lived in towns, by 1970 the proportion was 60 per cent; whereas the divorce rate in 1960 was 1.3 per thousand population, the corresponding rate for 1970 was 2.6.[30]

In spite of all these improvements, the living standards of the Soviet people leave much to be desired. Medvedev has this to say referring to the situation in the 1970s.

> Even today there are tens of millions of people who are experiencing serious material hardship, working for pay that is substantially below the minimum standard . . . At present millions of people live in uncomfortable quarters, in overcrowded rooms, in basements, waiting their turn to get apartments.[31]

On the political front the Brezhnev period has witnessed a move towards conservatism, with the result that the hopes engendered during the Khrushchev reforms for a substantial return to democratic socialism have largely disappeared. Even Lenin's notion of democratic centralism – 'freedom in discussion – unity in action'[32] – does not prevail. Lenin's thesis was necessary in the uncertain, poverty-stricken and war-ridden years of the early 1920s, but it should be redundant in the affluent years of the 1970s when the Soviet Union, according to Brezhnev, has reached the advanced stage of socialism, i.e. the stage preceding communism when the state as an oppressive apparatus should be withering away, according to Marxism-Leninism.[33]

An assessment of the achievement of socialist aims

We said at the beginning of this chapter that the first main aim of the new socialist Soviet state was the nationalisation of the means of production and distribution. The main reasons for the change were to abolish social class exploitation, to facilitate economic planning and hence to increase economic growth. By the end of the 1930s all the means of production and distribution had been nationalised and Stalin was able to claim that socialism had been achieved 'in the main' and that, as a result, exploitation of one social class by another had been abolished. He insisted that the transition to communism was difficult and long but he played down the importance of the social divisions still remaining in the Soviet Union. We shall return to this theme in the last chapter. Here we simply want to note that though social classes in the Marxist sense have been abolished in the Soviet Union, socio-economic groups have remained and they have had similar but not identical implications for the distribution of power, privilege and life chances with those of social classes in capitalist societies.

The Soviet model of economic development, in spite of its many faults, has been of immense importance to the world and it has been adopted in varying degrees by developed and developing socialist and capitalist nations. Government planning is today a common feature of all countries, including the capitalist world. The recent changes in Soviet planning allowing for more local initiative, for greater incentives and for more attention to consumers' wishes have met with success in stimulating industrial productivity but they have raised more sharply the issues of political and governmental power. Decentralisation in industry without decentralisation of government administration and without the loosening up of hierarchical authority relationships in administration is problematic. In the long run this contradiction may prove impossible. The recent decentralisation of industry is in line with Marxist ideals but the emphasis on the economic incentives for greater productivity are a step towards capitalist practice.

In terms of economic growth there is no doubt of the impressive progress that has been made. In a period of sixty years the Soviet Union has transformed itself from a backward, agrarian society to a major industrial power in the world. Its rate of growth has been unparalleled in history — undoubtedly a major achievement by any standards. But this overall growth hides uneven trends. The growth of heavy industry has been phenomenal; the growth of consumer goods has not been so substantial and the growth of agricultural produce has been rather poor in spite of increased mechanisation of farming. Part of the reason for this lies in the fact that there are fewer people engaged in agriculture, but part of it must lie in the attitudes of farm workers towards collectivised farming. It is for this reason that productivity in the private plots of land is so much higher than in collective farms.

Nationalisation of the means of production was also seen as prerequisite to the reduction of income inequalities. In one sense such a reduction has taken place through the confiscation of large private capital and the impossibility within the Soviet economic system of amassing private wealth that can be used to exploit others. But this has not abolished income inequalities nor even reduced them substantially.

In an attempt to warn against utopian solutions, Marx postulated that during the transition stage from capitalism to communism, i.e. during socialism, the governing principle should be from each according to his ability, to each according to his work. Like all general principles it has been interpreted differently by Soviet governments over the years. Three such different interpretations can be discerned, each with its own ideology and pattern of income distribution. During Lenin's leadership, egalitarianism was accepted even though with caution. The emphasis was in reducing wage differentials apart from the very small group of expert technical scientific workers who, for the time being, were paid disproportionately high wages in relation to the rest of the population. Excluding the specialists, the differential between the highest and the lowest wages was set at 1:2.1 in 1918; it narrowed down to 1:1.75 in 1919 and it increased after 1921 with the New Economic Policy. During Stalin's rule, egalitarianism was attacked as both utopian and criminal because it was linked with political groupings opposing Stalin. Wage inequalities were praised and increased substantially. The post-Stalin leadership of Khrushchev and Brezhnev has taken up a middle position. It disapproves of both extreme inequalities and equality of earnings from work. It has argued that with increased education and specialisation among the labour force the justification for paying very unequal wages has declined. People's work contribution has become more similar and hence merits more similar remuneration. Thus the principle 'to each according to his work' is still the official guideline, but has been interpreted as an argument for reducing wage inequalities. There has also been some recognition that there is injustice in paying the highest wages and salaries for those jobs which are the most fulfilling, creative and satisfying.

Wages in Soviet industry can be divided into three main categories in descending order; for the engineering technical personnel, for skilled and unskilled manual workers, and for the non-manual employees. Wages of the first group are about 30 per cent higher than those of the second group which in turn are 20 per cent higher than those of the third group.[34] These general comparisons, however, mask greater inequalities within each group. Thus among the first group, the wages of the top elite group of managers and directors of firms and enterprises are well above the rest. Among the workers, wages are higher for the skilled than the unskilled and for those employed in heavy than in light industry. Indeed, the wages of certain groups of workers — coal miners and steel workers — are higher than the wages of most categories of technical-engineering personnel. The lowest wages are those for some groups of the unskilled and some groups of the non-manual employees i.e. cleaners and office workers who happen to be predominantly women. Yanowitch provides data from a Soviet study in Leningrad in 1970 which showed that the monthly wages of directors of large industrial enterprises were eight times higher than those of cleaners.[35]

Earnings in collective farms are lower than those in state employment even after taking into account income from private plots. Within the collective farm community, however, there are wage inequalities which are as substantial as those found in industry. If anything, such inequalities are more substantial because the gradations between the top and the bottom paid are fewer. Women, again, are disproportionately represented among the low-paid jobs.

These wage inequalities are compounded by other material inequalities — fringe benefits and housing — the exact amounts of which are either not known or are difficult to estimate. Briefly, income inequality in the Soviet Union has declined recently and it appears that it is lower than that found in advanced capitalist countries in terms of gross earnings. The position, however, may not be all that different in terms of net earnings because direct taxation is lower in the Soviet Union than it is in any advanced capitalist country. As the above discussion showed, however, wage differentials in the Soviet Union are not along the same lines as those in advanced capitalist societies. Levels of industrial and managerial skills are the main criteria in the Soviet Union while the manual/non-manual dichotomy is the distinguishing criterion in advanced capitalist societies.[36] Lane, however, makes the interesting point that this difference is deceptive. People live in families and the size of the family of non-manual workers is smaller than that of manual workers. Moreover, male manual workers tend to marry semi-skilled or unskilled women while non-manual workers tend to marry women who are of about the same socio-economic category. The result of these two tendencies is that income per head in the family runs in a hierarchy 'from non-manual through manual to agricultural workers'.[37]

The nationalisation of the means of production and distribution was seen before the Revolution as the prerequisite step towards the democratisation of authority in industry and other enterprises. Lenin acknowledged that the self-government of the masses is a central feature of socialism. Engels, too, was explicit that the taking over of enterprises by the state is not necessarily a socialist measure. Otherwise, he warned, 'Napoleon and Metternich would rank among the founders of socialism' and 'The Royal Maritime Company, the Royal Porcelain Manufacture and even the regimental tailors in the army would be socialist institutions'.[38] In other words, whether nationalisation leads to socialism or not depends on who controls it and for what purpose. Thus public participation in government affairs and workers' participation in the running of their enterprises is a central feature of a socialist society, as stated at the beginning of this chapter.

By no stretch of the imagination can one argue that public or workers' participation exists today in the Soviet Union in the real sense of the word, i.e. the public or the workers playing a substantial or dominant role in the decision-making process. The government administrative machinery operates on hierarchical lines, with the local soviets being the local government unit responsible for the administration of such diverse services as education, social security, housing, health, restaurants, butcher and grocery shops, etc. Their responsibilities go well beyond those of local councils in capitalist societies — the first of two main differences between them. The second difference is that the number of professional, full-time administrative staff at the disposal of the local soviets is far smaller than it is in capitalist societies. A great deal of reliance is placed on the help of citizen volunteer groups operating on a functional basis. There is, therefore, enough evidence to suggest that participation at the local level is very substantial. Matthews estimated that the average participation rate shown by various Soviet studies is 40 per cent of the people in the samples.[39] But such participation is clearly pragmatic, facilitating and symbolic and does not exercise any substantial influence on government policy-making decisions.[40] Soviet authorities, moreover, claim that since administrators are answerable to the party and since the party is controlled by the people, the government administrative machinery is controlled by the people in this way as well. Such an argument is 'very thin indeed'[41] in Mary McAuley's words. Many administrators are party members anyhow and the evidence does not show, either, that the public controls decision-making in the party.

In brief, the Soviet administrative structure has most of the features of the government bureaucracies of capitalist societies in spite of its greater reliance on elected and on volunteer groups at the local level.

Workers' participation has gone through three different stages in the Soviet Union. During Lenin's leadership, there was a mixture of workers' control and workers' participation in industry for the reasons discussed earlier in this chapter. Stalin's era witnessed the growth and universal application of a very rigid form of the principle of 'one-man

27

management'. According to this principle, the factory or the enterprise is organised on hierarchical lines of authority but each sub-unit is under the control of a single executive who has full responsibility for the work of that unit and who is answerable to his superior. Thus both authority and responsibility are hierarchically organised. It was a system of administration that could be justified on grounds of efficiency at a time when the Soviet work force was largely semi-literate and newly arrived from the countryside. The growth of education and technical skills as well as the stabilisation of the work force have rendered this form of administration less suitable to optimal industrial efficiency. There have, therefore, been signs in recent years that the Soviet Union has begun to humanise – but not abandon – the 'one-man management' principle. It is a movement parallel to the 'human relations' school in capitalist societies which seeks to take into account the psychological and informal aspects of work in order to make management more efficient. As Yanowitch points out, a 'non-authoritarian style of management is encouraged, while the substance of managerial powers – the exclusion of workers from significant decision-making – remains intact'.[42] Though these changes in the context of the 1965 economic reforms, discussed earlier, are a welcome relaxation of the Stalinist model of administration and management, they are still essentially different from the type of workers' participation that Marx and Engels envisaged.

The general conclusion of this chapter is that the Soviet Union today exhibits a socialist form of ownership of the means of production but capitalist elements still dominate its system of income and goods distribution as well as its administrative structures in government and work. Moreover, there is no strong evidence to suggest that over the sixty-year period under review there has been any clear tendency towards either greater democratisation of decision-making or greater equality of income distribution, in spite of recent worthwhile improvements in both of these these fields.

We said at the beginning of this chapter that a materialist explanation of the development of economic and social policy makes sense in the case of the Soviet Union. One of the constant themes running through the writings of Marx and Engels was that an advanced stage of economic development in capitalism was necessary not only before a socialist revolution was possible but also before a classless society could be achieved after the Revolution.

> No social order ever perishes before all productive forces for which there is room in it have developed; and new, higher relations of production never appear before the material conditions of their existence have matured in the womb of the old society itself.[43]

It is true that the Bolshevik Revolution took place in an economically underdeveloped country but this does not contradict Marx's argument. Indeed, it lends support to it because in spite of the Bolshevik Revolution, the capitalist order remained after the Revolution and, as we indicated in this chapter, it still exists in the fields of economic distribution and power sharing. Marx and Engels were quite clear that advanced economic development for a socialist revolution was absolutely necessary in practical terms 'for the reason that without it only *want* is made general and with *want* the struggle for necessities and all the old filthy business would necessarily be reproduced'.[44] This describes very well the events after the Bolshevik Revolution even though the involvement of the Soviet Union in the First World War and the Civil War that followed exacerbated the desperate economic situation that prevailed.

A low level of economic development means much more than scarcity of material goods, important though that is. It means an equally low level of ideological development with the result that socialist policies are not easily acceptable to the general public. A perfect example of this was the attempt during the 1920s to bring about equality between men and women. Such a policy was resisted not only by most men but it was also found excessively modern by most women. How could such a policy become a reality anyhow in a country of mass unemployment or under-employment? Thus ideological factors are usually congruent with material factors and they influence each other.

A low level of economic development also means that the size of the proletariat is small, with the result that the Revolution comes about without the active support of the majority of the population. Lenin's emphasis on the importance of a united, disciplined Communist party acting as the vanguard of the working class was a reflection of the small size of the working class in Russia. The Revolution could only come about through tactical manoeuvring, intelligent political campaigning and authoritarian leadership. This situation was again exacerbated because of the Civil War that resulted in the death of a large number of dedicated socialist industrial workers. Lenin's views on the disciplined organisation of the party, and its role in leading the Revolution had clear repercussions on events after the Revolution. The party, small in size, could only change the face of the Russian society by acting often unilaterally, and in authoritarian ways. Thus the Leninist doctrine of the elite party leading the workers during the Revolution had clear implications for the course of events after the Revolution.

The personalities of Soviet leaders also played a part in shaping events after the Revolution. Lenin's authority was unquestioned in the party. His stature as a theorist, as a tactician and as a leader provided him with enough security to rely on democratic centralism as a form of government. Stalin's position in the party leadership during the first eight years, however, was always in question. He was not a great theoretician, he had not travelled outside Russia and there were several other members in the leadership of the party claiming the right to become the leader. His insecure position as a leader, coupled with his parochial background, made it difficult for him to rely on democratic centralism. The decision of the party to proceed with heavy industrialisation at a fast rate and the peasants' understandable wish to retain and improve the gains they made since the Revolution provided the first test for Stalin as a leader and, as we have seen, he reacted in the well-known repressive ways that set the pattern for the entire period he was the dictator of the Soviet Union. Thus material, ideological and personal factors coalesced to produce Stalinism. It was not a phenomenon explainable only in the terms of the personality of Stalin himself, as Khrushchev claimed in 1956. Nor is Stalinism an inevitable consequence of any socialist transformation of capitalist societies. As Ellenstein points out, Stalinism 'was a phenomenon restricted in terms of time and place, and not an historical necessity universally true of socialism, whether past, present or future'.[45] Dictatorship is not the prerogative of either socialism or capitalism. It cuts across economic systems as such recent examples as Hitler, Mussolini, Franco, etc., indicate.

2

Social security

During the transition stage from capitalism to communism, i.e. the socialist stage, the total product of society would be divided into three main funds, according to Marx. The first fund would be used to pay workers according to their work; and the second to pay for the expansion of production and for the depreciation of industrial buildings, machinery, and so on. It was out of the third fund that government administration and social services would be financed. The following three deductions would be made out of the third fund:

> Firstly: the general costs of administration not directly appertaining to production. This part will, from the outset, be very significantly limited in comparison with the present society. It will diminish commensurately with the development of the new society. Secondly: the amount set aside for needs communally satisfied, such as schools, health services, etc. This part will, from the outset, be significantly greater than in the present society. It will grow commensurately with the development of the new society. Thirdly: a fund for people unable to work, etc., in short for what today comes under so-called poor relief.[1]

The second and the third main funds would have priority over the first in the sense that only after the necessary deductions for these two funds from the total product of society were made would the remainder be divided among workers in the form of wages. Marx envisaged a socialist society following from an advanced capitalist society where the total

31

product of society would be abundant to meet the demands of the three main funds.

TABLE 2.1
Public expenditure as % of GDP (UK and USA)
or of net material product (USSR)

	USSR			UK			USA		
	1960	1966	1970	1960	1966	1970	1960	1966	1970
Education	5.8	7.3	6.8	5.3*	5.1	5.0	5.3*	5.3	6.4
Health	3.3	4.1	4.1	3.3	3.7	4.0	0.7	0.8+	0.8+
Social security	6.9	7.5	7.8	7.5	8.9	10.0	6.1	7.1	9.7
Housing	4.5	5.0	4.5	1.3	1.6	1.7	0.16	0.09	0.07
TOTAL:	20.5	23.9	23.2	17.4	19.3	20.7	12.3	13.3	17.0

*Refer to National Income not GDP. + Excludes medicare (caid)
Sources: ILO, The Cost of Social Security, 1967-71, Geneva, 1976 (for social security and health).
UNESCO, Statistical Yearbook, 1977, Paris, 1978 (for education).
United Nations, Annual Bulletin of Building Statistics for Europe, New York, 1967 and 1970 (for housing in USA and UK).
R.A. Clarke, Soviet Economic Facts, 1917-1970, Macmillan, London, 1972 pp. 7, 13 (for housing in USSR).

The interpretation of comparative data is always fraught with difficulties, particularly when, as in Table 2.1, east European and capitalist societies are involved. The use of the net material product instead of the gross domestic product overestimates slightly the proportion of national wealth spent on the social services in the Soviet Union in relation to the United States and the UK. Nevertheless Table 2.1 suggests that the USSR and the UK spend a similar proportion of their national wealth on the four social services — a proportion that is higher than that of the more affluent United States. These figures, however, refer to government expenditure and not to the total expenditure including private spending in the social services which is higher in the United States than in the other two countries. Moreover, the proportion of national wealth spent by the government and privately on any social service is no safe indication of the quality of service provided to the consumers. It may reflect, for example, the level of salaries paid to the professionals employed to run the service. The low salaries of medical personnel in the USSR, for example, result in a low proportion of the national wealth being spent on the health services. Judged by other criteria, the Soviet health service compares most favourably with countries which spend a higher proportion of their national wealth on their health services.

Marxism and social security

Neither Marx nor Engels wrote anything about the detailed provisions of social security. It is to Lenin that we must turn for some discussion of the nature of a socialist social security system. In his address to the Sixth All-Russian Conference of the Russian Social Democratic Party in Prague in 1912, he set out the following principles for a socialist social security system:

(i) It should provide assistance in all cases of incapacity, including old age, accidents, illness, death of the breadwinner, as well as maternity and birth benefits.

(ii) It should cover *all* wage earners and their families.

(iii) The benefits should equal *full* earnings and *all* costs should be borne by employers and the state.

(iv) There should be uniform insurance organisations (rather than organisations by risk) of a territorial type and under the full management of the insured workers.[2]

We shall be discussing the political context within which this statement was made in the next section; we shall also discuss the extent to which these principles have been met in the Soviet Union in the final section of this chapter. Here we confine our discussion to a brief examination of the rationale and implications of each of these principles. Lenin acknowledged that the interregnum of socialism would be long and hard in the Soviet Union. During this stage, people would depend for their living on their work and hence the notion of risks when people's income from work would not be forthcoming. Though he listed the risks as he saw them at that time, he left the list open for other risks to be added. The important implication, however, is that not all situations resulting in loss of income would necessarily be covered by social security. He left out unemployment, for example, though this was included in a bill presented to the Duma by the Bolsheviks in 1914. Lenin's list of risks was progressive for Russia but it was conventional by western European standards. It was, indeed, very similar to Bismarck's list for Germany.

Lenin's caution on the risks to be covered is matched by his view as to which population groups should be covered. He was quite explicit that only wage-earners and their families could be covered, leaving out the vast majority of the population in Russia who were either peasants working for themselves or self-employed artisans in the towns. Working for an employer was the main criterion for social security coverage. What he did not make clear, however, was whether the mere fact that a person was covered was enough to qualify him for benefits or whether certain conditions regarding the length of employment had also to be satisfied before a wage-earner could qualify for benefits. Practice varied during the 1920s, though length of employment gradually emerged as a necessary qualifying condition for benefits.

The principle that benefits should equal full earnings is socialist in nature only if earnings are not too unequal. Indeed, this was part of Lenin's thinking and earnings inequalities were reduced during the 1920s. How socialist, however, is the principle that the cost of social security should be borne by employers and the state, thus freeing workers from direct contributions? If Lenin was writing about a socialist social security system within advanced capitalism he committed the same error as other early writers on social security, by believing that contributions paid by employers and the state somehow were not borne by the workers in the end. The available evidence today strongly suggests that employers' contributions are passed on to the consumers in terms of higher prices and lower wages and they have, on the whole, a regressive effect on income distribution. The effect of employers' contributions in a socialist state is different and will be discussed in the final section of this chapter. It appears that Lenin supported this form of social security finance because of its political appeal to workers who saw it as a means of income redistribution from the employers to the workers.

Finally, the method of administration envisaged was to be uniform, national in scope and participatory in nature. It is only the latter aspect that distinguishes a socialist from a capitalist form of administration. This was in line with Lenin's thinking on workers' participation. As is generally known, however, Lenin was not consistent on this theme. In his *State and Revolution,* written in 1917, he advocated the extensive use of workers' participation, while in some of his earlier works, notably in *What is to be Done?* written in 1905, he saw the Bolshevik party acting as the leader of the working class during and after the Revolution in political as well as administrative affairs. As we pointed out in the previous chapter, Lenin's approach to workers' participation after the Revolution was cautious and, we argued, also realistic, in the socio-economic conditions of that time. These then were the Leninist principles of social security and, as we shall see in the remaining sections of this chapter, they have met with varying success since the October Revolution. Lacking from Lenin's principles was any recognition that the social security system could play a part in dealing with low incomes from work, and among families with children. Also lacking was any mention of what would happen to all those who, for one reason or another, fell through the insurance net. As we shall see later, these are still the main two gaps in the Soviet system of social security today. These two criticisms of Lenin's work support the suggestion that his ideas on social security were similar to those of reformers in capitalist countries at that time for they, too, omitted these two eventualities from their plans.

The development of social security

The inadequacy of social security provision under Czarism at the beginning of this century provided both Bolsheviks and Mensheviks with live political ammunition. While the latter, however, campaigned for gradual improvements within a reformed capitalist system, the former insisted on very radical changes which could not possibly be accommodated within the capitalist system of Russia. Lenin, in particular, saw clearly the value of social reform campaigns in increasing the political consciousness of the working class both for immediate revolutionary purposes and for long-term educational purposes as a preparation for socialism.

Like many other European countries at the beginning of this century, Russia relied primarily on public assistance for the relief of poverty. Local authorities were responsible for poor relief but they lacked the necessary funds. Madison estimates that a modest provision of poor relief would have cost the zemstvos 300 million roubles in 1912 instead of the 4.5 million they spent in that year.[3] As was also common in many countries at that time, poverty was attributed to the moral failings of the individual. The philosophy and practice of poor relief was thus openly harsh, and stigmatised the poor.

Insurance benefits were equally inadequate. Widespread industrial unrest preceded the Industrial Accidents Act 1903, which provided compensation to workers for accidents at work. It was, however, inadequate in many ways: it excluded workers in small establishments, it disqualified workers whose accidents were deemed to be due to their negligence, it made no provisions for compulsory insurance and it was excessively legalistic. Soviet literature today cites numerous examples of individual injustice resulting from this legislation that are meant to show the progress achieved by the Soviet Union since the Revolution. These examples are not, however, unique to Czarist Russia; they were common occurrences in other European countries where similar legislation was in force at that time.

Political reforms, continuing industrial unrest and general dissatisfaction with the 1903 act led to the second important piece of social security legislation prior to the Revolution — the Health and Accidents

Act 1912. The act was a significant advance but in the political situation prevailing in Russia at that time it was inadequate. It failed to match the aspirations of the politically conscious urban working class. The act provided for cash benefits for accidents at work financed by employers, and for sickness, maternity and death benefits financed jointly by employers and employees. Again, the coverage was limited to one-sixth of the labour force according to official Soviet estimates,[4] or one-quarter of the labour force according to Madison.[5] The act made no provisions for old-age pensions or for unemployment benefit.

The Bolsheviks opposed the legislation vigorously and systematically. Speaking to the Sixth Conference of the Russian Social Democrats in Prague in 1912, Lenin referred to the 1912 legislation as 'an unworthy bill with a beggarly rate of compensation'. He insisted that the Duma should improve the legislation it was considering along the five principles discussed above. If the Duma refused to modify the 1912 bill, Lenin advocated continued political and industrial pressure. The legislation should be turned into a live political issue, particularly among the unskilled industrial workers who were excluded by the bill and among whom the Bolsheviks had most power. Social security became a platform not merely of reformist political activity but of revolutionary change, because Lenin insisted that a comprehensive social security system was not possible under capitalism as it prevailed in Russia. 'An insurance reform really corresponding to the interests of the workers can only be accomplished after the final overthrow of Tzarism and the achievement of conditions indispensable for the free class struggle of the proletariat.'[6] In 1914 the Bolsheviks drafted a bill that was more radical than Lenin's principles and presented it to the Duma as a replacement of the 1912 legislation. Predictably, the bill was unacceptable, not only to the Czarist government but also the provisional government that took over after the February Revolution. When the Bolsheviks took over the government they had no option but to implement a comprehensive system of social insurance, for they had campaigned so long and so fervently for such provision. The spate of proclamations, decrees and regulations emanating from government and party sources in the years immediately after the Revolution is evidence of the pressure of economic, political and military events with which the new government was trying desperately to cope as best it could. As Dewar puts it, Bolsheviks 'were feeling their way by a process of trial and error that clearly shows the pressure of overmastering circumstances upon doctrine'.[7]

We noted in the last chapter that the government's proposals for the reform of social security were not utopian or extremist but rather progressive and realistic. The first law on social insurance, 11 December 1917, provided unemployment benefit while the second law,

29 December 1917, provided for sickness and maternity benefit and for
a death grant. These benefits were to be provided to wage-earners only,
regardless of length of previous employment. They were to be financed
by employers for the time being and they were equal to the average
wage of the locality, provided they did not exceed the previous earnings
of the unemployed worker. The administration of the scheme was placed
in the hands of a system of decentralised funds run by representatives of
the trade unions and of the insured people. The vast majority of the
population, i.e. the peasants, were excluded from the scheme. This
cautious approach was swept away by the events of the Civil War. In an
attempt to secure the loyalty and support of the peasantry, the government extended its social security programme very substantially and well
beyond its economic means. Thus on 31 October 1918, social insurance
programmes were expanded both in terms of risks and population
groups. Social insurance became known as social security and was extended to cover all population groups including the peasantry. It was
also substantially extended to cover all the major risks – unemployment,
sickness, maternity, invalidity, old age, widowhood and burial costs. It
is worth pointing out that old-age pensions were provided on the assumption that old age brought invalidity with it rather than a recognition that
old people should retire from work at a certain age if they so wished.
The amount of benefit was calculated in the same way as under the
previous legislation. The whole scheme was to be financed as before,
mainly out of employers' contributions complemented with private
property confiscated by the state and turned over to insurance funds.
The revolutionary appeal of the new scheme, however, began to lose
strength as the government was forced to nationalise all industry during
the war communism period of 1918-21. It was no longer possible to
argue that wealth was being taken away from employers to be given to
the employees. Rather it became a matter of whether the nationalised
industry, individually and collectively, could pay for the various benefits. Since industrial production fell so dramatically during this period,
it is no surprise that social security legislation remained largely a dead
letter. 'The insurance for peasants, artisans and home workers never
materialised and even for wage earners and salaried employees it was
impossible to implement the social insurance laws to any significant
extent', writes Madison, referring to the 1918 legislation.[8] As with
wages, social security benefits had often to be paid in kind to cope with
inflation. Priority also had to be given to the war victims, according to a
Russian official view.

> Material assistance to the families of soldiers who fell on the battle-
> field was of special importance at this time. In 1920, a million
> persons were in receipt of a pension; two thirds of these were soldiers

and their families and only one third workers, employees, their families and other citizens.[9]

As the government became increasingly responsible for the finance of the scheme, it also assumed more responsibility for its administration. The funds that were administered by representatives of trade unions and of the insured people were abolished and government departments assumed the responsibility for administering social insurance.

The initiation of the New Economic Policy meant a return to the more realistic social security programmes introduced before the war communism period. Firstly, as from 1921, the coverage of social security was confined to wage-earners. Self-employed people like artisans or peasants were encouraged to join special mutual aid societies. Thus wage-earners were compulsorily covered by the state insurance scheme while the rest, i.e. the majority of the population, were merely encouraged to join mutual aid societies whose funds were derived from various inadequate sources including contributions from the members themselves. Secondly, the payment of benefit to wage-earners was made conditional on their satisfying certain conditions. This was particularly important for the unemployed whose numbers in the early 1920s were quite high. Thus after the decree of October 1921, unemployment benefit was not available to all the unemployed as it was, in theory at least, under the 1918 legislation, but only to skilled workers who had no other means of support and to unskilled workers with three years' employment record — a stipulation which would have excluded most of them in the employment conditions of the time. Thirdly, both the level of benefit and its duration varied according to the risk it covered. The sick were treated more favourably than the unemployed and the long-term disabled. It was a policy which was influenced by labour market considerations. Rimlinger quotes figures from Minkoff's work which estimated that 'the average monthly pension paid in the years 1924 to 1928 ranged from 31 per cent to 36 per cent of the average monthly wage, whereas temporary disability benefits were about 95 per cent of the average wage'.[10]

As economic conditions began to improve under the New Economic Policy, social security doctrine began to be matched more with social security practice as far as wage-earners were concerned. Gradually the coverage for wage-earners increased so that the state scheme covered 5½ million people in 1924, 8½ million in 1926 and almost 11 million in 1928. This was due partly to legal extensions of the scheme's coverage and to the rise in the size of the labour force itself. The end of the New Economic Policy also saw the introduction of old-age pensions in 1928. They were payable to men and women aged 60 and 55 respectively who had employment records of twenty-five years. Prior to that, only the disabled elderly were covered. In the absence of data it is difficult to know whether this change, admirable though it was in the long term, increased the number of the elderly who qualified immediately. It is interesting, however, that though life expectancy in the Soviet Union has increased from 44 to 70 years between 1928 and today, retirement ages for both men and women have remained the same.

The New Economic Policy was followed as we saw in the last chapter by the first Five Year Plan which involved a relentless drive towards heavy industrialisation and collectivisation of agriculture. Inevitably this economic policy affected the social security system. The general effect was to make insurance benefits subservient to the drive towards industrialisation. The tone of this new relationship between insurance benefits and labour was best expressed by N. Shvernik, the Commissar of Labour, in his address to the Trade Union Congress in 1932:

> Bureaucracy and egalitarianism must be eradicated from social insurance. We must re-construct the whole social insurance practice in order to give the most privileged treatment to shock workers and to those with long service. The fight against labour turnover must be put into the forefront. We shall handle social insurance as a weapon in the struggle to attach workers to their enterprises and strike hard at loafers, malingerers and disorganizers of work.[11]

This new relationship between social insurance and labour was designed to achieve three inter-related objectives which, in turn, would facilitate industrial growth. First, to increase the supply of labour. The drive towards heavy industrialisation depended on adequate supplies of labour. The massive exodus from the countryside to the towns and the rise in the number of women workers were the two main sources for the additional labour that was needed at this time. The social insurance programme played its part in a variety of ways. The abolition of unemployment benefit in 1930 was perhaps the most important. After that date, absence from work was only acceptable to the management if the worker was ill and there was a medical certificate to prove it. Trade unions were responsible for finding employment for redundant workers though not necessarily in their trade or at their place of residence. The length of maternity benefits was reduced from sixteen weeks to nine weeks in 1938. A greater effort was made to encourage old-age pensioners to stay on at work by allowing them to keep part of their pension and, as from 1938, the entire pension in addition to their earnings from work. They were also influenced by the fact that pensions were eroded by inflation. In these and other ways social insurance attempted to assist in the government drive towards a larger industrial labour force. Second, the new social insurance policy was geared towards increasing labour discipline. Bearing in mind the influx of large numbers of peasant workers in industry, labour discipline was of particular importance to the government's industrialisation drive. The Labour Code was changed to facilitate industrial discipline. Starting in 1927 a series of measures were introduced whereby absence from work without good cause could lead to dismissal from work, eviction from any company housing and loss of other privileges the worker enjoyed as an employee of a particular firm. Work books were issued to workers in 1938 which were used to record the number and type of jobs held, and the reasons for changing jobs etc., so that management could more easily identify inadequate workers. The climax of these measures was reached in 1940, when a worker leaving his job without permission could be taken to court and sent to prison. Social insurance contributed to the drive by making entitlement to benefits dependent on the length of employment and, in some cases, on the length of uninterrupted employment. We saw earlier how entitlement to old-age pensions was made dependent on an employment record of twenty-five years. This principle was extended to sickness benefit in 1929 in a mild form and stiffened in subsequent years. The same applied to maternity benefits. Thus length of employment gradually became a condition to insurance benefit eligibility. Moreover, the Soviet Union extended further the criterion of work requirement by adding to it the requirement of uninterrupted employment. Starting with a decree in 1931 and culminating in the legislation of 1938, uninterrupted employment in the same enterprise became the main determinant of the amount of insurance benefits a worker could receive. Third, social insurance was modified to be more in line with the government's industrial priorities. People employed in industries that were central to the fulfilment of the Five Year Plans, or in hazardous or underground employment, could qualify for benefits more easily, could receive higher benefits, and were in general more favourably treated by the social insurance system than other workers.

These policy changes were accompanied by important administrative changes that were considered essential to the new role of social insurance. Until the beginning of the 1930s, social insurance was administered by government departments organised on a regional and local basis. The new role of social insurance demanded that its administration should facilitate the new policies for labour discipline, incentives and rewards. The existing administrative machinery was accused of failing to respond to this challenge and of being too concerned with the letter of the law. As Abramson put it, the existing social insurance funds

> were accused of treating all insured persons in the same way and making no distinction between workers whose work was essential to the success of the Plan, such as shock workers, and other workers, of

acting bureaucratically without contact with the working masses and of failing to fight against malingering and the constant changing of their place of work by some insured persons.[12]

In other words, the administrative system of social insurance was not following the party line and had to be changed. The decree of 1931 and 1933 transferred the administration of social insurance from government departments to the trade unions with their central, regional and local committees. The new system meant that trade union officials and members would implement social insurance in line with the party spirit on industrialisation. The local committees became a very important part of the new administration in both the payment of benefits and in the reduction of malingering. To emphasise the new importance of trade unions in social insurance, trade union members were paid higher sickness benefits than other workers. This administrative structure persists to the present day, as we shall discuss later in this chapter.

The successful completion of the Five Year Plans meant an expansion of the number of persons covered by insurance schemes: this number rose from 10.8 million in 1928 to 25.6 million in 1936 and 31.2 million in 1940. The largest proportion of this rise was the result of the increase of the number of employees but a small proportion was due to the actual extension of the scheme itself. Thus in 1937, old-age pensions were provided for salaried workers rather than for manual workers only, as was the case until then. The main population group left outside the insurance scheme were collective farmers who still had to rely on the inadequate scheme of mutual aid societies. Only certain personnel employed full-time by the collective farms were insured and these formed a very small minority of the labour force of collective farms.[13] Expenditure of social insurance grew even faster than the number of insured persons and a large proportion of this expenditure came from government funds rather than from individual firms and industries. Thus, in spite of its harsher image, the social insurance system began to be effective compared with the situation in the early 1920s, when the scheme was under a progressive ideology but lacked the resources to put ideology into practice.

The Second World War and its aftermath saw no substantial changes in social security apart from the area of family allowances. The system of mothers' subsidies introduced in 1936 for families with seven or more children was substantially extended in 1944 for demographic reasons relating to the low birth rates. The new scheme provided for lump-sum payments to a mother for the third and subsequent child, the amount of the grant increasing with each child. In addition to the lump-sum payments, monthly allowances were introduced for the fourth and subsequent children. The allowance was paid only for the ages 1-5 years of the qualifying children and they increased with each subsequent child. These allowances were paid on a more generous basis for unmarried mothers as will be discussed later in this chapter, for the scheme has remained largely the same over the years. It was a complicated scheme attempting to encourage the birth rate and to reduce any possibilities of discouraging women from working.

Changes in social security came with the death of Stalin as they did in other aspects of economic and social policy. The years between the end of the war and the death of Stalin in 1953 had been used, as we saw in the last chapter, to make the Soviet Union second only to the United States in terms of industrial and military power. One of the issues that Khrushchev singled out in his famous speech was the improvement of social security. The State Pension Law of 1956 was confined to workers and employees, thus excluding collective farmers and other self-employed persons. Nevertheless, it 'represented a genuine leap forwards' according to Madison — a view supported by all commentators on Soviet social security.[14] In general economic terms, the reform diverted some of the resources that had previously been used for industrialisation towards consumption by those out of the labour market. Four main changes were achieved through the 1956 legislation. First, the coverage of persons was extended to cover most workers and employees and their dependants. Second, the rates of benefits were substantially increased. Madison estimates that on average 'old age pensions rose 100 per cent, invalidity pensions 50 per cent and pensions for loss of the family breadwinner 64 per cent'.[15] Only family allowances were not increased. Third, benefits were made more egalitarian as between the low paid and the highly paid. The minimum pension was raised far more than the maximum pension. Fourth, the regulations concerning the coverage of the various risks included in the scheme were streamlined to reduce anomalies. Thus the new Soviet social security became comprehensive both in terms of people in the industrial sector and risks. Government funds were to be used to supplement contributions from employers. The reforms were inspired by a mixture of economic, political and welfare considerations. The emphasis was slightly different from that prevailing in the social security legislation under Stalin in the sense that the regulations were not as heavily dominated by the demands of the labour market and of the unremitting drive for heavy industrialisation.

Collective farmers were offered considerably improved social security protection under the legislation of 1964 which came into force the following year. The contrast between social security for workers and for collective farmers had become so glaring after the reforms of 1956 that it was a matter of time before something was done. The reforms of 1964 made sense not only on political and humanitarian grounds but on economic considerations as well. The government's efforts to increase agricultural production and to stem the rural migration to towns were incongruous in the light of the striking neglect of farmers in need of social security benefits. Until 1964, each farm had to make its own mutual aid provisions for its members who were old, disabled or sick. The result was that the rich farms made better provisions than other farms but even they provided benefits only to the needy who had no relatives to help them. The scheme was a form of public assistance providing lump sums in cases of desperate need. The 1964 reforms provided old age, disability, sickness and maternity benefits on a comprehensive basis to all collective farmers. The scheme was to be financed on a national basis by contributions from each farm which were to be supplemented by state grants. The level of benefits was lower than that for workers, partly because of the differences in the wages of the two groups and partly because of pension regulations.

Although no major reforms have been introduced since 1964, a number of important changes have been made, designed first to improve the position of collective farmers and the low paid, and second to give greater emphasis to the welfare rather than the economic aspects of social security. Under the first category, the improvement of the minimum wage vis-à-vis the average wage meant a corresponding improvement in the benefits of the low paid. It was also a recognition of the fact that low wages are responsible for poverty among the employed section of Soviet society. The successive improvements of the minimum amount of pension and the introduction of an income-tested family allowance scheme in 1974 were also designed to deal with poverty. A series of other measures were designed to improve the position of collective farmers: their retirement age was dropped by five years in 1967 to bring it in line with that of the workers; in 1970, the rules for the payment of sickness benefit to collective farmers were made almost the same as those applying to workers; and in 1971, similar changes were introduced to the rules relating to the payment of pensions. Under the second category, the two most important changes were the abolition of the length of employment as a condition for maternity benefit eligibility in 1973 and the change in the qualifying conditions for sickness benefit in 1975, so that those with three or more children can now receive their full earnings irrespective of their length of employment period. These and other changes are indications that the Soviet authorities have realised that a strict insurance scheme cannot abolish the problem of poverty. We shall return to this theme in the final section of this chapter.

The insurance system today

The social security system of the Soviet Union, like that of other countries, is very complex because it attempts to satisfy the varying needs and demands of different population groups at a level which the country can afford and in a way which the country can accept politically. The discussion in this section will look at the main features of the system — leaving out a great deal of the detailed discussion on rules and regulations. Table 2.2 gives a breakdown of expenditure on the various benefits.

TABLE 2.2
Composition of social security expenditure

Type of benefit	1960 % of total	1970 % of total
Sickness and maternity benefit	21.8	25.5
Retirement and disability pensions	73.0	72.6
Family allowances	5.2	1.9
TOTAL:	100.0	100.0

Source: ILO, *The Cost of Social Security 1966-1971,* Geneva, 1976.

Retirement pensions
Retirement pensions are by far the most expensive benefit in the country's social security system. The first general qualifying condition is that a person must have reached a certain age — 60 for men and 55 for women. The second is that a certain work record prior to retirement must have been achieved. For the full pension a record of 25 years of employment for men and 20 years for women is required. For the minimum pension, the length of employment required is 5 years for both sexes. Lengths of employment period between the minimum and the maximum qualify for corresponding amounts of pension. Since the Soviet Union requires no insurance contributions from the insured population, there is no contribution condition as such for qualifying for

44

old-age pensions or for any other social security benefits. The third general qualifying condition is that the person must have retired from work, though this condition is waived for many groups of workers. The result of these qualifying conditions is that the majority of the Soviet population today qualify for a retirement pension, particularly since years of employment include service in the armed forces and, where the individual had been in employment, years spent in higher education. The population groups likely not to qualify are women who enter employment late in their life, people who never enter the labour force because of some form of disability, those who work part-time who are mainly women, and some ex-collective farmers whose overall employment record may be satisfactory but who have not worked long enough in either the state or collective farm sector. These general qualifying conditions, however, are modified in a variety of ways designed to reward the person's individual contribution to the economic welfare of society and to encourage the working population to take up employment in difficult occupations or regions. Thus men who have worked under conditions deemed dangerous, i.e. underground or unhealthy, can retire at the age of 50. Men or women employed in occupations deemed arduous can retire at the age of 55 and 50 respectively. For both the dangerous and the arduous early retirement qualification, people must have worked for at least half of the years needed to qualify for a pension in those occupations. Men who have worked for at least 20 years and women for 15 years in the north or other regions of the country with severe climatic conditions can retire 5 years earlier. Women who have brought up five or more children to the age of 8 and who have worked for at least 15 years can retire at the age of 50. Blind men and women who have worked for 15 and 10 years respectively can retire 10 years earlier. These are some of the main ways in which the retirement age is lowered in accordance with the person's previous employment history.

The retirement qualification is also waived in different ways for different population groups. For both social and economic reasons, Soviet workers are encouraged to continue working beyond retirement age. The expectation of life at pensionable age is 16 years for men and 25 years for women, with the result that pensioners constituted 16 per cent of the entire Soviet population in 1970, three-quarters of whom were women. The rise in the proportion of the elderly and the relative improvement of retirement pensions over the years has meant a greater financial burden on the country's resources. For political and other reasons, the Soviet Union finds it difficult to ease the problem by raising retirement ages.

The 1964 act abolished the earnings rule for all persons who continue working beyond retirement age on collective farms or state farms. It was a measure motivated by both welfare and economic considerations

— an effort to stem the tide of rural emigration to the towns. The 1956 act, which related to workers and salary earners, was less generous and it was modified several times during the 1960s. An Order of the Council of Ministers of the USSR in December 1969 consolidated previous legislation and relaxed considerably the earnings rule for workers. The order provides for the payment of the whole pension in addition to wages in some occupations and for 50 per cent of the pension in other occupations. For those employed in the difficult climatic regions of the country, the 50 per cent entitlement is raised to 75 per cent. Production workers, foremen, postmen, rural school teachers, retail trade workers, etc., can keep their whole pension. Pensioners who had been employed in dangerous or arduous occupations can keep half of their earnings from work.[16] In all cases, however, if the combined sum of the pension and earnings from work exceeds 300 roubles a month, the earnings rule is applied and the pension is reduced accordingly. It is difficult in the absence of published statistics to know the effect of this ruling but, bearing in mind that the average wage was 150 roubles per month in the mid-1970s, it seems unlikely to affect many working pensioners.

People who continue working beyond retirement age not only receive their wages but they also qualify for a small addition to their pension when they eventually retire. In spite of all these measures, the proportion of all the elderly at work in 1975 was only 25 per cent though 50 per cent of those reaching retirement age in that year stayed on at work. Clearly the proportion of pensioners at work is high during the immediate post-retirement years but it declines thereafter. It is also clear that the improvement in the level of pensions is one of the main reasons for the decline in the proportion of the elderly at work. In 1956 the proportion of the elderly at work was 60 per cent but, following the improvements in pensions of that year, the corresponding proportion dropped to 20 per cent in 1958.[17] The proportion declined to 9 per cent in 1961 and rose in the late 1960s and 1970s following the relaxation of the earnings rule. Efforts are also being made to increase the range of suitable employment for pensioners with reduced working capacity. In an interesting article a Soviet author acknowledges the problems involved in increasing the proportion of the elderly at work.

The relatively high level of pensions is not conducive to large scale labour force participation by the elderly, particularly since the absence of working conditions corresponding to their special needs could harm their health. It is to a great extent by creating such conditions that a larger number of pensioners with reduced working capacity will be encouraged to continue working.[18]

Retirement pensions are related to previous gross earnings. Those who satisfy the employment conditions to the full receive a pension which is a proportion of their average earnings over the last year of employment or the best five consecutive years among the last ten years, whichever is the higher. By basing the amount of pension on recent earnings it is hoped to provide a pension which is closely related to the pensioner's standard of living. The percentage of earnings received in pension, however, ranged from 100 per cent for those whose earnings are very low to 50 per cent for those whose earnings are higher than about three-quarters of the average wage. Pensioners who were employed in dangerous occupations receive a 5 per cent addition to their pension. Those who satisfy only the minimum employment conditions receive a reduced pension — 25 per cent of the pension they would have received had they satisfied the full criteria. Similarly, people who satisfy employment criteria between the minimum and the full receive pensions according to their number of years of employment. In addition to the pension that a person qualifies for, there are two supplements. Those who work beyond the retirement age receive a small addition to their pension. Secondly, those with dependants who are not in employment or who do not receive a pension on their own work record receive fixed additions to their pension — 10 per cent of the pension for one dependant and 15 per cent for two or more dependants. These are very modest additions when compared with the situation in Great Britain, where a pensioner receives a 60 per cent addition to his pension for a dependent adult — usually a spouse.

How adequate are retirement pensions in the USSR? It is safe to state that most people in employment, apart from married women working part-time and the ex-collective farmers, qualify for the full pension. Since the level of pension is not totally inversely related to the level of previous earnings and since there are minimum and maximum levels, pension inequalities are lower than income inequalities during working life. Thus the minimum pension is about one-third of the average wage, whilst the maximum pension is about 90 per cent of the average wage. The average pension that people qualify for is now about 50 per cent of the average wage. Bearing in mind that there are no occupational pensions in the Soviet Union, retirement pensioners have to rely primarily on their state pension if they are not working. It is thus clear that pensioners who were in low-paid occupations must receive pensions which are even less adequate for a decent standard of living than their wages were, unless they continue working. Those who continue working can find themselves for a few years at least better off than before they retired. As Mandell points out, it is usually low-paid women who can benefit most from this situation.

The most important practical meaning of the job-plus-full-pension provision is that large numbers of women who came into the labor force from the countryside with only three or four years of schooling before or during World War II, and who never upgraded themselves above the minimum wage, are able to double their income attaining a living standard they never previously knew.[19]

The three main weaknesses of the Soviet pension scheme are that the minimum pension is too low when compared with the average wage; that allowances for dependants are too slight; and, above all, that pensions are not raised automatically in line with the rise in either prices or wages. The minimum pension is raised from time to time but this does not affect those pensions above the minimum which are still inadequate in amount. The rise in wages over the years must mean that pensions in payment must vary in amount considerably since the pension formula leans heavily on previous earnings, even after taking into account the fact that there is a minimum and a maximum pension. It is true that prices and wages do not rise so sharply in the Soviet Union as in capitalist countries, but even then the hardship suffered by the very old pensioners may be considerable, especially bearing in mind the improved longevity of old people. Another outcome of the present system is that pensions of highly-paid workers of an early generation may end up by being smaller than those of low-paid workers who retired recently.

Disability pensions

'Pension entitlement in the USSR has its origin in labour', comments a Soviet author.[20] This principle applies to all types of pensions and other insurance benefits not only in the USSR but in all other countries as well in different ways. It follows naturally from the fact that insurance benefits are designed not only to provide an income to a person out of work but also to ensure that this is done in such ways that the needs of the labour market are safeguarded. It is only when the needs of the labour market dominate that benefits become unduly complicated and this is the case with disability pensions in the Soviet Union. The payment of a disability pension depends on five main factors. First, the person's previous earnings from work. The pension formula is weighted in favour of the low paid as it is for retirement pensions. Second, the degree of disability. Disabled pensions are divided into three classes depending on the severity of the disability suffered. Class 1 includes totally disabled people requiring constant attendance. Class 2 other totally disabled persons, and class 3 the partially disabled. Classes 1 and 2 qualify for the same pension but an addition of 15 per cent of the pension is made for class 1 persons to pay for their care. The first two classes not only qualify for a higher pension than class 3 but they also receive supplements for any dependants they may have in similar ways to retirement pensioners. Third, the number of years of employment prior to disability. The qualifying period of employment is related to the age of the worker when disability occurred. The younger the worker the fewer the years of previous employment required, and vice versa — the older the worker, the greater the number of years of employment required to qualify for disability pension. Thus, at age 25, three years of employment are required while at age 55 sixteen years are needed. No qualifying years of employment are needed if disability occurred before the age of 20 if the person was in the labour force. In spite of this complexity the number of qualifying years of employment required is not excessive and most disabled people would qualify. Fourth, whether the disability was the result of an accident at work or of an occupational disease, or whether it was the result of an ordinary illness or accident. Industrial disability is treated more favourably than civil disability; no employment qualifying period is required and the amount of pension paid is higher. Thus pensions for industrial disability range from 65 per cent to 100 per cent of wages, depending on the disablement class; pensions for civil disability range from 45 per cent to 85 per cent of wages. In addition there is no earnings rule for the industrially disabled, while pensions of other disabled persons are reduced according to the size of their wages, if any. Fifth, the type of employment a person was in when disability occurred can affect the size of the pension for both industrial and civil disability. People employed in underground, unhealthy or very difficult occupations receive a small supplement to their pension.

In all these ways entitlement to disability pensions as well as the size of the pensions are affected by the person's place in the labour force. This rather intricate and sharp connection of pensions to work has meant that the disabled are treated less favourably than the elderly. Thus none of the totally disabled, unless they suffer from industrial disability, receive a pension equivalent to 100 per cent of their previous wages as can be the case for the low-paid worker in retirement. Similar observations apply to the highly paid and other workers. Madison summarises this as follows: 'For the average worker the pension he would receive in case of total disability would be about two thirds of what he would be entitled to as an old age pension beneficiary.'[21] This unfavourable treatment of the disabled vis-à-vis the elderly is due to the fear that generous treatment of the disabled, particularly of the partially disabled, can undermine work incentives. It is, of course, a feature of the social security system of most countries.

Survivors' benefits

Soviet legislation defines very broadly the family circle of persons who can be entitled to a pension as a result of the death of the family bread-winner. It can cover brothers, sisters, parents, as well as spouses and children. In this discussion, however, we shall refer only to widows' benefits for they are by far the most common and most important ones.

A widow is entitled to a benefit for herself only if she is looking after a child under the age of 8 or if she becomes disabled within five years of the death of her husband or reaches retirement age within the same period. In other words, unless a widow has children under the age of 8, she is unlikely to qualify for a pension and even when she does qualify she will lose the pension for herself when the child reaches the age of 8. The child's pension, however, continues to be paid until the child reaches the age of 16 or until the child completes full-time education or indefinitely where the child becomes disabled before that age. The implicit assumption of the scheme is that widows should start going out to work as soon as possible. The right to a pension simply because a woman is the widow of an insured person is not recognised as such. It is an attitude reminiscent of the Beveridge Report in the UK which commented that: 'There is no reason why a childless widow should get a pension for life; if she is able to work, she should work.'[22]

Apart from benefits for widows whose husbands died as a result of an occupational disease or an industrial accident, other widows' benefits are subject to a satisfactory employment record on the part of the deceased husband. The employment qualifying conditions are the same as those for a retirement or disability pension. Thus a widow will receive a pension for herself and her children if, at the time he died, the husband was either receiving or was eligible for a retirement or disability pension. Thus most widows with children under the age of 8 will qualify for a benefit.

The amount of pension is related to either the retirement or disability pension but it is lower than either. The cause of death, the nature of employment and the earnings of the deceased husband will affect the size of the pension. It is thus difficult to be precise about the size of widows' pensions. Nevertheless, a widow whose husband died as a result of an ordinary illness and who was receiving the average wage will qualify for a pension for herself equivalent to 20 per cent of the average wage or about one-third of the retirement pension of her deceased husband. The same widow with two children under the age of 8 will receive a total benefit which only equals the retirement pension of her husband. Clearly widows must establish a right to their own retirement pension through their own work if they are to reduce the risk of spending their old age in poverty.

This emphasis on widows going to work and maintaining themselves and their children is also reflected in the rule that widows' benefits, excepting industrial widows' benefits, are lost when the widow takes up paid employment. It is an attempt to encourage widows not only to go out to work but to take up full employment. On the positive side, provisions for nursery facilities in towns with means-tested fees make it that much less difficult for widows to go out to work and to look after their young children as well. The financial position of other one-parent families is even more insecure than that of widows, for there is no general benefit for them apart from the special scheme of child allowances discussed below. A divorced or separated husband is expected to contribute 25 per cent of his earnings to his ex-wife if she looks after one child, one-third of his earnings for two children and one-half for three or more children. Only a court order can reduce these amounts, and this is usually in cases where the father has a new family. The fact that all people in employment are state employees makes the enforcement of maintenance orders easier than it is in capitalist societies. On the other hand, remarriage rates are high and the possibilities of the maintenance amounts being reduced are correspondingly high. In the absence of any data it is difficult to know how useful this system of maintenance orders is to one-parent families.

Sickness benefit
Sickness benefit is earnings related and it is paid according to four main conditions. First, the cause of incapacity, i.e. occupational or non-occupational. Benefit for occupational sickness or accident is 100 per cent of the previous wage without further qualifications. Benefit for non-occupational sickness or accident depends on the other three factors. Both types of sickness benefit are paid from the first day of absence from work until the sick person is well enough to return to work or until he is deemed to be disabled, in which case the benefit will be paid according to the regulations discussed earlier. Second, the benefit rate is related to the length of uninterrupted employment. The term 'uninterrupted' means employment with one or more employers which did not involve unemployment of more than one month. Clearly this is intended both to promote and to reward stability of employment. People with continuous employment of over 8 years receive 100 per cent of their earnings from work; 5-8 years 80 per cent; 3-5 years 60 per cent; 3 years or less 50 per cent. People aged under 18 years receive 60 per cent of their earnings irrespective of length of employment. The sickness period does not constitute a breach of continuous employment but it is rather considered as part of employment. On the whole, these are generous conditions for generous benefits.

Third, the rate of benefit takes into account family responsibilities. In families where there are three or more children under the age of 16, or 18 if a student, sickness benefit amounts to 100 per cent of previous earnings. Fourth, non-trade union members receive only one-half of the benefit they are entitled to. This is not an important disqualification, however, since practically all workers belong to trade unions. Benefit rates for collective farmers are 10 per cent lower, partly because of the greater revenue they have from their private plots of land than other workers. Moreover, sickness benefit for collective farmers is restricted to four months continuous incapacity or otherwise to five months in any calendar year. Sickness benefit in the Soviet Union has always been closely linked with the person's employment history. Not only is the amount of benefit related to the length of service but workers who are dismissed for labour indiscipline must serve six months' continuous service in their new employment before they can qualify for sickness benefit. On the positive side, sickness benefit is also paid sometimes to people who have to be absent from work in order to look after their family for seven to ten days. Similarly, sickness benefit is paid to workers who, due to illness, were transferred to low-paid jobs. In such cases, the amount of benefit is enough to cover the difference between the old and the new wage for a period of two months. In both negative and positive ways, sickness benefit tries to deal with employment and labour discipline issues. Medical certificates are necessary as proof of illness. A certificate is valid for the first three days after which the patient's doctor can issue a further certificate for three more days. After that certification is granted by senior doctors involving frequent medical examinations. As Ryan points out, this hierarchical form of certification is designed to reduce absenteeism from work but inevitably such a strict control of certification will cause irritation to members of both the medical profession and the general public.[23] Ryan's data from several local studies also show that the number of days lost through sickness absenteeism was higher in 1970 than in 1960 suggesting that stricter certification is no panacea to work absenteeism.

Maternity benefits
Regulations for the payment of maternity benefit were relaxed considerably in 1973 with the result that income insecurity, as a result of childbirth, has been reduced in the Soviet Union. All women workers, irrespective of length of employment, receive a maternity allowance for eight weeks prior to and eight weeks after the birth of their child. In cases of twin birth or of complicated confinements the period is extended by two weeks. The amount of maternity allowance is equal to

100 per cent of the woman's earnings from work. The scheme applies to both workers and collective farmers.

In addition to the paid maternity leave, women are entitled to unpaid leave until the child's first birthday. Though this may not be particularly useful to all women, it is important to those who would find it difficult to obtain any employment or employment of equivalent status. Currently, the Soviet Union is considering whether to follow the example of some of the other east European countries – Czechoslovakia, Hungary and the GDR – which pay a small monthly allowance for one year to mothers who decide to stay off work and look after their child. This will reduce some of the obvious pressures on women to return to work so soon after the birth of their child. To be effective, however, the allowance has to be higher than that currently paid in the other eastern European countries and this has clear cost implications. A maternity grant is also provided for the birth of each child to low-paid employees who satisfy certain easy employment conditions. The amount of the grant is so small that it does not by any means cover the usual expenditure incurred by the birth of a child.

TABLE 2.3
Child allowances

	Grant at birth	Monthly allowance
For the first and second child	-	-
" " third "	20 roubles	-
" " fourth "	65	4
" " fifth "	85	6
" " sixth "	100	7
" " seventh and eighth"	125	10
" " ninth and tenth "	175	12.5
" " eleventh and subsequent child	250	15

Source: K. Boitsov, Benefits for Mothers and Children, *International Social Security Review,* vol. XVII, nos 8-9 August-September 1964.

Child allowances
The child allowances scheme introduced in the 1940s is still in force today in spite of its obvious drawbacks. It consists of a combination of grants and monthly allowances of very modest amounts heavily weighted in favour of large families. Even for such families, however, the allow-

ances are grossly inadequate and they are paid only during the child's first five years. It is assumed that after that both parents will be in employment to support their children. The amounts shown in Table 2.3 were in force in the early 1960s as well as in the mid-1970s.

Unmarried mothers are paid additional allowances to the above: 5 roubles for one child, 7.50 roubles for two children and 10 roubles for three or more children. These additional allowances continue until the child's 12th birthday.

The decline in the number of children per family since the last war had meant that a large proportion of families, particularly in the towns, had less than three children and were not therefore entitled to monthly allowances. Many such families were of low-paid workers. It was partly for this reason that the family income supplement was introduced in 1974. It provides a supplement of 12 roubles per month per child until the child's 8th birthday to those families whose per capita income is less than 50 roubles a month. The new scheme 'virtually doubled the number of children covered – the proportion rising to 37% of all children under age eight – and involved a fivefold increase in total expenditure'.[24] Welcome though this scheme is for the low-paid families, the amount of the allowance is still too small and it stops too early in the child's life.

Public assistance today

Public assistance schemes perform different functions in different societies. They can act as a 'topping-up' system for cases where insurance benefits may, for a variety of reasons, be inadequate. They can act in a temporary 'substitute' capacity where a person may have exhausted his right to a short-term insurance benefit. Or they can act in a permanent or semi-permanent 'replacement' capacity where a person may not have qualified for an insurance benefit. The extent to which assistance is being used in advanced industrial societies may be an indication both of the inadequacies of the insurance system, as well as the humane attitude of society towards its weakest members. Societies with good insurance schemes can also have comprehensive assistance schemes for those who, for a variety of reasons, fall through the insurance net.

The Soviet insurance scheme is clearly comprehensive but it undoubtedly leaves a variety of groups either partially covered or not covered at all. For these groups a comprehensive public assistance scheme is necessary to provide allowances according to their circumstances. No such scheme exists in the Soviet Union. Spouses, parents, children and grandchildren are legally required to support their relatives who are in financial need. Thus old or disabled people in need must be supported by their family; only if this is not possible will the state provide help. A

Soviet authority put it this way when discussing retirement pensions:

> If a person has not completed the requisite minimum period of
> service, his family may be compelled by law to provide for his main-
> tenance in his old age. If he has no relative who can help him he may
> receive benefits in cash or kind under the social assistance pro-
> gramme.[25]

In the case of deserted wives or divorced wives with children, the husband is legally expected to maintain them, though there are no statistics
to show how effective the scheme is.

Assistance is the responsibility not of the central government but of
the individual republics or, in the case of collective farmers, of the
collective farm. Inevitably there will be variations but, more important,
the benefits provided are of residual amounts. For old people lump-sum
grants are paid from time to time to meet exceptional needs. Disabled
people of categories 1 and 2 are entitled to small monthly allowances
paid out of republic funds – again if there are no liable relatives. The
scheme is so inadequate that it is hardly mentioned in official publications on social security.

Old and disabled people in need can apply for admission to institutions. Very often old age and disability coincide and many of the
inmates of institutions are the infirm elderly. The availability of institutional facilities is inadequate on a national basis and most of them are
concentrated in the Russian Republic. As Madison observes, 'waiting
lists of those seeking entry into institutions are common in most
republics'.[26]

An assessment of the system

Social security in the Soviet Union has expanded considerably since the
Revolution. But has this expansion been along the lines laid down by
Lenin in his speech which was quoted at the beginning of this chapter?
Lenin's first principle of a socialist social security system was that it
should cover all types of incapacity which lead to an interruption or
cessation of earnings. His list of risks was the same as that used by
social reformers in western European societies and which was partly
implemented by some of these countries at that time. With the exception of unemployment, the Soviet system of social security today
provides for all the risks in Lenin's list.

Unemployment benefit was abolished in the Soviet Union in 1930,
partly as a result of the success of the first Five Year Plan in reducing
unemployment, but largely as a result of the government's drive to

increase work incentives and labour discipline. Unemployment has come to be dealt with by the country's economic planning policies rather than by its social security system. The Soviet constitution guarantees everyone the right to a job and it likewise expects everyone to work unless there are officially acceptable reasons. To some observers this is a harsh and dictatorial policy; to others it is a realistic and humane attempt by a government to harness the work potential of all its members to the benefit of all. Such a policy means in practice that apart from frictional and voluntary unemployment, people need not fear being out of work, even at the cost of industrial efficiency at times.

Contrary to a widely held view, Soviet workers do not have to stay at their jobs and direction of labour is confined to graduates of higher education for periods up to two years. Lack of enthusiasm for work exists in the Soviet Union too, as the following letter to *Pravda*, 4 December 1978, shows:

Zakharchenko is a mechanic by training, a vocational technical school graduate. But since 1971 his work record has been dismal. He has done stints at the local tobacco experimental station, a few days at a time. A couple of times he has joined moonlighters on odd jobs that paid well — digging a well, building a fence. But basically he lives on his mother's and grandmother's farm wages which are rather generous nowadays (a total of 423 roubles in September). And the warm Crimean climate is there for the having, of course, whether one works or not.

Some five years ago, Slavik Zakharchenko became a husband and father, but no change in his attitude ensued: he only switched his dependence to his wife. Before long he moved back home but he didn't register his whereabouts or take a job and his wife has sought alimony payments in vain ever since.

During the harvest season this year, the farms in Bakhchisarai District brought more than 2,000 city dwellers out to help with the work. Zakharchenko, meanwhile, headed for Leningrad to visit and have a good time. True he has been warned repeatedly to find employment, and repeatedly and politely he has promised he will. But he knows that officials are lax and administrative wheels turn slowly: Not one of the eighty Party members in the village, for example, has made an issue of his parasitic life-style.

(Concerned readers report about many other Zakharchenkos around the country, often with abandoned wives and children. There are letters from Frunze, Kharkov Province, Rostov-on-Don, Chimkent, and Voroshilovgrad Province).[27]

Labour turnover defined as the number of workers sacked for

industrial misconduct or who left their job voluntarily has increased
over the years from 15 per cent of the work force in industry in 1950,
to 21 per cent in 1970 with wide regional and occupational variations.
The length of unemployment is not nationally known but different
studies have shown that it can be substantial for a small proportion of
the unemployed. Powell cites evidence from a study in Lithuania in the
mid-1960s which showed the following picture:

> Researchers found that only 11.3% of those who changed their place
> of work did so without a break in employment. One-fourth (24.6%)
> of those who changed jobs were out of work for a week, while
> slightly more (25.4%) were unemployed for a period of one week to
> one month. An even larger number (29.7%) were without jobs for
> periods varying between one month and a year. 9% were unemployed
> for more than a year.[28]

The larger part of labour turnover is for voluntary reasons associated
with either the workplace or family problems, etc. Koszegi summarises
the evidence from a study in the Ukraine which showed that 38.3 per
cent of workers who left their jobs did so because of dissatisfaction with
working conditions; 15 per cent because of dissatisfaction with pay and
the remaining 46.7 per cent because of personal problems at home.[29]
The rise in educational standards, the improvement in wages and the
shortages of labour will most probably combine to increase even
further the extent of voluntary unemployment. The absence of unemployment benefit will inevitably cause hardship to some of the unemployed and will force others to take up jobs they do not like. All that
exists to deal with economic insecurity is the payment of training allowances for a period of three months to redundant workers who agree to
be retrained.

These are the weaknesses of the Soviet method of dealing with the
unemployed. Unlike capitalist societies, however, it does not use unemployment as a means of managing the economy. The position in
advanced capitalist societies where thousands of workers are thrown out
of work and are offered unemployment benefit grudgingly in order to
improve industrial efficiency and private profits is equally undesirable,
if not more so. In a comparison of social security in socialist and capitalist societies, Minkoff and Turgeon conclude as follows with regard to
unemployment benefit:

> When one considers the treatment of the unemployed in the capitalist
> countries, any criticism made of the Soviet arrangement pales into in-
> significance. Jobs are preferable to monetary benefits in all respects,
> as many Westerners are sadly learning today — preferable in terms

of human dignity, feeling of self-worth and psychological well-being.[30]

Neither eastern nor western European societies have yet found a way of combining full employment with industrial efficiency and with a humane and generous treatment of the unemployed.

Table 2.4 summaries the main ways in which the Soviet system of social security attempts to strengthen the efficiency of the labour market. A similar table can be constructed for capitalist countries as well. Both types of countries are afraid that a generous treatment of the unemployed can undermine work incentives in spite of the failure of social science research to uncover such a relationship.

TABLE 2.4 Social security and the labour market

Aim	Positive measures	Negative measures
Distribution of labour	Easier qualifying conditions and higher amounts of benefit for those working in certain jobs or in certain parts of the country	Absence of unemployment and of assistance benefits
Discipline of labour		Qualifying conditions for benefits. Use of trade unions as administrative agents. Absence of unemployment and assistance benefits.
Quality of labour	Training and re-training benefits	
Quantity of labour	Payment of full or part of retirement pension in addition to earnings from work. Retraining benefits.	Absence of unemployment and assistance benefits. Low benefits for widows.

Though Lenin's list of risks for social security has been largely implemented, the system of social security has failed to respond to changes in society which create new risks needing social security provision. Perhaps the most potential addition to the list of risks for social security provision other than widowhood is family break-up. About one-tenth of all families in the Soviet Union are one-parent families according to the

1970 census, and the size of the group is likely to increase particularly in the urban areas. The absence of an adequate assistance scheme makes the financial situation of such families even more difficult. The Soviet Union today places as much emphasis on the family as any advanced capitalist society and the prospects of making adequate provision for one-parent families are, therefore, equally slim.

Lenin's second principle was that all wage-earners should be covered by the country's social security system. After many ups-and-downs and about-turns, the Soviet social security system has come to fulfil this principle. Though there are no omissions as such there are, however, exclusions which are inevitable once the payment of benefit is dependent on the satisfaction of certain employment conditions. As was pointed out earlier in this chapter, these conditions are, on the whole, generous and most people will meet them. There must, however, be a small number of people who either do not qualify for one of the various benefits or who qualify for reduced benefits. This is an inherent problem of all social insurance systems today, however comprehensive they may appear in statute. The recent changes in the rules governing the payment of maternity benefit are a welcome break from the stranglehold of the insurance principle. If this were to be extended to cover all benefits — it already covers industrial injury as well — it would be a major innovation and a socialist one at that. It would make the Soviet system of social security truly different from that of welfare capitalist countries.

We have already referred to the early abandonment of Lenin's principle that benefits should equal a person's wages. Such a principle is only socialist in nature if wages are not too unequal, as they are in the Soviet Union today. The present method of calculating the level of benefits is similar to that of welfare capitalist societies in that it attempts to reconcile conflicting principles. On the one hand it attempts to reflect previous wages, but on the other it attempts to reduce inequalities in benefits by weighting the benefit formula in favour of the low paid. The distinctive feature of the Soviet system is that it also attempts to reflect the demands of the labour market by providing slightly higher benefits for people in difficult and unhealthy occupations. It is this aspect among others that led Rimlinger to declare that 'No other country has exploited to such a high degree the engineered dependence of the individual on the state and turned welfare programs into such blatant instruments of political propaganda'.[31] Such a view ignores the fact that capitalist societies too use the social security system in similar ways and they also provide a range of occupational benefits which are designed to perform the economic and political functions of the state social security system. The main difference is that while the Soviet system rewards labour in difficult and unhealthy occupations, the occupational schemes of capitalism reward middle-class and white-collar labour.

The Soviet social security system, in line with Lenin's principles, expects no contributions from the insured population. The insurance scheme for workers and employees is financed from a central fund made up of contributions by enterprises amounting to between 4.4 per cent and 9 per cent payroll, according to the enterprise. The receipts of this fund are always insufficient to meet the necessary expenditure and they are supplemented by the state to the tune of 50 per cent of all expenditures. The system for collective farmers is financed out of two central funds, both heavily subsidised by the state. The first fund covers expenditure on old-age and disability pensions and its income is derived from contributions from collective farms amounting to 5 per cent of each farm's gross annual income. The state subsidy to this fund has increased recently – an indication of the relative improvement of pensions for collective farmers. In 1965, 62 per cent of its income was derived from contributions by collective farms; the remaining 38 per cent from state subsidies. In 1970 the figures were 40 per cent and 60 per cent respectively.[32]

Sickness and maternity benefits are financed out of a separate fund made up of contributions at the rate of 2.4 per cent of the sum paid in wages by each collective farm but with no subsidy from the state. In brief, social security in the Soviet Union is financed equally by all employing enterprises and by the government on a pay-as-you-go basis.

There appears to be little serious discussion on the vertically distributive effects, if any, of this form of financing. It seems to be taken for granted that social services, by the mere fact that they try to meet people's needs on a universal basis, are reducing income inequalities. Thus Rzhanitsina, starting from the basic premise that in a socialist society 'the fundamental form of distribution is remuneration in accordance with the quantity and quality of work done' proceeds to argue that the operation of the social services reduces the inequalities of the wage system.[33] Yet it is not all that clear that the method of finance of social security encourages vertical redistribution of income. The state subsidy amounting to about 50 per cent of the total expenditure has, at best, neutral effects. In 1965, only 7.5 per cent of government revenues were from direct taxation, which is not very progressive in nature; 37.8 per cent were from indirect taxation which is regressive; 30.2 per cent from the profits of state enterprises which is progressive and the remaining 24.5 per cent from a variety of undifferentiated sources.[34] The redistributive nature of a social security system depends also on the type of benefits provided. Bearing in mind that benefits are earnings-related, that the better paid live longer to draw retirement pensions and that there is no unemployment and assistance benefits which usually benefit the low paid, the overall conclusion must be that the Soviet social security system is either regressive or neutral. The main advantage of the system of finance of the Soviet social security system is that it is administratively simpler than the system of insurance contributions adopted by capitalist societies.

In a society where all enterprises are nationalised, the arguments for financing social security partly out of employers' contributions are even less convincing than they are in capitalist societies. Presumably it is felt that employers' contributions encourage greater public awareness of costs and active participation in the running of the scheme. Such advantages, however, must be seen in conjunction with the greater administrative costs that the scheme involves compared with a scheme financed completely by the central government on similar lines to education, health, defence and other services.

Lenin's last principle of social security was that workers should pay a full part in its management. It was part of the wider theme of workers' control of industry which was one of the main Marxist themes of the October Revolution. What exists in the Soviet Union today is a complex bureaucratic government system with substantial trade union participation. The State Committee for Labour and Wages is the central body which interprets decisions of the Soviet government and issues directives which are binding to the fifteen Republic Ministries of Social Welfare. These ministries operate through regional, district and local offices. The trade unions are involved at the central as well as regional level, but particularly at the local level. All enterprises with 100 or more employees have to set up social insurance commissions made up of elected trade union members. At smaller enterprises, the existing factory and local trade union committees do the necessary work. Members of these local commissions are not paid and they do their work over and above their normal working hours. They attend very short training courses and they rely on the advice of full-time and paid union officials.

Apart from this hierarchical structure, there is a horizontal structure distinguishing long-term pensions for the old and the disabled from short-term benefits for sickness and maternity. The administration of the latter is the total responsibility of the trade unions. The local social insurance commissions decide both on the entitlement and the amount of benefit, and they keep in touch with the sick in order to be of service and to minimise abuse of the system. Pensions for the old and the disabled are determined and paid out by the Ministry of Social Welfare through its hierarchical structures. The trade unions at the local level help applicants to fill in the relevant forms, produce the necessary documents and also take part in decisions on eligibility to pensions. There is a separate system for collective farmers but this is run on similar principles. Clearly workers do not control the administration of the social security system. They only assist in its administration. Moreover, workers do not decide directly on the structure or provision of the social security system; they only elect representatives who decide on their behalf. It is a system of state managerialism similar to those in capitalist societies but with greater involvement of trade union members at the local level.

Finally, there is the question of poverty. The most important aim of the social security system of any advanced industrial country, whether welfare capitalist or state socialist, is to ensure that everyone's income does not fall below a certain level acceptable to that country. The calculation of the poverty line in the Soviet Union has been along the traditional lines of Rowntree and Beveridge in this country and of the United States Social Security Administration. It is based on the decision of experts and professionals as to what goods, what quantity and what quality of such goods are necessary to achieve a certain standard of living. A number of western writers have used this level to estimate the extent of poverty in the Soviet Union since there are no published data directly on this issue.

Poverty among the families of wage-earners is a serious problem. Adopting the official poverty line of 50 roubles per month per person and making allowances for additional income from private agricultural plots, McAuley estimated on the basis of Soviet statistics that in 1967 'some 61% of the Kolkhozniki and 24% − 26% of state employees and their dependants were below the line'.[35] Adopting the same poverty line, i.e. 50 roubles per person per month for 1965, Matthews estimated from Soviet research studies that 'by the mid-sixties a third or more of the Soviet working class could be thought of as "poor" by accepted Soviet standards'.[36] These may be approximate figures but they give an indication of the magnitude of the problem among the working population. They also raise the question of the relative generosity of the poverty line that has been used to measure the extent of poverty. In 1965, for example, the monthly average wage of all state employees was 96.5 roubles, while the minimum wage was only 40 roubles. The figures were lower for collective farmers. In such circumstances the adoption of a per capita income of 50 roubles per month as the poverty line was excessively generous and would inevitably have led to the above findings of massive poverty among wage-earners. In Britain, the government poverty line for one person constitutes only 20 per cent of average earnings and using such a measure the extent of poverty in the Soviet Union is halved. The use, however, of poverty lines that bear the same proportional relationship to average earnings in different countries creates as many problems as it solves for comparative social policy studies. It can lead to the artificial conclusion that the extent of poverty in advanced industrial societies and in developing societies is not very different.[37] Soviet writers recognise the existence of the problem of inadequate pay to meet family needs even though they do not use the concept of poverty. Thus Buzlyakov acknowledges that, in spite of all the progress made, material insecurity still exists. 'Surveys show that this material insecurity is due to the following factors: level of wages of the working members of the family, the numbers of working members and the number of dependants, particularly children.'[38]

The Soviet Union has attempted to deal with the problem of the working poor mainly by increasing the number of wives at work and by improving its child allowances scheme. About 80 per cent of women aged 16-55 are in employment but the proportion is lower among mothers with young children. It is among this group of families that poverty is most likely to be found. It seems unlikely that there is much more that could be done by way of female employment to reduce poverty among working families. It is to the system of child allowances that one must look for a solution as far as the working poor are concerned. As was pointed out earlier in this chapter, these allowances are only a modest beginning and they need to be improved substantially before they can become an effective anti-poverty measure.

Apart from poverty among the working population there is the question of poverty among the non-working section of the population — the aged, the disabled, and so on. As mentioned earlier, though the coverage of the various insurance schemes is high, it is nevertheless inevitable that a small number of people will be missed out or will qualify for only a proportion of the benefit. More important, however, is the fact that even those who qualify for the full benefit may receive an amount which is lower than that needed to reach the poverty line. This is particularly the case for those on very long-term benefits since there is no automatic adjustment of benefits to either prices or wages. Thus Madison concludes that: 'At least one half of all pensioners will have to exist on a per capita income level of less than 50 roubles a month, that is below the official "minimum of material well-being".'[39] The position can only be the same or very similar among other long-term beneficiaries. The absence of an adequate and comprehensive assistance scheme to act as a safety net for those who fall through the insurance net is the most inadequate aspect of the Soviet social security scheme. Without such a safety net, poverty among the non-working section of the population is inevitable. The Soviet Union is thus in need of an anti-poverty policy, both as regards the working and the non-working section of the population.

3

Education

Education systems in industrial societies can claim four main aims: to develop all the abilities and interests of children and young people; to promote the economic growth of the country; to influence the distribution of life chances; and to encourage the transmission of those values, attitudes and beliefs that form the dominant ideology of the country. Excessive emphasis on any one of these aims can have adverse effects on the fulfilment of the others. An educational system, for example, which is so designed and administered that it is too closely tied to the country's efforts to increase economic growth can be so constraining that it does not allow enough scope for the development of those abilities and interests that are not directly related to economic growth. Vice versa, an educational system that makes provision for the fulfilment of all types of abilities equally can reduce the amount of educational resources devoted to economic growth. Similarly, excessive emphasis on transmitting the dominant culture intact can act as a conservative force reducing the impetus for modernisation that is part and parcel of the drive towards greater economic development. Different countries have adopted different solutions to these dilemmas and their solutions have changed during the course of their history. The aims of social policy, however, should not be confused with its consequences. What an education system aims at achieving and what it actually achieves in practice are not usually identical.

The educational systems of different countries place different emphasis on each of these four main aims and they also adopt different methods in the pursuit of these aims. The discussion that follows illustrates this in the case of the Soviet Union.

Marxism and education

Though Marx and Engels did not write at length about the nature of education in a socialist society, they made several references to education in their many writings. From these and from their other writings it can be suggested that education under socialism should be universal, secular, polytechnical, participatory and environmentalist.

The concept of universal education is full of ambiguities. In its purest form it can mean that all the education facilities should be open to all without any obstacle — academic or financial. It can also mean that education should be free and compulsory up to a certain age, after which it becomes either free or selective but, in either case, not compulsory. A higher-education system which is free and open to all, irrespective of educational achievements, is substantially different from one which is free but academically selective. An academically selective higher-education system is almost bound to be more accessible to young people from middle-class than other family backgrounds. It is a good example of the inter-relationship between social institutions: so long as children are brought up in families they will be affected to a large extent by their family background, irrespective of the political system.

Marx and Engels were against religion for two main reasons. As an institution, the church under capitalism and feudalism had been part of the upper classes, resisting economic, political and social changes that favoured the lower classes. Religion tended to emphasise divine rather than scientific, idealistic rather than materialistic, explanations of events, processes and problems in society. Such types of explanation not only hindered scientific progress and economic growth but they also tended to make people less actively dissatisfied with their living conditions and hence to undermine working-class radicalism. Thus schools run by the church, or religious teaching in any schools under socialism, would hinder scientific progress and impede the socialisation of the young in socialist ideology. Marx and Engels expected that in a fully socialist society, religion would gradually disappear. This, however, would come about not only gradually but peacefully too, because, as Engels observed 'persecution is the best means of strengthening undesirable convictions. This much is certain: The only service that can still be rendered to God today is to make atheism a compulsory dogma'.[1] As the discussion below indicates, the Soviet Union has abolished religious teaching in schools but religion still flourishes in spite of the hostility of the government towards the church.

The third feature of education under socialism was polytechnicism. The Marxist notion of polytechnical education was part of the emerging emphasis during the nineteenth century on the value of vocational education. The classical Greek view of education as expressed by Plato and

65

Aristotle dominated European thinking and practice for centuries, and consisted of three main strands: education was necessary for the few only in society; it should, therefore, be liberal in nature emphasising abstract thinking of a broad non-specialist kind; and where practical education was necessary, it was not worthy of free men. This view of education was being challenged during the nineteenth century as a result of the spread of political rights and the process of industrialisation. Nevertheless, the ideal of an educated person remained that of the all-round, amateur gentleman. As Holmes points out, there were good material reasons as well as ideology that backed up this notion of education.

> To the force of ideas were, of course, added the facts of life.
> Manual work was brutish for the most part. The professional classes
> enjoyed political power and social status. Naturally the education
> which prepared young men for positions of advantage in society
> was in greater demand than that which led to drudgery, or at best,
> acceptance as a craftsman into a guild.[2]

Marx and Engels, individually and jointly, made several references to the significance of polytechnical education under socialism. Though their various references do not add up to a fully-fledged theory of polytechnical education, they do suggest strongly that the notion of polytechnical education consisted of two inter-related strands — the moral education of people in socialist societies and the encouragement of economic development. The following quotation not only indicates these two inter-related strands but it also shows Marx's indebtedness to Robert Owen's education experiments in Scotland during the early part of the nineteenth century.

> From the factory system budded, as Robert Owen has shown us in
> detail, the germ of the education of the future, an education that
> will, in the case of every child over a given age, combine productive
> labour with instruction and gymnastics, not only as one of the
> methods of adding to the efficiency of production, but as the only
> method of producing fully developed human beings.[3]

The Marxist notion of polytechnical education is inextricably linked to the broader question of the division of labour and the distinction between mental and manual labour. Polytechnical education would help to reduce the division of labour and gradually to do away with the distinction between mental and manual labour which is the ultimate feature of a truly socialist society.

Education will enable young people quickly to acquaint themselves with the whole system of production, it will enable them to pass in turn from one branch of industry to another according to social needs or the bidding of their own inclinations. It will, therefore, abolish one-sidedness in development imposed on all by the present division of labour. Thus a communistically organised society will be able to provide its members with the opportunity to utilise their comprehensively developed abilities in a comprehensive way.[4]

Similarly, Marx felt that this type of education was superior to that practised under capitalism. 'The combination of paid productive labour, mental education, bodily exercise and polytechnical training, will raise the working class far above the level of the higher and middle classes.'[5]

In spite of their strong emphasis on polytechnical education, Marx and Engels did not spell out the organisational aspects of this form of education. The result of this has been that polytechnical education in the Soviet Union has taken several forms, some of which are only marginally related to the twin strands of polytechnicism.

The emphasis on democracy and participation in schools stems not from anything that Marx and Engels wrote specifically for education but from their writings in two other areas. We have already referred to their views that workers' participation is a central feature of socialism and communism. It can justifiably be argued that they would have supported a similar form of administration in schools because of their analysis of how society functions. Their writings on the nature of man in socialist and communist societies would also have necessitated a participating form of school administration. They saw men and women in a communist society as altruistic and self-determining, without any major conflict between individual and collective interests. Such a personality could only be shaped if people had an opportunity from a very early age to participate, to have a say, in decisions affecting their everyday life.

A democratic-participatory form of schooling is not peculiar to Marxism. Many non-Marxist educational theorists outside Russia — Dewey, Montessori, Dalton, and others — and various Russian authors — Herzen, Belinsky, Ushinsky, Pisarev, Tolstoy, and others — expressed similar ideas and in more specific ways relating directly to education. It is for this reason that the writings of these non-Russian authors became so popular in the Soviet Union before the Revolution and during the 1920s.

The Marxist view of human abilities does not ignore the fact that people are born with different physiological tendencies but it insists that these are mere tendencies which can blossom or not depending on the environment. It is a dialectical materialistic view of human development which sees genetic tendencies and environmental factors constantly influencing each other. Thus the same inborn tendencies can result in different abilities depending on the environmental factors. But these inborn tendencies are not very differently distributed among infants. As Marx put it, 'The original difference between a porter and a philosopher is less great than between a watch-dog and a greyhound. The gap between them exists through the division of labour'.[6]

The concept of environmental factors is interpreted broadly to signify not only physical conditions but cultural influences as well. Moreover, both physical and cultural factors are seen in an historical perspective — influenced by the past and ever changing. Referring to Raphael's talents as a painter, Marx wrote

> Raphael, like any other artist, was conditioned by the technical advances of art that were made before his time; by the organisation of society and the division of labor in his locality; and finally, by the division of labor in all the countries with which his locality was in contact. It depends entirely on the demand for his work whether an individual like Raphael develops his talents; and this demand itself depends on the division of labor and the cultural conditions of men which develop from it.[7]

Thus the concept of ability has both an environmental and an historical character.

The next section discusses how Marx's ideas have been changed to suit the demands of economic, social and political situations. It is also worth pointing out at this stage that the Soviet Union inherited the Czarist education system and did not start with a clean slate. Inevitably, Marxist ideas had to be grafted on existing thought and practice. This, however, does not mean that there was no break with the past and that Soviet education is merely a continuation of Czarist education. Hans has expressed the view of continuity by insisting that Soviet education is not Soviet at all. Rather, 'Russian it was and Russian it remains'.[8] The view taken here is that, though the influences of Russian history and education cannot be ignored, Soviet education has developed along different lines than it would have done had Czarism continued, or rather, had the Bolshevik Revolution not taken place. As Judge has argued, the reason why changes were introduced after the Bolshevik revolution was 'primarily in order to make a Soviet system based on Marxist-Leninist principles. The very nature of the Soviet educational system has been determined by the ideology'.[9] Marxist ideology on education has not obviously been implemented in its entirety but it has exerted an overwhelming influence on the nature of the Soviet education system.

Historical development

In spite of some progress in the decades preceding the October Revolution, Russia was still a country of mass illiteracy with an outdated and class-biased education system. The literacy rate had risen from 21 per cent in 1897 to 40 per cent in 1914 and the Primary Education Act of 1908 promised free and compulsory education for the ages 8-11 to be achieved by 1922. The student population in secondary schools and in universities trebled between 1885 and 1915 and several new universities were established. The rate of progress was, however, slow and class-biased. It was too slow to satisfy the rising aspirations, and its class bias was blatant enough to attract the criticism of both revolutionaries, educational reformers and students. Moreover, progress in education was being made in the face of opposition from the established order. It was part of the class struggle that was ushering in piecemeal reforms in various aspects of life. Educational work, wrote the Webbs,

> was scarcely encouraged by the Czar, the Holy Synod and the bureaucracy, and was tolerated only as a class system on old-fashioned lines, designed mainly for the production of enough doctors, lawyers, teachers, clerical officials and other specialists for the use of the Court and the government, the nobility and the wealthy. The idea of educating the mass of the population, even as far as reading and writing, found no favour with the autocracy.[10]

A series of decrees starting from a few days after the Revolution through to the end of 1918 transformed the legal basis, the goals and the whole ethos of the education system. As with other government policies, intent never matched reality and wide variations existed throughout the country. Nevertheless, most of the reforms proved real enough in the long run and were aimed at achieving four main objectives. Universalism was the first objective. The decrees of August and October 1918 made primary, secondary and higher education free and accessible to all. Primary education was compulsory while the other two forms of education were simply made free to all. In this way it was hoped to create a unified education ladder from primary to higher education accessible to everyone irrespective of home background, sex or race. Private schools were abolished. 'The whole system of schools', writes Tomiak, 'from kindergarten to university was declared to constitute one school, one unbroken ladder'.[11] It was at this time that the Soviet Union inaugurated what may be nowadays called policies of positive discrimination. Having made entrance to universities open and free to all without any entrance examinations, it proceeded to set up in 1919 Workers' Faculties in the form of three-or four-year courses, designed to

69

prepare semi-literate workers who wished to enter university. That these courses were successful is shown by the fact that in 1925 '38.5% of all students enrolled in the universities had come from the Workers' Faculties'.[12] At the same time upper-class applicants were denied entry to universities in an effort to change substantially and rapidly the class origin and the political ideology of the intelligentsia.

The provision of universal, free and compulsory primary and secondary education, even if fully implemented, would have taken decades to solve the problem of adult illiteracy. In December 1919 a massive literacy campaign was therefore inaugurated with the personal support of Lenin, starting with the Russian Republic and spreading gradually to other parts of the Soviet Union. The literacy campaign was not only necessary for educational reasons but for political and economic considerations. A literate nation is one of the prerequisites for the building of socialism. In Lenin's words: 'An illiterate person stands outside; he must first be taught the ABC. Without this, there can be no politics; without this there are only rumours, gossip, tales, prejudices, but no politics.'[13] In spite of the vigour and the enthusiasm behind the literacy campaigns it was not until the late 1930s that the Soviet Union could show with statistics that illiteracy had been eradicated.

The second objective of the immediate post-revolution reforms was to democratise the entire educational system at all levels. The prime beneficiary of these changes was to be the individual child who would be able to develop its abilities and potentialities according to its own wishes and self-perceived interests. Both teaching methods, subject content and relationships with teachers were changed. The influence of such western European and American writers as Pestalozzi, Montessori, Dalton, Dewey and others was clear and openly admitted and appreciated by the Russians. There was also the influence of the various nineteenth century Russian education theorists mentioned earlier whose progressive ideas were similar to those of European writers. 'These Russian educators of the third quarter of the nineteenth century even contended that the school should be a place where children would be happy', writes Counts, summarising their contributions to the school experiments of the Soviet Union in the 1920s.[14] Separate subject teaching was abolished in favour of the 'project' or 'complex' method whereby children learned their history, geography, grammar, mathematics, languages, etc. through their involvement in specific projects. Pupils took a very active part in running school affairs. They were encouraged to treat their teachers as friends, calling them by their first names, rather than as distant learned disciplinarians. Individual assessment was abolished in favour of class assessment. They were expected to criticise and report on their teachers for either propagating old ideas or using old teaching methods. Children were encouraged to think and behave, not for their own individual interests as such, but as members of a group, of a class, of a socialist society. These experiments have been described as humanistic, progressive, romantic or, in the words of the Webbs, as 'joyous Bedlam', 'in which the pupils learned all sorts of things and the cleverest among them not a little, but seldom the formal lessons common to other countries'.[15] Whereas western European societies experimented with these ideas, the Soviet Union seemed anxious to apply them untested on a nation-wide basis. In practice, however, these experiments were resisted or ignored by many teachers and a large section of the public and their application was on a restricted scale, mainly in large towns.

The third objective of the educational reforms was to replace the purely academic education that prevailed in primary and secondary schools with polytechnical education. Lenin, however, though a strong supporter of this form of education was aware that the conditions were not favourable for its full implementation. In 1917 he pointed out that because of 'current, present-day deplorable reality . . . only a number of steps to polytechnical education, feasible at present' could be implemented.[16] Moreover, the uncertainty about the exact meaning of polytechnical education meant that primary and secondary schools experimented in a variety of ways, all designed to create a new attitude to mental and manual labour. Thus schools established workshops and laboratories often with the help of local industry. School children sometimes spent part of their time working in local factories or farms, or they took an active interest in local affairs and helped out where possible — in literacy campaigns for example. Kreusler's summary of the different approaches to polytechnical education during this period is indicative of this confusion.

> The meaning of polytechnicism changed several times. At the beginning it was doing any kind of manual labor necessary for the upkeep of the school, such as cleaning and repair work. For a time it was self-service; then it was participation in communal affairs; and finally it became a course in labor combined with practice in the craft shops organised in the schools.[17]

Finally, the educational changes were designed to instil into the younger generation the new communist ideology. To make this possible the close link between church and state and between schools and church was broken in 1918. Religious education in schools was banned in 1921, monasteries and church schools were closed and the new school textbooks were hostile to religion. This, coupled with the demise of Czardom and all its trappings, left the scene open to communist propaganda in schools. Politics entered into every aspect of school activity.

71

Each project and each separate course was to be permeated with ideological principles, and there was to be no purely academic activity. Activities which could not be fitted easily into this frame-work, such as playing with toys in pre-school institutions, were de-emphasised. Visitors to Soviet schools during this period remarked upon the festooning of school walls with political slogans and posters and some noted with discomfort that 'objective education' had given way to political propaganda.[18]

The politicisation of schools was also facilitated by the new family policy and the encouragement given by the state to the notion that children owed allegiance first and foremost to the state. Schools were also closely connected with the newly created youth movement — the Komsomol for those aged 16 and over, the Young Pioneers for the ages 10-16 and the Little Octoberists for children aged 8-11 years. The youth movement was in turn linked to the Communist party so that schools, directly and indirectly, explicitly and implicitly, came under the control and the daily influence of the party. All societies use their schools to socialise their children in the dominant ideology. What was striking, though understandable, in the new Soviet society was the extent to which political socialisation and party indoctrination dominated school activities. The school was openly used in the struggle against the old order and in the effort to create a new socialist society.

The 1920s were a period of experimentation and change in education as well as a period in which achievement lagged far behind official pronouncement. There were not enough buildings and many of those that existed were inadequate. Similarly, there were not enough teachers and many of the employed teachers were untrained. In the chaotic situation and the severe economic crisis of the early 1920s, the number of schools and pupils actually dropped. It was in the late 1920s that progress began even though school premises were still used in shifts and this practice continued well into the 1930s. The same problem existed in the other areas of reform. The central government lacked the authority, the administrative machinery and the resources to apply uniformly its policies for democratisation, polytechnical education and party domination of schools. As a general rule, village schools remained conservative while city schools indulged in many forms of experimentation. The country was a patchwork of varying standards, practices and ideologies varying from the traditional to the unorthodox.

The first Five Year Plan marked the beginning of important changes in educational policy. During the early years of the first Five Year Plan, polytechnical education was boosted. The new emphasis on rapid industrialisation and collectivisation provided opportunities for school children not only to work in factories and farms as part of their education but also to help out with the fulfilment of the production targets laid down under the Five Year Plan. As time went on, however, the increased involvement of school children in production began to have counter-effects and by 1931 a reaction was emerging against the new educational ideas. Four main reasons accounted for this reaction. First, enough evidence was being brought forward by diverse sources that the 'project' and 'complex' methods of teaching in schools were failing to teach children the basic skills in reading, writing and arithmatic. Schools may manage to make children happy but if they do not teach the three Rs in a society anxious to promote economic growth they fail in their economic role. Second, polytechnical education was causing too many administrative problems to both schools and industries and the educational return was not considered worthwhile. Industries had to make arrangements to educate school children either on a day basis or on shorter sessions and the economic costs of these arrangements were too heavy. Schools also complained that the equipment supplied to them by local factories for the school workshops was outdated with the result that children were taught out-of-date skills. Third, teachers complained that the free-discipline methods used in schools meant that they had to spend an excessive part of their time trying to cope with unruly children. These problems were aggravated by the lax family policy and the war victims, both of which created a large number of children deserted, neglected or undisciplined. Finally, and perhaps most importantly, the drive towards industrialisation initiated by the first Five Year Plan showed up the inadequacies and incongruities of the education system. The inadequacies were that the school did not teach the three Rs well; that it did not teach scientific subjects well in spite of all the emphasis on polytechnical education; managers complained that the lack of individual school assessment meant that they had no way of knowing the standards of school leavers; similar complaints were also voiced by university authorities. The incongruities of the school system were that it was operating on principles and values that were diametrically opposed to those used in industry. Labour discipline, individual effort and reward according to individual work were the guiding principles of the new drive towards industrialisation. These were not compatible with the free, participatory and collective life of schools. In such a clash of ideals there was no doubt that it was the value system and the practices of the school that had to change. Moreover, the drive towards industrialisation meant a national plan carried out in all parts of the country which was seen as incompatible with local autonomy and the experimentation in schools which led to variations and unpredictability.

Of the four objectives of education reform mentioned earlier, two were strengthened — universalism and political socialisation — and two were abandoned or modified – democratisation and polytechnicisation, following the various decrees of the Central Committee of the Communist party on education during the early 1930s. The improvement in the country's economic position meant that the government could implement some of its decrees on universal education. Thus compulsory school attendance was introduced in 1930 for children aged 8-12 in rural areas and 8-14 in all urban and industrial areas. In 1943 compulsory education was introduced from the age of 7 instead of 8. Thus this period saw the consolidation of primary education both in law and in practice, particularly in the rural areas where educational facilities were so inadequate prior to the Revolution. The political socialisation of children directly through the school and through the youth movement continued as before. In fact the more rigorous school regime that was enforced in the 1930s meant a more sustained form of political socialisation of children. Similarly, the ascendancy of Stalin meant that the political culture of the youth movement was more rigid, divesting itself of the permitted differences of opinion of the 1920s. Thus both in school and in the youth movement children were under a more single-minded political ideology than before. Opposition to religious influence on the young was sustained and strengthened. The decree of 1929 codified previous regulations and prohibited the teaching of any religious subjects in all types of schools. The first Five Year Plan made it obvious that the country needed more scientists, technologists, engineers and scientifically educated workers. The Central Committee of the Communist party recognised this in 1929 and took the step of directing higher-educational institutions to begin selecting through academic competition. The open-door policy to higher education was firmly shut to the academically unqualified.

Primary and secondary schools were subject to a series of decrees that put an end to the notion of participatory democracy and polytechnical education. The decree of September 1931 set the pattern of future changes. It points out that the main weakness of the school system is the 'fact that school instruction fails to give a sufficient body of general knowledge' with the result that it fails to 'prepare for the technicums and higher schools fully literate people with a good command of the basic sciences (physics, chemistry, mathematics, native language, geography and others)'.[19] The decree then directs education authorities to remedy these deficiencies. The next step was to bring back the traditional authority of the headmaster and the teachers. The decree of 1932 stressed the importance of discipline in schools and the vital role of the teacher in enforcing discipline. Participation by children in running the school, let alone responsibility for correcting and reporting on teachers, was abandoned. Discipline was seen as important not only for its own sake, but as important to real learning. The return of traditional teaching necessitated the use of prescribed textbooks. The decree of 1933 revoked previous teaching methods and directed the use of prescribed textbooks as the basis for teaching. This meant not only uniformity in what was being taught but it also made certain the teaching of political ideology in such subjects as history, geography, etc. Uniformity in teaching necessitated uniformity in assessment. Thus 1935 saw the introduction of a uniform system of assessment of pupils ranging from the 'very bad' to the 'excellent'. Pupils graduating from the secondary school with the mark of 'excellent' could proceed to higher education without further entrance examinations. The notion of poly-technical education as understood in the 1920s was whittled away by all these changes and was officially abolished in 1937. This, however, did not mean a turn away from scientific knowledge. Rather, emphasis was placed on teaching the sciences at school in a conventional manner.

> Polytechnicism was reinterpreted to mean simply the study of the scientific subjects upon which industry is based, such as mathematics, physics, and chemistry. The curriculum of the Soviet schools contin-ues to be heavily weighted in the direction of the natural and physical sciences.[20]

It was also during this period that the work of the Soviet educationist A.S. Makarenko with delinquent and abandoned children became best known even though it began in the late 1920s. He placed a great deal of emphasis both on humane discipline and on the use of the group in re-forming and educating children in his school. Lack of discipline was considered as undesirable as excessive discipline. The group, the collect-ivity, was the medium through which pupils were educated, praised, rewarded, punished, disciplined and socialised. Makarenko's methods received widespread support and they influenced the 'Rules for Pupils' that were published in 1943. As Kreusler observes, these rules were incorporated in a new code in 1972 which 'reflects the techniques based on group activities and the traditions which developed in the course of three decades'.[21]

The changes of the 1930s have been usually described by western observers as the decline of progressive education, as a turn towards reac-tion or as a return to Czarist education. Apart from the political and scientific aspects of education the Soviet Union was, in fact, attempting to base its educational system on principles not too dissimilar to those of western European societies. The emphasis on formal teaching, on discipline and on assessment was a general feature of schools in capital-ist European countries of this period. Having decided to adopt a policy of rapid industrialisation concentrating on heavy industry, on lines very similar to the western European model, the Soviet Union had likewise to provide a school system which inculcated scientific knowledge in an orderly and predictable manner. It was amidst all these educational changes and all the other economic and political changes that the constitution of the Soviet Union was published in 1936, proclaiming that all citizens have the right to education.

> This right is ensured by universal and compulsory education; by free education up to and including the seventh grade; by a system of stipends for students of higher educational establishments who excel in their studies; by instruction in schools being conducted in the native language and by the organisation in the factories, state farms, machine and tractor stations and collective farms of free vocational, technical and agronomic training for the working people.[22]

The new drive towards curriculum uniformity, pupil discipline and rigorous assessment was maintained throughout the war and immediately after it. Thus in 1943 'socialistic' competition in schools was abolished, co-education in secondary schools was ended (to be reintroduced in 1954) and the 'Rules for School Children' were published. In 1944 a system of silver and gold medals as prizes for excellent work at the end of the ten-year school was introduced, entitling the receivers to automatic entry to higher education – a system which was discontinued in 1950. Finally, the system of repeating classes was introduced in 1946 and has remained in force to the present day. In the same year the 'Rules for Internal Order' were approved for teachers and other workers in the school. The two sets of rules for pupils and staff established what is acceptable and non-acceptable behaviour and what sanctions were to be applied when necessary. They are exceptionally strict by western European standards and they are in total contrast to the participatory regime of Soviet schools in the 1920s. Nevertheless, they reduce substantially the ambiguity that exists in advanced capitalist societies concerning the role of teachers and pupils.

War devastations meant that many schools were destroyed and others were closed with the children being evacuated to the eastern districts of the Soviet Union. A great deal of attention was given to military training in schools and to the inculcation of military, patriotic values. New types of evening schools were established in 1943 for young workers and peasants who missed out on their education on account of the war. Perhaps the most unanticipated measure was the introduction of modest tuition fees in 1940 for the last three classes of the secondary school and for higher-educational establishments. Children whose fathers were in the armed forces, war orphans, children of sick and disabled parents and, above all, children with excellent school achievement, were exempted from these fees. In spite of these exemptions, however, tuition fees must have had the effect of solidifying the Soviet social structure since it was the children of working-class parents who could not pay and who were consequently excluded from higher education. The official reason for the introduction of fees was that most parents could afford to contribute towards the education of their children. The extra income would be used by the government to improve educational provision. Widmayer adds another explanation:

> Probably a more compelling motive was the desire to bring as many new workers as possible into industry by discouraging the intellectually dull pupils from continuing general education and obliging them to enter trade schools which prepare for productive jobs in a relatively short period of time.[23]

The period between the end of the war and the death of Stalin contains no important changes in education policy. But it was a period when 'education in the Soviet Union expanded rapidly'.[24] Expenditure on education increased, school attendance rose and higher education expanded. It was a period of consolidation and expansion rather than of change and experimentation. It contained, however, the seeds of fermentation which led to changes soon after the death of Stalin. Already in 1952, at the nineteenth Congress of the Communist party, complaints were being voiced against the academic nature of education and the lapse of polytechnical education. Soon after, it was becoming clear that the expansion of secondary education was creating strains for higher education. Too many secondary graduates were chasing too few places in higher education, with the result that frustration and bribery set in. In a situation where academic secondary education is prominent and places for higher education are scarce it is inevitable that family background will play a more vital role than it normally does in deciding who secures a place in higher education. It should not have come as a surprise, therefore, when Khrushchev produced statistics in 1958 to show that a working-class and particularly a peasant-family background was highly detrimental to a young person's chances of reaching full-time higher education, particularly entrance to the prestigious universities of Moscow and Leningrad.

It was out of these strains and stresses that the Khrushchev education reforms of 1958 originated. The reforms had been widely reported in advance and had been preceded by a few measures which indicated the way policy was moving. In 1955 entrance regulations to full-time higher education were changed to the benefit of people at work. Applicants who had worked for at least two years had a quota of places allocated to them, thus freeing them from direct competition with applicants straight from school. In 1956 the system of fees for the upper grades of secondary schools was abolished thus making the whole system of education free.

The malaise, as Khrushchev saw it, went beyond the educational system itself to affect the whole way of life in a society struggling to achieve socialism.

> We still have a sharp distinction between mental and manual work . . . This is fundamentally wrong and runs counter to our teaching and aspirations. As a rule, boys and girls who have finished secondary school consider that the only acceptable path in life for them is to continue their education at higher schools. . . . Some of them consider work beneath their dignity. This scornful and lordly attitude is to be found also in some families. . . . Such an incorrect situation . . . can no longer be tolerated. In socialist society, work must be valued for its usefulness, must be stimulated not only by its remuneration but also by the high respect of our Soviet public. It must be constantly inculcated in the young people that . . . work is a vital necessity for every Soviet person.[25]

Briefly, five inter-related reasons are thought to account for Khrushchev's reforms: they were intended to provide industry and agriculture with much needed labour; to ease the pressures on full-time higher-education places; to reduce the growing gap between the proletariat and the intelligentsia or between manual and mental labour; to reduce the influence of family background on higher education; and to help students to choose a career. They are a mixture of economic, political and ideological considerations, all very difficult to achieve and all conferring different benefits to different socio-economic groups in society. Khrushchev's proposals were substantially different from the legislation that emerged later in 1958. Schwartz and Keech point out that Khrushchev's suggestions aimed at replacing full-time post-secondary education with part-time study combined with work.

> After finishing a seven or eight-year primary school, said Khrushchev, every young person should enter the labor force. Those who wished to prepare themselves for higher education could continue their studies in evening and correspondence schools. Successful students would receive two or three days released time from work to facilitate studying.[26]

The same substitution of full-time with part-time study would also take place in higher education, though not to the same extent. Only the first two or three years of higher education would be expected to be provided on part-time study while the remainder would be on a full-time basis.

The 1958 reforms made, in fact, far less drastic changes. Full-time post-secondary education continued though it was supplemented with work for short periods. The changes introduced by the reforms were as follows. First, compulsory education was to be extended by one year, i.e. ages 7-15 instead of 7-14. Second, those wishing to continue their secondary education beyond the age of 15 had three avenues open to them, all of which could theoretically lead to higher education. (a) Through a network of schools providing part-time education after working hours to young workers and farmers. (b) Through full-time secondary education lasting three years where academic teaching would be combined with work in a factory or farm. The third year was usually taken up by full-time employment. (c) Through technical schools on a full-time or part-time basis, again combining academic and practical work. Third, an extension of evening and correspondence courses in higher education and a reduction of full-time higher education.

Opposition to Khrushchev's proposals came from various quarters and it took various forms. Boiter summarises this opposition as follows:

The most vocal opposition comes from the teaching profession itself, and, somewhat surprising, it still finds cautious expression in Soviet pedagogical literature. Next, the managers of the Soviet economy are unenthusiastic about, if not openly hostile to, the parts of the reform which directly affect their enterprises. Then comes the students and parents of students, whose attitudes even Khrushchev does not try to conceal.[27]

In spite of the substantial watering down of Khrushchev's proposals, the 1958 legislation had some of the desired effect. Thus the proportion of evening and correspondence students in higher education increased from 50 per cent in 1959-60, to 60 per cent in 1965-66, whilst the proportion of full-time students declined accordingly. Also the proportion of students accepted for full-time higher education who had satisfied the work criteria increased, so that by 1964 it accounted for 64 per cent of all entrants in that year. The reforms, however, did not reduce the influence of family background on full-time higher education. It seemed that the children of the middle classes adapted themselves to the new situation and maintained their privileged position as regards entry to full-time higher education. Khrushchev's downfall inevitably meant that opposition to the reforms of 1958 increased. Apart from the objections raised earlier, new ones were being put forward in the form of 'evidence' accumulated since the introduction of the reforms. Evidence was being produced to show that failure rates and drop-out rates in higher education had risen, that standards were falling and, even worse, that young workers and farmers were not taking up places in

79

evening and correspondence courses. The scene was thus set for the dismantling of the 1958 reforms. In 1964 the three-year full-time secondary education following compulsory education was reduced to two years, leaving out the year designed for practical work. For the other forms of secondary education, practical training and work were substantially reduced. The advantages awarded to full-time higher-education applicants with work experience were reduced in 1967 with the result that their proportion fell to 30 per cent for the full-time student intake of 1967.

In spite of these changes official policy still remains committed to polytechnical education, though the emphasis now is on scientific education within schools rather than work experience outside the schools. Concern with inequality in higher education also continues but official policy as to how to deal with the problem has changed. Instead of giving preferential treatment to applicants with substantial work experience, the policy now is to provide 8-10 months' preparatory courses in higher-educational establishments for demobilised soldiers and children of peasants and workers. Their aim is similar to the Workers' Faculties of the 1920s, i.e. to prepare young people from modest backgrounds and with political commitment for higher education.

Pospielovsky states, however, that official reports show that 'at practically all the 191 institutions of higher learning where the preparatory courses were established, children of white collar workers and intellectuals have been accepted'.[28] Whatever the reasons for this the result is that the disadvantaged position of peasants and working-class applicants is unlikely to change. This situation is accentuated by the fact that middle-class applicants make much greater use of private tutors than working-class applicants. A recent study, quoted by Matthews, showed that 'about 20% of all first year students had enjoyed this, but the incidence was very much higher amongst students of "white collar" backgrounds'.[29]

A recent development that is likely to exacerbate the problems of academicism in education and inequality of opportunity even further is the expansion of the system of special schools for gifted children. Such schools for children with special aptitudes in music and dancing have long been established in the Soviet Union. The Khrushchev reforms, however, seemed to have given birth to schools for children gifted in mathematics, physics and chemistry. These schools are very selective, they are attached to universities, they take children at the age of 14 and they prepare them for university education. The success rate of these schools in university entrance examinations is superior to that of other secondary schools. Clearly this development goes against such socialist policies as polytechnical education and equality of opportunity to all children. As Tomiak remarks, the existence of such schools 'makes it clear . . . that political and scientific imperatives do not always coincide with each other'.[30]

Apart from all these changes the Brezhnev period has been one of consolidation, expansion and a few other minor reforms. The emphasis has been on improving the standard of existing services by providing more human and physical resources and making such services universally available, where relevant. Education for the age group 7-15 is now free and compulsory and it is hoped to extend the upper age by two years by the 1980s. Already substantial progress has been made in this direction, since 80 per cent of all pupils leaving school at 15 continue their education up to the age of 18 in the various types of secondary schools. The substantial expansion of nursery education has made possible the reduction of the elementary school from four to three years (ages 7-10) and the corresponding expansion of the secondary school from four to five years (ages 10-15) thus allowing more time for the study of theoretical scientific knowledge and its technological application. As the proportion of young people staying on at school until the age of 18 has risen, the pressure on higher education places has increased, for the latter has not expanded at an equally fast rate.

Description of the education system

TABLE 3.1
Number of persons attending different educational establishments

	1940	1970	1976
	(Million persons)		
Kindergarten and nurseries	1.95	9.28	11.85
General education schools	35.6	49.4	46.5
Specialised secondary schools	1.0	4.4	4.6
Higher education establishments	0.8	4.6	5.0
Vocational training schools	0.7	2.6	3.5
Skill upgrading courses	9.5	18.8	33.5

Source: Government of the Soviet Union, *USSR, 1977, Sixty Soviet Years,* Novosti Press Agency, Moscow, 1977, p.142.

The four main components of the school system are pre-school education, primary schools, secondary schools and higher education. Several of the activities of trade unions and of the youth movement have a direct educational value but these will be excluded from this discussion because education, so defined, assumes broader perspectives than this chapter envisages. Table 3.1 gives an indication of the expansion of all forms of education since the last war. Of special significance, too, is the sharp upturn in the number of young people attending vocational schools during the 1970s, though such figures are prone to be based on loose definitions that change over time.

Pre-school education

There is no doubt about the enormous growth of this sector over the last sixty years. In pre-revolutionary times the few pre-school institutions that existed were located in the large cities and served the children of the middle and upper classes. In spite of the enthusiasm of the early leaders of the Soviet Union little was done to increase such facilities during the 1920s. The growth of urbanisation and industrialisation, the rise in the proportion of married women with children at work and the improved economic position of the country are the main factors explaining the recent growth of pre-school education. Even now, however, demand exceeds supply in most parts of the country. Provision is more adequate in the large cities catering for 50 per cent to 80 per cent of the relevant age groups; it is less adequate in smaller urban areas and in rural districts in spite of the substantial effort by collective farms to improve on the situation recently. Exact figures are difficult to come by. Thus Madison estimated that in 1970 'only 50% of all urban children were attending pre-school facilities, while the figure for rural children was a low 30%'.[31] Jacoby, on the other hand, writing in 1974 estimated that 'fewer than one third of all Soviet children attend a state nursery or kindergarten'.[32]

Pre-school education is neither free nor compulsory. Parents have to pay modest fees varying according to their income. Official statistics indicate that the cost borne by the parents

does not exceed 15% to 25% of the actual cost of the child's care and 2% to 3% of the parents' earnings. A total of 25% of all children (children of handicapped parents, children from large families and children of unmarried mothers) are maintained in nurseries and kindergartens free of charge.[33]

Most pre-school institutions are provided either by the state or by enterprises or farms. They are usually run on a permanent basis though some are run at special times of the year when there is a strong demand for them, such as during the summer in rural areas.

Pre-school establishments are of two kinds: nurseries for children of 6 months to 3 years and kindergartens for children aged 3 to 7 years.

Nurseries are supervised by the Ministry of Health and they provide mainly play facilities for children. Kindergartens are supervised by the Ministry of Education and they attempt to provide some basic educational skills as well as social training in accordance with socialist principles. Soviet authorities recognise the importance of pre-school education, not only in economic terms but also for social and political considerations. Now that the family has been accepted as a desirable form of institution, pre-school education is seen as reinforcing rather than replacing family values. An official statement expresses this thus:

> An extensive development of the network of pre-school institutions, a strict scientific organisation of the collective education of children and successful achievements to this end in no way reduce the role of the family in the education of children. The family is, and remains the most important cell of society where a future citizen is moulded.[34]

In spite of the apparently impressive figures for pre-school attendance, two factors must be borne in mind in assessing their real significance. In the first place compulsory education starts at the rather late age of 7 years; and in the second place most of the children attending such establishments are in the age group 3-6 years. Jacoby thus estimates that only '10% of all children are enrolled in day care centres before age three'.[35] This is due partly to the prevailing ideology on the importance of mother care during infancy and to the social security provisions for maternity benefit and maternity leave discussed in the previous chapter. Thus demand for places is higher for children after the age of 3 years than the global figures indicate. The lower importance placed on establishments for children up to 3 years is also shown by the fact that 'most of the staff members have no specialised education beyond high school',[36] compared with the situation for the establishments of older pre-school children, where staff must have completed a two-year training course after high school. The staff in all pre-school establishments are women and their salaries, excepting those of the directors, are lower than the average wage of all industrial workers.

A recent article by a Soviet lecturer in pre-school education highlights the problems of the quality of individual care faced by pre-school institutions. The article, based on a large study of pre-school institutions, comments that complaints from parents 'about overcrowded conditions are entirely accurate. The instructresses and nannies wear themselves out just getting the children's shoes on, feeding them and keeping them clean and occupied. So that the fine points of character building are completely out of the question'.[37]

Compulsory education

Education is compulsory, free and universal for all children aged 7-15 years. The first three years constitute primary education and the remaining five years form secondary education. This division into primary and secondary education is for administrative and teaching reasons and does not involve any selection at the end of primary schooling. In other words, education is based on comprehensive school lines without selection and without streaming. At the age of 15 a child can leave school and take up employment or he/she can stay on at different types of secondary schools until the age of 18. Since 1975 the explicit policy of the government has been to encourage young people to stay on at school until the age of 18 and 80 per cent do so but with wide variations particularly between urban and rural areas.

Schooling is for six days a week but for only half of each day — morning or afternoon. The number of hours per day is greater for secondary than for primary schools but still confined to only half of the day. Clearly this creates difficulties for children whose parents are in full-time employment and many schools have made provisions for looking after children after school hours or organising games and homework facilities, etc.

The centralised nature of Soviet education is evident in primary schools. The number and type of lessons that are taught each day for each year, the textbooks to be used, the teaching methods to be adopted, the assessment methods, etc., are all laid down by the Ministry of Education in the USSR, and enforced by the Ministry of Education of each Republic. Lessons last for 45 minutes and they are usually taught in a rather formal way. Children are required to do homework and the number of hours is laid down by the Ministry of Education as one hour for 7-year-olds, increasing to four hours for 15-year-olds. In practice, however, homework assignments take longer than the stipulated hours. Assessment is rigorously carried out and children who do not do well at the end of each school year can be given assignments to be done during the summer, before being allowed to proceed to the next class, or they can be required to repeat the class. Those who fail in one or two subjects can attend a summer school; they are then examined and promoted if they are successful. Otherwise they have to repeat the class together with those who fail in more than two subjects. There are no available figures on the incidence of repeating the class. In a way, the practice reflects the dominant view in educational psychology that all healthy children have the ability to achieve the necessary school standards if they are guided, helped or forced by their teachers. This should not conceal the fact that there are day- and boarding-schools for physically and mentally handicapped children.

In the primary school stage, teachers teach all subjects with the exception of music and physical education and they move up with their class. It is felt that this system makes relationships between teachers and pupils easier, more meaningful and more beneficial educationally. Assessment is also made of children's conduct and, in extreme cases of misconduct, children can be expelled from school. The 'Rules for Pupils' are used as guidelines and children are expected to abide by them. These require pupils to obey their teachers, work diligently, attend school regularly, concentrate in class, show respect to their parents and elders, to be attentive to old people, small children and the weak, to carry their record book always and generally to cherish the honour of their school. Misconduct in Soviet schools does not take the dimensions found in the urban schools of advanced capitalist countries because of the close discipline at home, at school, and in society at large.

The director of each school is responsible to the authorities for the proper conduct of the school. Parents' committees exist in all schools and their functions are designed to facilitate the smooth running of the school but they do not override the powers of the headmaster or the teachers. Parent-teacher meetings, however, are used to discuss not only broad educational and social issues but the progress of individual children as well, particularly those not doing well academically or misbehaving. Discussing such a session, Smith comments as follows:

> From Russian friends we heard that such criticism sessions were a regular ritual, dreaded and yet paradoxically looked forward to by both parents and children, as a source of considerable gossip afterwards as both parents and children swapped stories from family to family about what the classroom teacher said about everyone.[38]

Many schools are linked with individual industries or farms which provide such services as material assistance when necessary and where possible arrange for some form of vocational guidance for pupils etc. Each school also appoints an organiser of social activities for the pupils in the community as well as an organiser of the Young Pioneers' movement.

The range of subjects taught is wide and increases with age in the secondary school. Increasing emphasis is placed on scientific subjects and on foreign languages as the child gets older, particularly in the ninth and tenth grades. The curriculum is standard for the whole of the Soviet Union but it would be naive to infer from this that this uniformity prevails also in the results achieved. There are so many other variables affecting achievement — number and training of teachers, school buildings, equipment, social class background of school, etc. — that the influence of a uniform curriculum on geographical variation of educational standards is impossible to assess.

In rural areas, primary schools may be housed separately from secondary schools. The number of such schools, however, has been diminishing rapidly as the policy has been to house primary and secondary schools in the same building in order to rationalise resources, to strengthen the view that primary and secondary education are parts of the same process rather than two separate entities, and to provide a better service.

At the end of the eighth grade, i.e. at the age of 15, all children sit the final examinations. After compulsory education, pupils can either take up full employment when they can still continue their education part-time or they can register as students in one of the following three types of educational establishment. First, they can continue with grades nine and ten of the secondary school which are often found in the same buildings as the eight-year school. These two grades provide an exacting curriculum which is seen as an extension of previous education and as a preparation for university entrance examinations. Indeed, those who pass the final leaving examination at the age of 18 are awarded a certificate which entitles them to apply to any university for a place, though whether they are actually admitted or not depends on their performance at the entrance examination of the particular university. Second, students can proceed to full-time specialised education in one of the specialised technicums. Courses are designed to prepare students for specific professions and hence emphasis is given on both theoretical and practical work. Electricians, statisticians, librarians, nurses, primary school teachers and other such professional groups receive their education and training in technicums. Competition for places in some of the nationally-known technicums is very stiff indeed. Courses last for four years for those coming straight from the eight-year school, while for those coming from the tenth grade of the secondary school, courses last only two years. At the completion of the course students receive both a professional qualification and a certificate of secondary education which entitles them to apply for admission to universities. Most students, however, go straight into the job for which they qualified. Students receive state scholarships and those who have to live away from their families are provided with accommodation in government hostels for students. Third, they can apply for admission to a vocational technical school for full-time study of different courses varying in length from six months to three years. These courses prepare students for factory work or for a variety of industrial occupations or for agriculture. Examples of such occupations are radio and TV mechanics, electricians, fitters, bricklayers, miners, tractor drivers, etc. The emphasis of such courses is on the practical aspect of the particular occupation though there is some teaching on its theoretical aspects as well as teaching on general arts and social science subjects. Full-time students receive government scholarships and they are paid for their work during the practical part of their course by the employing enterprise. The increasing mechanisation of work in the Soviet Union has meant a substantial increase in the technical schools during the last ten years.

According to Yanowitch, the proportion of graduates from the eight-year school taking up the various options open to them is as follows:

entry to ninth grade of general-secondary school	60.1%
entry to specialised-secondary school	11.1%
full-time work or vocational school:	28.9%
work	12.5%
vocational school	16.4%[39]

Higher education

Higher education consists mainly of universities, polytechnics and monotechnic institutes in economics, law, pedagogy, medicine, agriculture and arts. All higher-education establishments are centrally administered by the Ministry of Higher and Secondary Specialised Education of the USSR and of each Republic. Decisions about the total number of students and the number of students in each subject are taken centrally in consultation with other government departments to safeguard an adequate flow of graduates for the different sectors of the economy and the needs of the nation. Higher education is closely tied to the needs of the labour market.

All higher education is free and students receive grants, usually from the government but sometimes from industrial enterprises or collective farms. The amount of the grant is lower than the minimum wage and many students have to supplement their grant, either from working part-time or from private sources, in spite of the fact that many live in government hostels where the fee is low. Many other students live at home with their families or in private lodgings. The amount of the grant varies a great deal. Students receive higher grants as they proceed yearly through their degree courses; grants from enterprises and farms are higher than government grants; students in some subjects receive higher grants than other students; students' progress affects the amount of their grant, with the result that students who fail their year receive no grant though they are allowed to repeat the year.

Qualified applicants for higher education have to sit the entrance examination arranged by each institution. These examinations are both written and oral and they vary in difficulty from one institution to another. Students who fail the examination in one institution can apply again in the following year or they can apply to other institutions, though there is no centralised system of information regarding vacancies. The number of places available for any one subject, the number of applicants, the restrictions – if any – on the number of students to be admitted from different parts of the country, recommendations from local communist parties and the student's personal school record are some of the many factors that affect an applicant's chances of success at the entrance examination. In spite of the relative expansion in higher education, demand still exceeds supply. The scarcity of places varies from place to place – ranging from one in three, to one in thirty in some of the highly prestigious institutions.

Courses last from 4 to 5½ years, depending on the subject: thus history lasts 4 years; agriculture 4½; engineering 5; and medicine 5½ or 6 years. Teaching is heavy on all courses and students are expected to work very hard to pass the examinations at the end of each year. All students, whatever their subject, have to attend classes and pass examinations in political studies and a foreign language. This is not to give the impression that courses are wide-ranging; on the contrary, they are very specialised. Assessment is very exacting and rigorous based on essays, laboratory work, home assignments and written examinations. The fallout rate is not known exactly but in the 1960s was estimated at '22% for full-time courses and must have been higher at part-time ones'.[40]

On graduation, students are assigned to a job in their special field in any part of the Soviet Union for a period of two or three years. After that they are free to look for a job elsewhere if they so wish. Those who fail to turn up are liable to legal prosecution, though this does not happen often in spite of the frequent disregard of the assignment system. Some groups of graduates are exempted from the system of assignments for personal or family reasons – married couples are not separated, health reasons, graduates with dependent relatives, and so on. The system of assignment is considered necessary to meet the country's plans for economic development and to provide the required personnel for all parts of the country irrespective of their geographical or social position. It has also been argued that students having been educated at public expense have a moral duty to serve their country even at some personal cost and self-sacrifice.

All higher-education institutions after four or five years offer the same qualification – the degree with or without distinction. After the basic degree, students can study for three more years and produce some original research to receive the higher degree of Candidate of Sciences. Financial support from the government is far more generous for higher studies than for undergraduate work, sometimes being equivalent to a salary. The highest degree is Doctor of Sciences and it is awarded very rarely indeed. Only those with a Candidate of Sciences degree, who have worked for a few years and have conducted and published major original research, can qualify for a doctorate.

Part-time education in the form of evening courses, day-release courses or correspondence courses is a major feature of Soviet post-compulsory education. All forms of post-compulsory education with the exception of the ninth and tenth grades of the complete secondary school is amenable to one form or another of part-time education. The extent of part-time education varies from one branch of education to another. In higher education, 47 per cent of students were full-time, 15 per cent were registered for evening courses and 38 per cent were studying by correspondence in the academic year 1969-70. In the same year, the corresponding proportions for secondary specialised schools were 56 per cent, 16 per cent and 28 per cent respectively.[41] The situation is different for vocational technical schools, where students spend most of their time at work and are paid apprenticeship wages.

To facilitate evening and correspondence study, the authorities provide several services and benefits – longer holidays, day release with pay and reduction of shift work. In spite of these, the burden of combining work with study is very heavy and as a result the drop-out rate is very high. In theory the academic standards expected from part-time students are the same as those of full-time students and the degrees or diplomas they receive are of equal standing. In practice, however, part-time students are at a disadvantage compared with full-time students in a variety of ways – quantity and quality of teaching, use of library facilities, etc., and their qualifications carry less esteem than those gained by full-time students.

The Soviet Union has stressed part-time education for both ideological and pragmatic reasons. It has been seen as a means of reducing the gap between theory and practice, of reducing academic exclusiveness and snobbery. As we saw, the Khrushchev reforms were partly motivated by such considerations. The pragmatic reasons are obvious enough – reduction of education costs, less interference with the demands of the labour market, and an opportunity for higher education for many who could not be accommodated within the full-time education system. It is for this reason that the majority of part-time students are of working-class or peasant background.

An assessment of the system

In an earlier section we set out the five main features of education under socialism as seen by Marx and Engels: universalism, secularism, polytechnicism, democracy and environmentalism. In this section an attempt is made to evaluate the achievement of these features by the Soviet system of education.

Egalitarian universalism

The notion of universalism implies that education should be free and compulsory up to a certain age; that entry to education after that age is free and open to all who qualify; and that family and social background do not influence the chances of children and young persons from making use and benefiting equally, according to their abilities and desires, from the educational system. Used in this way, universalism is tantamount to the principle of equality of opportunity advocated by many social reformers of non-Marxist ideology.

The extension of primary and secondary education to all up to the age of 15 and the proposed further extension up to the age of 18 are substantial achievements in making education free and compulsory up to a certain age. The same can be said about the extension of pre-school education but with the important qualification that the extent of provision varies substantially between urban and rural areas. Marx, however, acknowledged that severe geographical variations would inevitably lead to inequalities. The existing urban/rural variations in pre-school provision in the Soviet Union cannot be attributed totally to geographical factors. There is room for substantial reductions in these inequalities and indeed policy plans for the future aim at such reductions.

In advanced industrial societies, however, the essence of universalism is its egalitarian streak. The achievement of compulsory and free primary and secondary education shifts the emphasis to the ability of higher education to reach all people with the necessary ability irrespective of family background. Egalitarian universalism is more powerful in the Soviet Union than in advanced capitalist societies for two reasons. First, the dominant psychological and educational theories over the years have maintained that innate intelligence is not correlated to socio-economic background. In other words, the children of working-class parents are as likely to be among the most able who can benefit from higher education as the children of the upper classes. It therefore follows that any disparities in the socio-economic composition of higher-education students cannot be attributed to innate intelligence. Egalitarian universalism demands that any such disparities should be rectified. Second, the absence of private enterprise means that positions of authority, prestige, and high reward have to be achieved largely through the educational system. Thus equality of opportunity in higher education is a much more crucial process in the Soviet Union than in any capitalist society. Official and other literature in the Soviet Union has always stressed equality of opportunity partly for ethical reasons and partly for economic reasons. It is the natural right of every person to benefit from education according to his aptitudes and abilities; and a society which achieves the fulfilment of people's abilities promotes economic growth as well. Nevertheless there can be tensions between these two justifications for the principle of equality of opportunity. If, for whatever reason, the abilities of certain groups of young people have not been developed as well as the abilities of others, is the government ethically bound to make special provisions for their entry to higher education? If it does, is it likely to promote or impede economic growth? It is this tension between the ethical and the economic imperatives that characterises Soviet higher-education policies.

To what extent, then, does family background influence a person's educational achievement? The available evidence shows that family background is correlated with achievement in primary and secondary schools, with aspirations for higher education, with early school leaving, and with entry to higher education. Lane cites evidence from a study in Novosibirsk which showed that while only 5 per cent of all children in primary and secondary schools received 'excellent' marks, the corresponding proportion for the children whose parents had received higher education was 11.4 per cent. Similarly, while only 30 per cent of all children received 'good' marks, the corresponding proportion for children whose parents had received higher education was 43 per cent.[42] Repeating the class is an indication of severe educational backwardness because every attempt is made by the schools to avoid it. Lane again cites evidence from another Soviet study which showed that 'only 3% of children of parents with higher education had to do so, compared to 16% of those whose parents had four years or less'.[43]

It comes, therefore, as no surprise to find that when children reach the compulsory school-leaving age at 15 they reach decisions about their future which correspond to their family background. There are numerous Soviet studies which show that children whose parents are classified as employees, and particularly specialist employees, are more likely than children from working-class backgrounds and even more likely than children from peasant backgrounds to stay on for the ninth and tenth grades of the secondary school which form the main avenue to university education. This, of course, also means that children from working-class and peasant backgrounds are far more likely than children from employee backgrounds either to leave school and take up employment or to carry on their education in specialised secondary schools or vocational schools. Of particular significance, however, is the evidence which shows that even working-class children whose academic standard at the compulsory school-leaving age is equivalent with or even higher than that of middle-class children are less likely to continue with the ninth grade. Yanowitch cites evidence from a Soviet study in Leningrad in 1968 which supports this. The influence of the home background, however, was greater with regard to the less academically able children. Indeed the influence was so great that the children whose parents were in jobs requiring higher education and who scored low at the end of the eighth grade were more likely to enter the ninth grade than the children of skilled or unskilled parents who had scored high at the end of the eighth grade. Clearly, educational achievement was less important than family background in deciding entry to the ninth grade. The end result of this selective process is, as Yanowitch points out, 'the direction of changes as we move from the eighth to the tenth grade is invariably the same: a declining component of working class children and an increasing share of children reared in families of non-manual occupational strata'.[44] In view of the size of the working class in the general population, however, the proportion of students who graduated from the tenth grade in Leningrad in 1968 was still substantial — 48.5 per cent of all graduates compared with 51.5 per cent with employee background.[45] Educational provision in Leningrad is one of the best in the Soviet Union and hence the chances of working-class children graduating from the tenth grade are higher than they are in other areas.

Before moving on to discuss the position in university education it is worth examining briefly the situation of technical schools, for they offer the opportunity of early attainment of semi-professional or low professional status. As one would expect, the composition of technical schools is mainly working class — 60-70 per cent — but this is only slightly above the proportion of the working class in the general population. It is the composition of vocational schools which train young people for manual occupations that is overwhelmingly working class — almost 90 per cent, a proportion which is well above the ratio of working class in the general population. The only young people from non-manual backgrounds in vocational schools are those who failed to enter the ninth grade or the technical colleges.

The careers of school leavers are partially related to their aspirations. The evidence suggests that the higher the socio-economic background of pupils, the greater the likelihood that aspirations will match the actual careers followed. Not only do pupils from employee-class backgrounds have higher aspirations than pupils from working-class backgrounds but they are much more likely to fulfil their aspirations. Table 3.2 illustrates this in a very dramatic way and though it refers to a local study there is no reason to believe that the situation will be very different in other parts of the country. There is no good reason to believe either that the situation may have changed since 1963 because competition for university education has not declined and in competitive situations of this kind, middle-class applicants are more likely to win over applicants with working-class backgrounds. There is substantial evidence, anyhow, which shows that the situation has not changed.

TABLE 3.2
*Plans of graduating students and their actual status following
graduation – Novosibirsk secondary schools, 1963*

Occupational background of father	Plans of graduating students			Actual status of graduates		
	Work	Combining work and study	Full-time study	Work	Combining work and study	Full-time study
	%	%	%	%	%	%
Specialists, urban	2	5	93	15	2	82
Specialists, rural	11	13	76	42	-	58
Workers in industry and construction	11	6	83	36	3	61
Workers in transportation and communication	-	18	82	55	-	45
Agricultural personnel –						
Non-specialists	10	14	76	90	-	10
Trade and service personnel	9	15	76	38	3	59
Others	12	38	50	63	12	25
TOTAL	7	10	83	37	2	61

Source: M. Yanowitch and N. Dodge, 'Social Class and Education:
Soviet Findings and Reactions', *Comparative Education Review*,
vol. 12, no. 3, October, 1968.

Clearly social inequalities prevail in university education as well.
Khrushchev's open admission of this fact in 1958 has made discussion
of the issue more possible with the result that there is today abundant
sociological evidence documenting the relationship between family background and university education. This social inequality in university education must be seen against the background of the increasing competition for university places. In spite of the substantial expansion of university education over the years, competition for university places has
intensified because the secondary-school graduate population has
increased much faster. Thus Soviet studies give the following picture:

Year   Percentage of secondary school graduates entered day-time higher education[46]
1940   80
1950   50
1960   25
1972   22

Heightened competition for university education over the years has

Education

meant that social inequality in higher education has not declined in spite of the expansion of higher education. Data for such comparisons are not only scarce but not very reliable and the figures of Table 3.3 should, therefore, be treated with caution. The figures for 1937 include students in teacher-training colleges which are more likely to include working-class students than universities. Nevertheless, the broad picture that emerges from these data is that while the proportion of working class children graduating from secondary schools was small in the 1950s and before, most of them proceeded to university education. Now the proportion graduating from secondary schools is high but many of them do not succeed in entering universities. Mass secondary education has created more frustration for working-class children than existed before.

TABLE 3.3
Status groups in the population and among students

	1937			1970	
Status group	Population	Student body	Status group	Population	Student body
	%	%		%	%
Non-manual	17.5	42.2	Employees	25.0	53.1
Manual	32.2	33.9	Workers	55.0	36.2
Peasants	46.4	21.7	Peasants	20.0	10.7
Others	3.9	2.2			

Sources: For 1937 figures: R.A. Feldmeiser, 'Social Status and Access to Higher Education', *Harvard Educational Review,* vol. 27, no. 2, Spring 1957.
For 1970 figures: M. Matthews, 'Soviet Students: Some Sociological Perspectives', *Soviet Studies,* vol. XXVII, no. 1, January 1975.

Finally, family background affects the choice of university. Applicants from middle-class backgrounds are more likely to be admitted to the prestigious universities of Moscow and Leningrad and to some of the equally prestigious institutes for the training of doctors, lawyers, and other professional groups.[47]

Soviet explanations of social inequality in education are in the traditional combination of economic and cultural factors. Low income and inadequate housing are the two main economic factors cited: they are said to affect early school-leaving, school homework, the purchase of books, the payment of private tutors for university entrance coaching, and so on. Since the institution of the family is now highly prized in the

Soviet Union it is openly acknowledged that families where the parents have higher educational attainments are more likely to provide an academically stimulating home environment and an ambition for higher education than other families.[48] Soviet sociology has not yet come to examine social inequality in education from the perspectives of organisational theory and the influences of the teaching profession. Nevertheless, the study of social inequality in schools is one of the main pre-occupations of Soviet sociology.

International comparisons in this field are notoriously unreliable. The definition of what constitutes the different socio-economic groups varies and so does the definition of higher education. The result is that international comparisons of the size of the working-class student body in universities are unreliable. With this proviso firmly in mind, the available data suggest that the Soviet Union compares favourably with western European countries. Parkin showed that the proportion of working-class students in universities in eight western European countries in 1960 varied from 5 per cent in the Netherlands and West Germany to 25 per cent in Norway and Britain.[49] One would expect the Soviet Union's proportion of university students from working-class backgrounds to be higher because in spite of the changes in its admission policies it has tried to discriminate positively in favour of applicants from working-class and peasant backgrounds. As was pointed out in a previous section of this chapter, the Soviet Union abandoned its straight quota for university entrance of applicants with work experience in favour of a new scheme, whereby the number of applicants admitted to universities with and without work experience was a fixed proportion of the number of applicants from those two categories. After a prolonged discussion it also initiated in 1960 the establishment of 'preparatory departments' attached to universities which provided special classes to working-class and peasant young people wishing to apply for entry to universities. Those who do well in these classes can enter a university without having to take the usual entrance examinations. In spite of the weaknesses of both of these policies of positive discrimination, they do provide some help and protection to working-class applicants in an increasingly competitive situation.

Secular education

The anti-religious, anti-ecclesiastical attitude of Marxism and of Soviet policies has made a significant impact on Soviet life and education. Though the church is now accepted as long as it operates within very narrow constraints and continues to support the existing political system, it has lost a large proportion of its support and power. This process always accompanies industrialisation but the decline of the

Russian church has been far beyond that experienced by advanced capitalist countries. Most of its support is now among the peasantry, the elderly and the women.[50] What is perhaps more interesting is not the decline of the church but the persistence of religious belief in spite of all the persecution and constraints placed on the church and religious belief.

The abolition of religious teaching in schools was motivated by the twin designs of freeing scientific teaching and thinking in education and of making room for the undisputed hegemony of socialist ideology. The teaching of science will be discussed in the subsequent section and thus we concentrate on the socialisation aspects of school in this section.

From very early days Soviet authorities have declared that one of the basic functions of schools at all levels is to inculcate into the new generation communist ideology. Schools in all societies inevitably attempt to socialise children with the dominant ideology. It would be both impossible and unacceptable to society for schools to be operating on a value system that is at odds with the dominant value system. The difference between the Soviet Union and any western European capitalist society is that Soviet education performs its political function openly, rigidly, systematically and comprehensively, compared with the seemingly haphazard, flexible and discreet way in which education performs the same function in a capitalist society.

Subjects in primary and secondary schools are always taught from an openly Marxist perspective. There is, however, no special course in politics until the last year of the complete secondary school when a course in social science is taught. An analysis of school textbooks in history, geography and social science by Cary has shown that both history and geography are taught in Marxist-Leninist ideology. History is more amenable to ideological treatment than geography. 'By explaining the development of societies in terms of historical materialism, instruction in history is supposed to suggest to children that their society can and will be transformed from a socialist into a communist one.'[51] As the children grow older, Marxism-Leninism becomes more apparent in textbooks of both history and geography, both as regards space allocated to it and as regards emphasis. Social science is taught in the last grade and its purpose is

> to arm students with the knowledge of the basic laws of development of nature and society, to teach them to link theory with the practice of communist construction, to instil the fundamentals of dialectical thinking and to inculcate firm convictions, will and other qualities.[52]

In addition to the formal teaching the whole environment of school attempts to bolster communist ideology. Slogans on the walls, the photographs of Lenin and sometimes of Marx and other communist leaders, the 'Rules for School children', the use of public holidays and so on, all directly and indirectly beam communist ideology to pupils and students. The role of teachers includes not only teaching but propagating in direct and indirect ways the socialist ideology. This is accepted by both the government and the teaching profession as part of the teacher's role. Thus the chief newspaper of the teaching profession declared that:

> The rearing of school children in the spirit of the Party Program and of the decision of the [Communist Party] Congress is not a short-term campaign. The teacher must not limit himself to a few lectures, talks or lessons. Shaping a Communist World outlook means pro-longed and constant work. All teachers, no matter what their subjects, are obliged to make their contribution to instilling a Communist World outlook in the youth.[53]

In higher education of all types, students are exposed to longer formal teaching on Marxism-Leninism. Whatever subject they may be studying, students have to attend classes every week on Marxism and on the history of the Communist party and they have to pass examinations on this teaching.

Extra-curricular activities, particularly membership of the Youth Movement, are designed to promote the same purpose for pupils and students. The youth movement is so closely related to educational establishments that it is almost an integral part of them. The Octobrists, for young children up to the age of 10, is not so formal an organisation as the other two for older boys and girls. It performs the usual leisure and social functions of such organisations and it acts as a preparation for the Young Pioneers for children aged 10-15. This is run on formal lines and on clear communist ideology. The oath of the Young Pioneer is 'to love my Soviet Motherland passionately and to live, learn and struggle as the great Lenin bade us and as the Communist Party teaches us'. Most children join, though membership is voluntary. Leaders for Young Pioneers may be full-time professionals or teachers on a part-time basis. The Komsomol for young people aged 15-27 is a much more political organisation and is more selective in its membership. Higher-education students are encouraged to join though many either do not or drop out after joining. Membership of Komsomol, however, carries clear advantages for students: it counts as one of the factors taken into consideration in the allocation of jobs to graduates and it is also vital for membership of the Communist party, a fact which is important and sometimes a necessary prerequisite for certain positions. The activities of Komsomol are primarily political and of a serious nature. Important political issues are discussed in Komsomol and Soviet leaders pay a great deal of attention to its work. It publishes its own journals and books and its organisation is modelled on the lines of the Communist party.

Finally, the values inculcated by the schools and the youth movement are reinforced by the mass media. Newspapers, radio, television, cinema, theatre, etc. are either directly or indirectly controlled by the government and the extent of conflict between the values propagated by the various institutions is thus minimised. In these ways Soviet authorities hope to reduce differences of ideology to the minimum and to the non-essential aspects of societal organisation. In trying to achieve cultural uniformity, however, they run the risk of putting a strait-jacket over scientific inquiry, particularly those aspects of scientific inquiry that have direct and immediate implications for the country's social, political and economic system.

It would be incorrect and misleading to give the impression that the socialisation of children in schools is confined to promoting loyalty to Marxism-Leninism. It has a much wider aim than this. The code of moral education recommended by the Soviet Academy of Pedagogical Sciences, the rules of the youth movement, the school rules and various official and non-official pronouncements propagate an ideology that stresses all the cardinal values of the Protestant ethic, most aspects of the Christian and of other religious codes. The social code advocated by the Soviet Academy, for example, stresses truthfulness, honesty, hard work, discipline, helpfulness, comradeship, good conduct, modesty and other such virtues. Character building in schools thus extends beyond the mere acquisition of abstract party doctrine, Soviet nationalism and anti-capitalist sentiments. It aims at creating individuals with a collective, socialist value system.

It is difficult to know how successful such an ambitious programme is in practice. Bronfenbrenner's observations and research investigations concluded that child socialisation meets with substantial success.

What impressed this observer, like others before him, about Soviet youngsters, especially those attending schools of the new type, was their 'good behaviour'. In their external actions they are well-mannered, attentive, and industrious. In informal conversations, they reveal a strong motivation to learn, a readiness to serve their society, and — in general — ironically enough for a culture committed to a materialistic philosophy, what can only be described as an idealistic attitude toward life. In keeping with this general orientation, relationships with parents, teachers, and upbringers are those of respectful but affectionate friendship. The discipline of the collective is accepted and regarded as justified, even when severe as judged by Western standards. On the basis not only of personal observations and reports from Soviet educators, but also from entries in the minutes of the Pioneer and Komsomol meetings which I had an opportunity to examine, it is apparent that instances of aggressiveness, violation of rules, or other anti-social behaviour are genuinely rare.[54]

Bronfenbrenner went further to compare the conduct of school children in the USSR, USA, Britain, West Germany and Switzerland and his results 'strongly indicate that collective upbringing does achieve some of its intended effects — at least at the school age level'.[55] In more detail, his results indicate that

> Soviet children are much less willing to engage in anti-social behaviour than their age-mates in three Western countries (the United States, England and West Germany). In addition, the effect of the peer group was quite different in the Soviet Union and the United States. When told that their classmates would know of their actions, American children were even more inclined to take part in misconduct. Soviet youngsters showed just the opposite tendency. In fact, their classmates were about as effective as parents and teachers in decreasing misbehaviour.[56]

Secondly, they showed that 'Soviet children, in the process of growing up, are confronted with fewer divergent views both within and outside the family and, in consequence, conform more completely to a more homogeneous set of standards'.[57]

At the university level there is some evidence to suggest that the students' commitment to Marxism-Leninism is not so monolithic or actively pursued as is officially claimed. Studies exploring students' reading interests reveal that political literature does badly compared with other types of literature; that student participation in Komsomol activities is not so high, and so on. Matthews summarises the position by claiming that 'the reaction of most students to politically orientated activities is one of passive indifference'.[58] While this may be an extreme position to take there is certainly enough evidence to substantiate the claim that the political socialisation of students is not as effective as it is officially claimed.

Finally, there appears to be a conflict between the collective, co-operative, unselfish value system inculcated by the school system and the individualistic competitive, self-orientated ethos of the educational ladder that leads to higher education, as well as the reward system from employment. Thus while the group is very important for the activities of pre-school and early-school children, its importance diminishes as the children grow older when they have to pass examinations that will decide their educational and professional career. Similarly, the emphasis at work on individual incentives is at best at variance and at worst a contradiction of the value system of early schooling. This conflict between the different dominant values of Soviet society is possible by the mere fact that values are vague and flexible enough to accommodate different interpretations. Nor, of course, is the Soviet Union unique in this. Indeed, it is one of the main features of all advanced industrial societies that they propagate the value of equality of opportunity while practising inequality that negates the fulfilment of the former.

Polytechnical education
The provision of polytechnical education is still official policy in the Soviet Union. This expressed faith in the value of polytechnical education is possible largely because of the reinterpretation of this type of education to mean mainly scientific and technical education. To understand how this has come about one needs to look at the tensions between the moral and the economic aspects of polytechnical education. Its moral aspects relate to the Marxist views of the desirability of work under socialism, the abolition of the differences between mental and manual labour and the abolition of the division of labour. In other words, polytechnical education is one of the main forces behind the creation of a socialist and a communist society.

The economic aspects of polytechnical education centre around the creation of an industrial society. Socialism, let alone communism, cannot be created in a society of scarcity. Abundance of services, consumer goods and other material necessities is a prerequisite to socialism and such an abundance can only be created by advanced technology. The type of educational system, however, that is needed to promote scientific knowledge and advanced technology is not always compatible with the educational system that aims at providing children with substantial work experience through a close link between school and the work place. In other words, a tension exists between the economic and the moral aspects of polytechnical education.

A similar tension is to be found between the need to create an all-round type of industrial worker being able to perform different jobs equally well and the demands of the economic system for specialised personnel. An educational system that produces specialists cannot, at the same time, produce all-round qualified workers. In this clash it was the second that had to be modified. Kreusler has this to say on this issue: 'The final goal of education, the development of an all-round personality, is a dream. The Soviet pedagogues think now that the objective should be the development of many-sided interests.'[59] It is an attempt at best to create polyspecialists, rather than generalists.

Even the abolition of the differences between mental and manual labour has been seen as only possible within an advanced technological society. In other words, it is tantamount to the abolition of manual labour and this can only be achieved with the advance of scientific knowledge and specialisation. This is not to suggest that the mere growth of scientific knowledge by itself leads to the abolition of manual labour but that it is a necessary prerequisite.

For all these reasons, the Soviet education system has come to lay a very strong emphasis on scientific education. In De Witt's words, 'first, last and always, the Soviet commitment to education is a commitment to scientific education, to technological education . . . .[60]' The curriculum of the secondary school is weighted toward scientific subjects; the provision of part-time study is mainly in the field of technical, scientific subjects; full-time higher education stresses science and technology more than the arts and social sciences, and so on.

Thus, in its efforts to find ways of implementing polytechnical education, the Soviet Union has been strongly influenced by the overriding consideration of creating an industrial society that will provide the material wealth for the building of socialism. The result has been an academic form of scientific and technological education providing the trained personnel for industry that is based both on the division of labour and on the superiority of mental over manual labour. Thus polytechnical education, as practised in the Soviet Union today, is very different from that envisaged by Marx. Perhaps it is the only form that is feasible in a rapidly developing industrial society.

Participation in education

The notion of participation is generally troublesome but particularly so in the field of education. It is both difficult to define and to implement. Does it refer to the sharing of power among the staff or does it extend beyond that to include power-sharing with the pupils, the parents and the community? For Price, participation in schools is part of the wider practice of participation in society, and it is an essential feature of democracy in a socialist society. It involves open government through general and informed discussion '*before* policies are formulated', and the 'rotation of positions of responsibility and control'.[61] It is no surprise that he reaches the conclusion that such participation does not exist in Soviet schools. An official Soviet publication states clearly that the headmaster of a school 'has the powers of one-man management' but he involves in discussion the rest of the staff in pedagogical problems.[62] It is a form of participation similar to that in industry discussed in chapter 1. The headmaster is ultimately responsible for any decisions affecting the school and any sharing of power with the rest of the staff must be seen in that context.

A similarly unequal relationship exists between the staff on one hand and the children's parents on the other. Parents' committees exist in all schools but their functions are mainly social or educational in the broadest sense of the word. Parents have no say in such matters as the hiring or firing of teachers, in the organisation of the school curriculum or in the running of the school. Apart from social functions and the raising of funds for specific school projects, parents' committees also help teachers deal with difficult parents. The same official publication states: 'An active parents' committee is a reliable support both in school affairs and in enhancing the school's links with the public at large.'[63] Thus the close co-operation that exists between home and school reinforces rather than questions the authority of teachers.

Heredity versus environment

The importance of the environment on a child's ability is one of the generally-accepted principles of Soviet education. Following Marx, most Soviet psychologists and educationists reject the idea that children can be divided at an early age into ability categories. Hence compulsory schooling is on comprehensive lines; special help is provided to slow learners, children can repeat the class, and so on. All these administrative measures imply that all children of normal ability can be educated together without detriment to any one ability group. IQ tests are rejected because they are 'founded on a fatalistic theory of aptitudes which considers human abilities pre-determined through heredity and unchangeable by environment'.[64] The same Soviet writer explains that the 'correct investigation of abilities is possible only if the child's activities are performed under his ordinary conditions of life . . . Such an investigation can be carried out by the teacher himself'.[65]

The recent growth of special schools in the arts, mathematics, physics, biology and languages for gifted children beyond the seventh or eighth grade is a partial violation of the environmentalist principle. Children attending such schools are three to four times as likely to enter universities as those in ordinary schools. On the other hand, these schools cater for only a minority — about 3 per cent — of all children in complete secondary schools and the family background of the children attending these schools is not too unrepresentative of Soviet society. Dunstan's recent study of these schools concluded as follows:

> To sum up, it may be said that schools for talented children offer them considerable career advantages but such benefits are not restricted to young people already in superior social circumstances at the time of entry, nor are these schools by any means the only paths to excellence open to the Soviet child.[66]

The achievements of the Soviet education system since the Revolution have been truly great. But they are achievements in areas where education systems of advanced capitalist societies have also been successful — the spread of literacy, the extension of compulsory education, the provision of free higher education to increasingly larger numbers and the improvement of standards in educational institutions.[67] These achievements have furthered the process of industrialisation on which the Soviet Union has placed so much emphasis. In spite of the failure of polytechnical education, the Soviet education system appears more effective in relating theory to practice than the education systems of many advanced capitalist societies. Equality of educational opportunity, however, has been as much an elusive concept in the Soviet Union as elsewhere, largely because the institution of the family and the value of competitive inequality are as strong there as elsewhere. Finally, Soviet schools have stressed a great deal their function of socialising the young, largely because the notion of freedom has to be seen more in collective than in individualistic terms in a society struggling to divest itself of its old capitalist value system in order to achieve its own brand of a socialist way of life.

4

HEALTH SERVICES IN THE SOVIET UNION

Marxism and health

In contrast to the outline available from Lenin's address to the Bolshevik party in Prague in 1912 on what constituted a socialist social security system,[1] we do not have a clear idea of what Lenin imagined a socialist health system would be. However, it seemed obvious to Marx that ill-health was linked with capitalism:

> take the blacksmith as a type ... we see the stress of work on that strong man, and what then is his position in the death rate of 31 per thousand per annum, or 11 above the mean of the male adults of the country in its entirety.[2]

And again:

> we dwell on only one point, the enormous mortality, during the first few years of their life, of the children of the operatives.[3]

These observations had been foreshadowed by Engels who set out to:

> prove that society in England daily and hourly commits what the working-men's organs, with perfect correctness, characterise as social murder, that it has placed the workers under conditions in which they can neither retain health nor live long.[4]

Not surprisingly Lenin took the same view:

Thousands and tens of thousands of men and women, who toil all their lives to create wealth for others, perish from starvation and constant malnutrition, die prematurely from diseases caused by horrible working conditions, by wretched housing and overwork.[5]

From this general position, ill-health was seen as arising not merely from social factors but explicitly from capitalism. Some Bolsheviks felt therefore that the October 1917 Revolution would lead to the elimination of disease and ultimately the withering away of clinical medicine (but not sanitary and preventive work), much as other bourgeois institutions such as the state and the family would disappear.[6] In any case, the socialisation of medicine would mean much more than its nationalisation:

the Leninist strategy was not only the one that changed the quantity and distribution of medical resources, but changed the nature of medicine as well. In that respect, revolutionary medicine meant then, as it would mean today, the democratisation and deprofessionalisation of medicine in which the content and practice of medicine was not defined by the Party member, the bureaucrat or the expert, but by the collectivity of the population.[7]

This strategy was not spelled out in detail by Lenin, although Ulam has argued that he had a 'veritable obsession about health and fitness'.[8] Rather it was N.A. Semashko, from 1907 to 1917 a medical associate of Lenin in enforced exile, who outlined the new health policy as the first Commissar of Health. The socialisation of medicine entailed the provision 'for everyone, at his earliest need, a free and well-qualified medical treatment'.[9] But in addition he gave heavy emphasis to the positive creation of a healthy population through early preventive intervention.

We can thus summarise the ideals of a Soviet socialist health system in the immediate post-revolutionary period as follows:

1 Comprehensive, qualified medical care.
2 Available to everyone in the population.
3 A single, unified service provided by the state.
4 A free service.
5 Extensive preventive care, with the aim of creating a healthy population.
6 Full workers' participation in the health service.

These principles were drawn up at the Congress of Medical-Sanitary Departments of Soviets of Workers', Peasants' and Soldiers' Deputies, 15 June 1918, which established the first People's Commissariat of

Health, headed by N.A. Semashko. According to Skorokhodov, three influential sources were drawn on:

> The People's Commissariat of Health borrowed the system of wide prophylactic measures from British health protection, its class character from German medical insurance, and free and generally accessible medicine from Russian Zemstvo medical services.[10]

To which we should add, of course, Marx and Lenin. Although still broadly followed, these aims have been seriously qualified since 1918, both in reaction to specific health needs of the population (for example the devastating epidemics during the period of war communism), and as a result of general political and socio-economic changes such as Stalin's drive towards rapid industrialisation.

Historical developments

In common with all pre-industrial societies, pre-revolutionary Russia suffered from a high mortality rate, and infectious diseases were endemic. The general mortality rate in 1913, about 30 per thousand, was similar to that of England in 1750 or India in the early twentieth century.[11] This appalling burden was not unrecognised by the Czarist regime which had encouraged the provision of limited medical care in the rural areas since the 1864 zemstvo (local government) reforms. Salaried physicians, assisted by feldshers (physician's assistant, from the German 'army surgeon'), provided limited care by touring the countryside on small circuits. By the 1890s sufficient rural physicians were available to staff permanently based dispensaries.

The provision of this service, although part of Alexander II's general plan of modernisation, was also stimulated by the realisation that disease recognised no class divisions: the health of the nobility was threatened by the prevalence of disease in the rural population. However, the distribution of physicians, the majority of whom were in private practice, remained grossly distorted. Even by 1913, while 82 per cent of the population lived in rural areas, only 13 per cent of physicians practised there. These 'zemstvo physicians' endured an unattractive rural life (as Chekhov, himself such a physician, has portrayed) through dedication to public service. But they also supported populist political ideals, recognising that political and economic reforms were essential to any effective improvement of rural health conditions.[12]

Despite their small number (about 3,000 in 1913) the zemstvo physicians exerted a considerable influence on medical thinking, particularly through the Society of Russian Physicians in memory of N.I.

Pirogov (the Pirogov Society, founded in 1885) — the most influential medical association to develop by the early twentieth century. This society wanted both medical, political and economic reforms but only in so far as they promoted the practice of medicine as it was developing in western Europe, for example through Bismarck's health insurance legislation of 1883 and Lloyd George's 1911 act. Indeed the Czarist government enacted its own equivalent piece of legislation in the 1912 Health and Accidents Act, although this provided little more than out-patient treatment.

With the growth in the overall number of physicians (from 10,000 to 23,000, 1864 to 1913) and their professional consolidation in the Pirogov Society, early twentieth-century medicine in Russia was following a typically European path. The February 1917 Revolution made way for a variety of bourgeois and professional groups, including the medical profession, to extend their influence over what was expected to be a new era of democratic capitalism. The Pirogov Society set about planning a health service dominated by the medical profession, in which medical ethics determined the doctor-patient relationship and a 'universal' service was in fact to give preference to those who were insured or could pay.[13]

Indeed the provisional government set up a Central Medical-Sanitary Council to provide centrally-planned, government-financed medical care under the control and supervision of the medical profession. In addition, the Pan-Russian Soviet of Professional Associations of Physicians was formed by the Pirogov Society in the spirit of the times (for although the provisional government was the legal holder of power, soviets of workers' deputies were spreading rapidly).[14] Thus the medical profession quickly began to strengthen its position in the health service, as it has done in all other industrial societies. But these plans were short lived. With the failure of the February Revolution and the assumption of power by the soviets in October the political context of the medical profession changed dramatically. Instead of consolidating its position it was to be transformed from 'a self-conscious, independent, vocal, politically oriented, and militant corporate entity to that of a docile and politically inert employee group'.[15] However, this claim over-emphasises the neutrality of the medical profession. It was in fact opposed to a genuinely socialist health-care system.

The immediate post-revolutionary years witnessed a struggle between policies based on the socialist health ideals of the Bolsheviks and considerable practical difficulties (including political opposition). Although feldshers could be relied upon to provide, as they had always done, health care to the rural population, the Bolsheviks had to use the existing urban-based physicians to cover the urban working class. Indeed they wished to invert the pre-existing distribution in favour of workers and party members, and away from the middle and upper classes who had supported private practice. This posed the problem of securing the co-operation of physicians, while requiring them to establish completely new medical priorities. The Pirogov Society was bitterly opposed to such interference, arguing that it was unethical to provide care on any basis other than (medically defined) need. Whether this opposition extended to medical sabotage is disputed, but it is clear that the Pirogovists sided with the Mensheviks and other opposition groups after 1917.[16]

The Bolsheviks' strategy was aided considerably by the virtual disappearance of clients for private practice between 1918 and 1921. More positively, they dissolved the Pirogov Society in 1918, and relied heavily on the existing health workers' unions to incorporate the physicians into the All-Russian Congress of Medical Workers which established the Medical Workers' Union in 1919.[17] In the same year the opening up of higher education and Workers' Faculties began to expand and proletarianise the medical profession in order to achieve a greater redistribution and wider coverage of medical care.

The establishment of a single union exacerbated the issue of quite who was to run the health service. Although the central Commissariat of Health had been set up in 1918, the Bolsheviks decided that health (and other) services should be run by the local soviets. However, the health workers' unions felt that they should direct all health institutions through their local branches. In addition, the spontaneous takeover of factories and other institutions, which had continued after October 1917, gave rise to regional and national workers' committees based on place of work. The resolution of these various interpretations of working-class control was soon to be determined by the objective conditions prevailing in Russia during the period of war communism, 1918-21. In addition to the general shift towards centralisation as a result of Civil War and economic blockade the health service faced acute epidemics of typhus, typhoid, smallpox, and relapsing fever. Table 4.1 shows that the number of cases of typhus rose dramatically:

TABLE 4.1
Typhus cases per 10,000 people, 1913-27[18]

	Year						
	1913	1918	1919	1920	1921	1922	1927
Cases of typhus per 10,000 population	7.3	21.9	265.3	393.9	54.0	109.6	4.0

Between 1916 and 1924, ten million people died of all epidemics.[19] Perhaps over dramatising the situation for political reasons, Lenin nevertheless proclaimed to the second Congress of Medical Workers: 'either the lice will defeat socialism, or socialism will defeat the lice.'[20] In these conditions the distinction between military and civilian services dissolved in the public health fight against epidemics, increasing the power of the centralised Commissariat of Health over the local soviets and the unions. However, it was not the health service which defeated the epidemics nor socialism, but the improved living standards generated by the end of war communism and the New Economic Policy of 1921. In a sense then the lice did help to force a strategic retreat on socialism.

The denationalisation of land and non-essential industrial enterprises at the heart of the NEP was paralleled in the health services by the resurgence of limited private practice, doctors having to choose either complete public or private work. Limited health resources and the desire to give priority to industrial and agricultural production resulted in health care being restricted to the insured, while a structure of regional services in the rural areas was created. These were the first steps taken towards fulfilling the ideals of 1918. They confirmed the power of the central Commissariat of Health since the unions (including the Medical Workers' Union) were now directly under the control of the party and the state,[21] but they also revealed the first compromises in the face of economic and political constraints.

Almost all the 1918 principles were altered. Despite a 300 per cent increase in doctors between 1917 and 1928 it proved difficult to persuade them to work in rural areas. Local soviets failed to provide housing and transport inducements, and the health service continued to be split into two: feldshers in rural areas, and doctors in towns.[22] The service was in addition beginning to split between the soviets, industrial and agricultural enterprises, and the Commissariat, while the direct participation of workers was never seriously encouraged. The main success was the change in emphasis towards preventive care, but this was as much the result of the necessary public health fight against epidemics as the result of general policy.

By the advent of the first Five Year Plan (1928-33), the objective conditions which had constrained health policy (war communism, epidemics and the shortage of resources) were less pressing. However, new political constraints appeared in the form of economic policy which carried the health services even further away from the original ideals. In fact these crucial decisions, taken after Lenin's death, were to determine the whole future development of Soviet society, including of course the health services. Stalin's radical shift in economic policy to the development of heavy industry and the collectivisation of land required, in addition to more extreme methods of coercion, a change in social policy. The health services were enjoined to 'wake up and fit in' with the new policies.[23]

The health services were now quite explicitly directed towards industrial effort. Health posts in industrial enterprises were the first priority, quadrupling for example in the first six months of 1932.[24] Second, with the increase in women at work a special health service section was developed for women and children. Third, a special branch was set up to organise and plan the sanitation of rapidly growing urban areas while the legacy of neglect in rural health care continued to be a problem: in 1933 the number of patients per doctor was 750 in towns, but 14,200 in the country.[25] This western-style division of the health services was consolidated by the division of medical studies into therapeutic and industrial medicine, pediatrics, and public health in 1938.

Associated with these specific developments other characteristics emerged and crystallised. Stalin rejected as idealism the idea that illness was only a result of capitalism. Heavy industrialisation might worsen health but this was a necessary sacrifice on the road to communism. However, the growth of industrial medicine was not entirely benign. Labour was in short supply, and a major task for the doctors was to ensure that only genuine illness justified a worker's absence. Indeed a Soviet textbook states:

> The most important objective of that period was the reduction of illness in the workers associated with temporary loss of fitness for work . . . the [medico-sanitary] units subordinated all their activity to the interests of fulfilling the production plans of the industrial enterprises . . .[26]

This attitude lead ultimately to the idea that 'Damage to the worker's health is not as serious as economic damages to production . . .'[27]

The reorientation of medicine from need to labour discipline was aided by the continuing drop in the status of medicine. In addition to the common unionisation of medical workers and the proletarianisation of medical school in the 1920s, doctors' pay fell to three-quarters of the average wage, and by one-third in real terms,[28] and the engineer became the new hero. As the status of medicine dropped so did the availability of instruments, drugs and buildings. Moreover, experiments common throughout education in the 1920s were abandoned, entrance exams were reintroduced in 1926, and medical education was taken out of universities. As a result partly of this general downgrading and because men were needed in heavy industry, women were actively encouraged to take up medicine. Between 1928 and 1934 they grew from 52 to 75 per cent of doctors, or as Navarro puts it: 'second-rate workers — women — were to perform second-rate jobs.'[29]

110

By 1936 the new constitution included the right to free health care, although charges for drugs introduced in the 1930s continue up to the present day. More importantly, the Ministry of Health was confirmed at this time as the supreme health authority — completing a process of centralisation which had begun almost twenty years earlier. In addition, the division of the service into three specialist areas and the complete absence of worker participation opened the way to increasing academic and technical dominance, and (as in the west) the influence of the hospital. This was confirmed when in 1947 polyclinics and in 1956 sanitary-epidemiological (public health) stations came under hospital control.

Apart from this there have been no major changes in health policy up to the present day. The general expansion of facilities continued up to 1940 (for example, the number of doctors reached seven times the 1917 level). The Second World War of course required the adaptation of health services to military requirements and the prevention of epidemics, as had the Civil War. Despite the destruction of many health facilities, including much of the pharmaceutical industry, 'there can be no doubt that victory was achieved, as a result, partly at any rate, of the rapid pre-war development and modernisation of the health services'.[30] In the post-war years, apart from making good these losses, general expansion of medical services continued. The main recent development has been the change of morbidity and mortality patterns 'away from that associated with agrarian communities to that of highly urbanised societies'.[31] The health services were not substantially affected by Khrushchev's reforms in other areas of social policy. His attempt to open up higher education to more workers had no more effect than similar policies in the 1920s, when the proportion of working-class medical school students never exceeded 50 per cent.

The 1969 Public Health Act 'On Measures for the Further Improvement of the Health Service and for the Development of National Medical Research' introduced no new policies, but merely confirmed existing practice, reiterated basic health-care principles, and outlined areas of possible expansion (general recreation and treatment facilities, free medicine, factory health inspection, industrial medical facilities and so on). The latest policy, 'On Measures for the Further Improvement of the People's Health Care System', was adopted by the CPSU central committee and Council of Ministers on 22 September 1977. This again heralds no new departures. The incentives for physicians to stay in rural practice are improved (up to three times urban salaries after ten years, plus the opportunity to buy a car, to buy food direct from state farms, and a free flat). Increased drug and medical technology production is planned, and in general an attempt will be made to raise quality rather than quantity.[32]

Health services today

The modern Soviet health service is by and large state-provided and free at the point of consumption. Access and distribution are determined by need, in accordance with central planning norms. In this section we shall examine the Soviet health service in three areas: needs, services, finance.

Needs
In any social service which is provided outside the market the definition of need is politically negotiated, often through professional service providers. The reduction in power of the medical profession soon after the Revolution enabled the state to exercise a more direct influence over medical-need definition than has been the experience in western countries. What factors determine legitimate medical needs for this service? These factors can be grouped broadly into the more objective and the more subjective. First, then, we can examine demography, morbidity and mortality. Demographic structure is vital in several ways. The Soviet Union has experienced a rapidly increasing elderly population, as have all industrialised countries, which absorbs a disproportionate amount of health care per capita. In contrast, despite variations between the European and Asian Republics, the birth rate is low and declining which reduces potential demand from the other 'heavy-user' section of the population — maternity and child care.[33] These changes, particularly the low birth rate,[34] have been accentuated by the steady urbanisation of the population, from 18 per cent in 1926 to 60 per cent in 1975.[35] A further factor offsetting the current ageing of the population is the distortion produced by the Soviet Union's experiences in the twentieth century (see Fig. 4.1).

The noticeable excess of females over males and considerable fluctuations in the size of population in each age group were caused by a variety of factors affecting both the birth and death rates. First, the First World War followed by the Civil War reduced birth rates, increased death rates, and resulted in a direct loss of 14 million people. The treaty of Brest-Litovsk ceded a further 26 million to central powers (A). Second, military losses in the Second World War were about 20 million, but there was also a gain of 20 million in annexed territory (B). Third, lost births as a result of the First World War and the Civil War (C), the collectivisation of agriculture (D), the prohibition and re-legalisation of abortion (E — 1936, G — 1955), and lost births as a result of the Second World War (F), all contributed further to distort the population structure.[36] All this has in effect temporarily reduced the size of cohorts entering old age (particularly male), which will result in a very sharp increase once these unusual cohorts have passed through the population: the currently low dependency ratio estimated to be 55-70 in 1980[37] will rise rapidly.

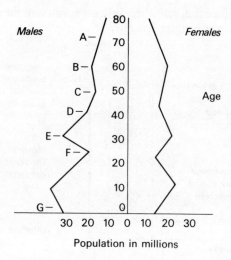

FIGURE 4.1
Population structure of the USSR[38]

Morbidity and mortality rates are closely linked with these demographic changes in so far as we can tell because the data are very patchy.[39] Since the Revolution life expectancy has doubled to 70 years, the most significant change being in early childhood mortality which has fallen from around 40 per cent to less than 1 per cent.[40] This dramatic change is reflected in the causes of death which are now predominantly those typical of an advanced industrial society; around 60 per cent of deaths are caused by cardiovascular diseases and cancer.[41] However, infectious diseases are still significant and tuberculosis hospitals are still being built: 'the current morbidity pattern in the U.S.S.R. creates certain demands that fortunately have become comparatively insignificant in this country with its higher standards of nutrition and housing, which reflect, in part, higher disposable income per person.'[42] In other words, non-medical developments such as higher levels of nutrition, available housing space, and a sanitary urban and industrial environment have both a direct and indirect (demographic) impact on medical needs.

We can summarise these objective determinants of medical need as typical of an industrialising country, similar to western Europe and North America, while exhibiting a residual problem of infectious disease and benefiting temporarily from an unusually low dependency ratio. However, medical needs are also crucially determined by more subjective factors, such as the competition for and availability of resources,

113

perceptions of medical scientists, political constraints on planning and the articulation of popular demands.

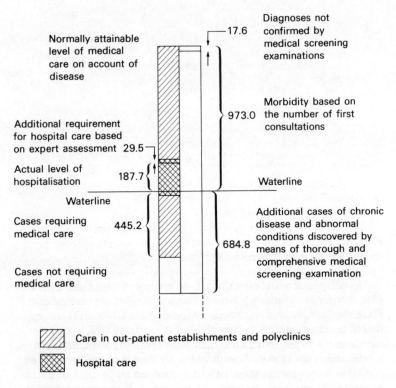

FIGURE 4.2
The iceberg of morbidity[43]*

*The figures shown are per 1000 population of the town of Aktjubinsk (Kazakh SSR).

As in other countries, a major determinant of legitimate medical need is the supply of medical resources. For example, the number of physicians (at around 30 per 10,000 of the population) is almost three times the provision for Britain and hence encourages the expansion of medical need to include extensive home visits (including certain 'social work' functions), comprehensive industrial health care, and, most notably, widespread screening of those at medical risk. Figure 4.2 illustrates the increase in medical needs generated by screening in the town Aktjubinsk (Kazakh SSR). When regular screening is extended from the present coverage of mothers, children and certain risk categories (dangerous work, TB, mental illness and so on) to the whole population, as is planned, this 'generated' need will increase still further.

The articulation and impact of popular demand for Soviet health care has been weak in the face of political constraints on resource allocation and the planning process. A director of a Moscow polyclinic told one of the authors that health education was raising expectations and that the press should not discuss new drugs and treatments in short supply. When asked how he contained demand he characterised many patients as slaves to fashion — currently requesting blood pressure measurement (about 100 patients a day) and recently wanting treatment for influenza. Hence such 'fashionable' demand only received junior nursing care. However, this relatively generous provision of polyclinics and dispensaries tends to expand demand for specialist hospital services which cannot so easily be met, despite a rate of hospital bed provision nearly 50 per cent higher than in Britain. Hence in terms of the quality of provision a great contrast exists between good primary-level care and poor hospitals (discussed in more detail below).

The influence of major interest groups concerned with health care in advanced industrial societies — the government (usually through a ministry of health), the medical professions, and the general population (as patients) — varies considerably. As we have seen in the Soviet Union the Ministry of Health had become by the early 1930s far more powerful than the medical profession or the patients. Through its regular central planning cycle it came to exercise a third and major influence on the definition of medical needs. Central control by the CPSU and its commitment to economic growth through heavy industrialisation resulted in medical needs being defined with a view to the reproduction of labour, the encouragement of labour discipline, and the dependence of the patient on specialist, technical caring by doctors. The mass involvement of the public in a democratic health service was seen as incompatible with these developments. Hence legitimate medical needs and the services to meet them were planned centrally by the academic Semashko Institute and implemented through a highly centralised control of budgets and exercise of administrative power over planning 'norms' and 'standards'.[44]

We can summarise these more subjective determinants of medical need as highly politically directed, while influenced to a lesser extent by the 'automatic' generation of needs through the supply of medicine itself and the demands of patients.

Services
The nature and extent of health services designed to meet medical needs in the Soviet Union are in general not unlike those of some

western countries: the dominance of doctors, the influence of technology and medical science located in large hospitals, and the regionalisation of primary and specialist care. Feted differences, such as the mass participation of the general public, the emphasis on preventive care (especially screening – the 'dispensation method'), the use of less qualified feldshers, and the lower status of doctors, turn out on closer examination to need serious qualification.

We may begin our discussion of the health services with some details of overall supply before examining structural differentiation. One of the most noted features is the generous supply of doctors and hospital beds by western standards. Table 4.2 gives some comparative figures.

TABLE 4.2
Hospital beds and doctors per 10,000 population,
USSR, USA, UK, 1974

	Doctors	*Beds*
USSR	29.6	115.8
USA	16.0	82.0
UK	13.0	87.0

This provision is still being rapidly expanded, with 40 doctors per 10,000 now seen as the optimum level. However, such figures, although they indicate overall provision, must be qualified in two ways. First the distribution of both doctors and beds is uneven geographically although it has improved since the Second World War (Table 4.3):

TABLE 4.3
Highest and lowest ratio of doctors and beds per 10,000 in Union Republics, 1950 and 1974[45]

	1950		*1974**	
Doctors				
	Georgia	26.7	Georgia	38.8
	Tadzhik	8.4	Tadzhik	19.6
Beds				
	Estonia	66.1	Russia	120.4
	(Russia	59.2)	(Estonia	111.0)
	(Georgia	54.6)	(Kirgiz	110.2)
	Kirgiz	40.3	Georgia	94.5

*All urban doctors per 10,000 population = 34.5
All rural doctors per 10,000 population = 17.9

The coefficient of variation of the distribution of doctors in the Soviet Union may be compared with that of the USA and England in Table 4.4:

TABLE 4.4
Coefficient of variation of distribution of doctors
in USSR, USA and England[46]
(By Union Republic, State, and Regional Health Authority)

USSR	1950	0.37
USSR	1974	0.19*
USA	1969	0.31
England	1975	0.15

*Since Russia and Ukraine have populations of 160 and 52 millions respectively, it may be better to omit them. The coefficient of variation of the remaining 13 Republics is similar, but slightly higher at 0.20 in 1974.

Given the tremendous geographical size and variation of the country, Table 4.4 shows the achievement of the Soviet Union in reducing inequality and hence the coefficient of variation since 1950 to well below the American figure. (The relatively low comparative figure for England reflects the twin effects of geography and central planning on the distribution of doctors.) Despite this improvement, however, as in other industrial societies urban areas are better served than rural areas (Table 4.3). Although the pre-revolutionary legacy of maldistribution was greater than now, it is still a problem for the Ministry of Health to persuade doctors to work in rural areas and considerable material incentives are now employed to try to even up the gap between town and country. Even so, the turnover of doctors in rural areas is high, 40 per cent staying less than four years,[47] and many doctors are straight from medical school in directed placements. A second qualification to be noted about overall supply is the quality of doctors and beds. The rapid expansion in medical education in the Soviet Union has not in fact been at the expense of quality. Competition to enter medical school is high (between 5 and 15 applicants per place, compared with 2 in the USA and 5 in the UK), and the length of training extensive (6 years plus postgraduate training, compared with 8 years in the USA and 5 in the UK).[48] However, the rapid expansion in the provision of hospital beds has not been matched by high quality. There is a problem of hospital infection, since virtually no disposable equipment is used and staff wear their ordinary clothes under gowns.[49] Anecdotal evidence suggests strongly that the physical state of hospitals is poor, with overcrowded wards and an acute shortage of drugs and equipment.[50]

This overall expansion in health services must be qualified not only in terms of gross distribution and quality, but also by the structural organisation and philosophy of the service. Since the Ministry of Health emerged as the administrative body in sole charge of health services in the twenty years after the Revolution, it has implemented policies set out by the party through the plans of the Semashko Institute (of the National Academy of Sciences), and provided centrally most of the budget for Republic and regional services. This highly central control is balanced by detailed administration at the regional level where the chief medical officer is responsible for all health services. Below this, at the district level, the chief physician, as head of the district hospital, co-ordinates polyclinics, dispensaries and public and industrial health services (see Appendix 1.3).

Within this structure the organisation of medical care itself embodies certain clear ideas. The most significant feature is the highly developed degree of specialisation. This can be traced back to the 1930s when health care was under increasing pressure to accommodate and assist the drive for industrialisation. This culminated in the division of medical studies in 1938 into three branches from the beginning of the student's education: general clinical and industrial medicine; maternity and child care; and public health. Such a division of labour, Navarro argues,[51] was clearly to meet industrial needs: the first sector for servicing and maintaining a productive work force; the second for reproducing the labour force efficiently; and the third for preventing illness which might reduce an already scarce labour supply. These demands give rise to considerable conflict for doctors who try both to meet the needs of the patient (for example, for him to stop working) and the needs of industry (to maintain production).

Specialisation runs right through primary-level health care such that industrial health points, general polyclinics, 'dispensaries' (in fact for screening and monitoring certain age groups, and illnesses), and sanitary-epidemiological or public health stations overlap with poor co-ordination. A patient may be registered with and receive treatment from both his neighbourhood and his factory polyclinic even when he no longer works there.[52] At secondary and higher levels hospitals become increasingly specialist, incorporating less prevalent illness, and teaching and research activities.

Since the Second World War, hospitals have gained a central position over polyclinics (in 1947) and public health (in 1956), in an already highly centralised system such that, as in Britain, many primary-level physicians feel they are merely referral agents. This reflects the dominant influence of academic medicine situated at regional and Republic level. For example, the Minister of Health recently stated that 'it is impossible to conceive that only a single doctor with a broad background could fully guarantee highly qualified care for patients suffering from a variety of illnesses which are frequently complicated to diagnose and treat'.[53] Such a view, in contrast to the major incidence of relatively simple and self-limiting illnesses brought to primary-level physicians, clearly indicates the interests and perceptions of medicine oriented towards academic specialisation rather than patient needs. Indeed Ryan describes how the proliferation of academic specialities had become virtually uncontrolled by the late 1960s, giving rise to 'excessively compartmentalised activity and a blinkered perception of the patient'.[54]

The growth of specialisation and the related dominance of academic medicine culminated in 1969 in the partial resurrection of a medical profession, including an oath along Hippocratic lines, though significantly this included references to communist morality and the Soviet government.[55] This development, in such sharp contrast to the bitter struggle surrounding the repression of the profession in 1918, indicates the strength of an industrial and academic orientation which has developed in the Soviet health service since the 1930s.

In contrast to this picture, Soviet writers emphasise other aspects of the health service in principle which are only partially realised in practice, precisely because of the above trends. The best known is the heavy emphasis on preventive health care. This tradition arose as a result of early theoretical ideas that disease was a product of capitalism, and hence that preventive health care would become sufficient as the need for clinical intervention withered away. In addition, post-revolutionary medicine had by force of circumstance to concentrate on public and preventive health care in the face of massive epidemics. Preventive health care embraces both an attitude running through all medicine and specific activities. Lisitsin argues that prevention is not merely sanitary health protection or control of infections, but rather 'the aggregate of social-economic and medical measures aimed at preventing disease and, what is even more important, at eliminating disease . . . [by] remaking man's environment . . .'[56] In other words, preventive health care includes wider aspects of social policy such as housing, income maintenance, and education. Yet the examples given are very familiar to western eyes — the establishment of maximum levels of harmful chemicals in the environment, vaccination, and the screening of populations at risk (the 'dispensarisation method'). The latter covers nearly 100 per cent of children and some 20 per cent of adults, plus certain specific categories of disease such as tuberculosis and mental illness, and it is hoped this will reach the total population before the end of the century.[57] This would of course be an exceptional achievement, but the current coverage does not in reality appear to be grossly different to the attention that mothers, children and the sick receive in Britain. Indeed, Ryan calculates that 'personal medical care accounted for . . . 94.6 per cent, whilst environmental health and physical education absorbed 4.2 and 0.6 per cent of the total [expenditure] .'[58]

A second distinctive feature highlighted by Soviet writers is the mass involvement of the public in health care. Lisitsin states that 'the extensive participation in health protection of all sections of the population has become one of the country's basic principles . . .'.[59] However, as examples he suggests merely that, in reporting to the supreme soviet, health commission chairmen represent 'sections of the population'. For additional examples he cites public councils in many health institutions, popular support for the Red Cross, and an annual health day (11 July), when 'physicians and public health organisers . . . give the population an account of their work'. It is very difficult to see how this adds up to 'extensive participation'. Rather it indicates the gap between theory and practice, and reinforces our interpretation of Soviet health care as centrally controlled to meet the requirements of industrialisation and the academic interests of medical scientists. Indeed Navarro has characterised its essential features as broadly similar to those in western Europe: industrial and scientific, where the consumer is a passive individual recipient of the service, and problems are to be solved in an apolitical managerial framework.[60] There is little room in such a system for mass participation and all too much room for political repression.[61]

A final feature is the nature of the health professions, particularly the use of less qualified medical staff (feldshers) and the high proportion of female doctors. Feldshers have been indispensable substitutes for doctors since the nineteenth century, particularly in rural areas. Since the majority of complaints that are presented for primary health care are relatively simple this may not affect the quality of provision, although research in the mid-1960s identified poor diagnoses and inappropriate referrals more often amongst feldshers.[62] In fact feldshers, although acting as doctor substitutes, are not distributed inversely to the distribution of doctors as might be expected. Republics short of doctors are also short of feldshers, the coefficient of correlation between the two staff-to-population ratios by Republic being 0.77 in 1950 and 0.84 in 1974.[63] The number of feldshers has grown as rapidly as the number of doctors since 1950, and there is now one feldsher to two doctors nationally (about half a million in total). Thus there is still great reliance on these medical workers, despite plans by several union Republics to restrict their work to emergencies only. Such plans are in line with the preference for highly qualified specialists in Soviet medicine. However, it is unlikely that feldshers will eventually disappear since they still provide more medical consultations than doctors in rural areas, and many feldshers ultimately qualify as full doctors through further education.[64]

An unusually high proportion of Soviet doctors are women (70 per cent), though this is lower than the all-time high of 77 per cent in 1950 and entrants to medical school are now roughly in equal proportions by sex. This feminisation is a further indication of the place of medicine in Soviety society, and the priorities that were set in the middle of the century. During this time rapid industrial expansion took clear preference over services such as medicine, which received less productive workers (women) and lower wages.[65] This interpretation gains strength from the observation that senior positions contain a much higher proportion of men (though not as high as in Britain and the USA) (Table 4.5). To summarise, we can conclude that despite a rapid and continued expansion of supply of doctors and hospital beds, and a commitment to preventive and popular health care, the pursuit by the CPSU of industrial growth has centralised and made hierarchical a health service shaped by academic medicine.

TABLE 4.5
Women in the health services[66]

	% women
Academy of Medical Sciences	10
Professor	20
Administrator	50
Surgeon	30
Primary-care doctor	90
Feldsher	85

Finance
The Soviet health service is financed almost entirely with central government funds (called 'social consumption funds'). These funds can be seen in the structural context of all government finance as discussed in chapter 2. Since 1958 government expenditure on health care has remained at a steady 4 per cent of the net material product, or nearly 20 per cent of all social consumption funds.[67] In addition another 1 per cent of NMP was spent by state enterprises, trade unions and collective farms, with a small contribution from social insurance funds and private payments.[68] Government finance is handled centrally by the Ministry of Health through union ministries and hence down into regional health facilities, where salaries take over 50 per cent of the budget, food about 10 per cent, and medicines about 8 per cent.

The 1 per cent of NMP not handled by the Ministry of Health provides some contentious issues in an otherwise highly-regulated system. Part of this income comes from charges for medicines, other than those supplied in hospitals which are free. Poor supply often results in patients purchasing their own drugs outside and bringing them into hospital. Despite a promise in 1969 to phase out these charges by 1980 there is no sign of this policy being implemented. Indeed, one of the authors was assured recently that charges were still necessary as a way of controlling demand. Another part of this non-government income comes from state enterprises and collective farms which can plough back part of their profits to provide better health services for their workers. As suggested above this occupational welfare in many cases duplicates and supports adult polyclinic provision. It functions both as an aid to labour incentive, attracting good workers and reducing turnover, and also to help labour discipline by scrutinising closely any absences from work excused on medical grounds. These services also extend to the provision of health sanatoria and resorts which, depending on circumstances, may be paid for in part by industrial enterprises, trade unions, and workers.

A more contentious source of non-government finance is private payment for health care. In any economy with a range of incomes, high earners may wish to purchase social services privately. In the Soviet Union this is frowned upon officially, but potential demand is actually met in two ways. First, there is a range of closed hospitals, dispensaries and polyclinics provided for privileged members of the party and government elite — the so-called 'fourth directorate' of the health service.[69] This removes a considerable part of potential demand for private medicine. Second, there is allowed, though discouraged through heavy taxation, private general practice, a few fee-paying polyclinics open to the public, and a scale of unofficial fees for 'tipping' ordinary medical staff. This latter situation is by far the most widespread and is sufficiently developed for a market to have emerged such that the rate of these additional fees is fairly stable: 4-5 roubles plus taxi fare for a home visit; 50 roubles for a post-operative gift to the surgeon; 150 roubles for extensive dental work; and so on.[70]

It is difficult to describe the Soviet health service today without implying certain judgments about its adequacy compared with its own and the original Bolshevik ideals and compared with other industrialised countries. Such an assessment can now be tackled explicitly in the final section of this chapter.

Assessment

Because the starting point we have chosen for each social service is a summary of the early Bolshevik ideals, it is appropriate to finish with an examination of their realisation, the extent to which they have been modified and the constraints on them.

The original ideals were remarkably similar to those of the British National Health Service: comprehensive, universal, free and

state-provided. In addition, preventive care and workers' participation
were to extend the meaning and administration of health care on the
basis of a Marxist view of illness. We can examine each of these six
principles for signs of their continued existence, and the extent of
their implementation.

The notion of comprehensive health care is difficult to circumscribe,
for it depends on the state of current knowledge. Most countries have
deferred to professional judgment in the expectation that this would
maximise the use of scientific knowledge. However, concern has recently
appeared in the west both from the point of view of the consumer[71] and
the social scientist[72] that such judgment and indeed the development of
science itself are powerfully influenced by economic and political constraints. In the Soviet Union, although the medical profession has no
independent political status, autonomous specialisation and technical
development has occurred and indeed been encouraged. As a result, the
technical division of primary care, the rapid growth in the provision of
doctors, and the administrative dominance of the hospitals (in the
western pattern) must also be subject to such criticism. In essence this
is that medical science is still geared to a nineteenth-century model of
illness, concerned with acute life-threatening disorders. Today these are
chiefly cancer and heart disease. Enormous investments are being made
in these areas (the source of much pride shown towards western visitors),
while investments in preventive care are less spectacular. In reality the
twentieth-century pattern of illness is of non life-threatening episodic
disorders which allow a fluctuating level of functioning (mental illness,
bronchitis, influenza, and back injuries). In this respect the early
emphasis on prevention in the Soviet Union was a great advance. However, this notion is even more difficult to pin down than comprehensiveness of provision, for it may be stretched to include substantial aspects
of the environment, such as housing and diet; and as far as mental illness is concerned, family life, social and occupational mobility, and so
on. It is difficult for this reason to measure investment in preventive
health care except by such narrow definitions as screening and health
check-ups. Nevertheless, as a principle it is still important and is identified in the Soviet Union more as an attitude than an activity within
health care.

As ideals, comprehensiveness and prevention are thus alive and well,
although it is now apparent that the original notions were so broad as to
make their evaluation difficult. In comparison with Britain the remarkable similarity of Soviet health care (in contrasting both countries again,
for example, with the USA) may be a result merely of central planning
and state provision. Hence we may conclude that the identification of an
important principle of medical science in the twentieth century — prevention — has not yet been extensively translated into practice.

The goal of universal coverage of the population, despite early allocation in favour of workers, obviously resonates with fundamental ideals of eliminating class differences, of resolving antagonisms between the city and the countryside, and so forth. This ideal, concerned as it is with the distribution of services and with problems of access, is more easily evaluated than the issue of what kind of medical care to develop. We can identify several basic dimensions of inequality here: social class, geography, age, sex and illness type. Access to services from the point of view of the consumer has not really been systematically studied in the Soviet Union. Data are scarce and often anecdotal. Overall distribution on the other hand can be more firmly, if more generally, mapped. Social class differences in health care occur in two respects. First there are some 'closed' polyclinics and hospitals available as a 'fourth department' of the health service to certain elite people such as party members. Of this special service only good hospital care really constitutes a privilege since access to good primary care is widely available to ordinary citizens. In addition, a small private market in medicine and the wide-spread custom of 'tipping' health professionals must disadvantage the poor. Second, workers receive additional health care at their place of work. In certain cases (railway workers)[73] this service is reported to be markedly superior; enough to attract external 'back door' demand. More generally a mere duplication of neighbourhood polyclinics is involved, with the occasional chance of a sanatorium stay at the sea-side or in the country − as much a holiday as anything.

Geographical inequality is more serious. Despite a commitment to urban-rural equality, the direction of doctors into the countryside is still a considerable problem. Although all Republics have substantially increased their supply since 1950 and the variation in distribution has decreased, the least urbanised Republics are universally less well provided-for. This pattern is accentuated by a parallel maldistribution of feldshers who, contrary to a widely held assumption, do not make up for shortages of doctors. The current solution is to encourage rural patients to travel to urban centres instead.

Additional inequalities by age, sex and type of illness are more difficult to assess. To the extent that maternity and child-health services are a specialist branch (all children are regularly screened), and old people no longer have access to industrial polyclinics, children are advantaged. However, this is offset by the noticeably higher birth rate in the poorer rural areas. The influence of sex, only recently recognised as significant in the west, is unlikely to disadvantage women so much in the Soviet Union since so many doctors (especially in primary care) are women. The influence of illness-type requires some measure of equivalence between qualitatively different needs such that, for example, we can decide whether mental-illness needs are served as well as heart-disease needs. This difficult issue, already alluded to earlier, can only be evaluated in such general terms as the emphasis on high technology, hospital based medicine and the low investment in preventive care. As such, Soviet medicine shares criticisms directed at western medicine and, as Mark Field has pointed out,[74] this contrasts sharply with the suspicion of specialisation and the use of traditional medicine in China.

It is clear that the original ideal of universal coverage has not yet been realised. In addition the ideal itself has been seriously compromised. Priorities in favour of certain elite members, workers, the young, and acute life-threatening illness have appeared. However, other deviations from the ideal such as urban-rural differences, are not accepted and considerable efforts have been made to overcome them. The limits to the success of these efforts and the appearance of favoured groups of health consumers can be related to certain long-term developments of Soviet society, particularly the overriding goal of industrialisation and the centralisation of political power which will be explored further below.

The ideal of free provision has been largely attained at the point of consumption. Drugs supplied in hospital and for serious and chronic illnesses are free, but have to be paid for otherwise (about 30 per cent of all prescriptions), and are relatively inexpensive. However, hospital supplies are sometimes unreliable and it is not unusual for patients or their relatives to purchase them outside. A further qualification is the widespread practice of tipping medical personnel. It is reported that this is common enough for stable rates to have become established[75] and non-payment can make life uncomfortable for the patient. Private practice is heavily taxed and not widely available. Similarly private polyclinics (perhaps 130 in all),[76] are very scarce compared with the state service. Of course, although the state is funding the service the resources are basically produced by Soviet workers, and hence this central financing represents a transfer rather than a net gain.

The last ideal, that the service should be uniform and state-provided, is again very general since state provision can be autocratic or democratic. It is relevant here to include the ideal of worker participation, for although the Soviet health service is state-provided and uniformly administered, the extent of participation is questionable. There are several ways this can occur. First, the existence of permanent public health commissions at all levels from the supreme soviet to local district soviets can call the health service to 'account' and exercise some 'effective control'[77] and hence offer participation through the normal representative channels of 'democratic centralism'. Second, trade unions monitor industrial safety and encourage workers to participate in health-promoting activities such as physical exercise and subsidised health resorts. Third, the party and the press can monitor and offer sometimes

biting criticism of any aspects of the health service which are not satisfactory. Fourth, this can sometimes lead to 'popular movements' for
health, such as the post-war efforts to avoid epidemics. More permanent
organisation of this voluntary activity comes through the Red Cross and
Red Crescent societies with 80 million members, official 'health days',
and public councils in health institutions.

Although these channels appear numerous their effect is difficult to
evaluate in real terms. There is no doubt that popular health education
and the promotion of physical culture and health resorts is widespread.
Yet this is also true of West Germany, where generous social insurance
and traditional attitudes have elevated such activities in the 'curehouse'
to a major industry. More telling is the specialisation of medicine and
centralisation of management in the Soviet health service, which it is
difficult to reconcile with real popular- and mass-participation. Hence
Navarro has been forced to the conclusion that the health service is
undemocratic, and that the only participation is that 'in which the
individual is a passive recipient and consumer of services — as in
bourgeois medicine'.[78] Similarly, Field has observed that in comparison
with

> the exciting experiments going on in medicine and public health;
> the emphasis on local, rural personnel, and de-emphasis of pro-
> fessionalism and expertise; the attempt to cope with difficult tasks
> by enlisting the active co-operation of lay personnel . . . [character-
> istic of China] the Soviet contemporary health scene is a deadly bore.
> Brezhnev's interest in and concern with medicine, public health and
> physical fitness . . . is close to zero. Attempts to involve the laity are
> minimal, though ideologically recognised as legitimate. The Soviet
> picture is that of a highly specialised, differentiated bureaucratic
> system, where routine and predictability have been elevated to a high
> art.[79]

We see then that the survival and implementation of the early ideals
has been partial. As a conclusion to this assessment we can suggest
briefly some of the constraints which are responsible. The role of state
intervention in this area is of crucial significance, placing constraints
round the health service in three ways. These are the production and
servicing of human capital, the consumption of health care as a desirable
good, and the control and legitimation of the social order. While these
are related to the health services in this chapter, they are explored more
generally for Soviet social policy in Appendix 2.

The idea that health care is an investment in one of the basic factors
of production has a long history. The introduction of public health
measures in Britain in the nineteenth century rested partly on such views

held by Chadwick. In the Soviet Union, Strumilin has long argued such a model for both health and education policy. Since all societies must produce their wealth and appropriate a surplus to be distributed more or less justly on collective provision, any measure which can either prolong or maintain the efficiency of productive labour may be seen as an investment. If this were the exclusive criterion for the use of health care, one would expect it to be at least primarily directed towards productive (and reproductive) labour. The development of specialist health services for industrial workers and mothers and children in the Soviet Union during Stalin's drive for industrialisation fits such a model well. However, it is not at all clear to what extent the health services do provide a good rate of return for such investment. It might be more efficient to build better housing or produce more food, neither of which the Soviet Union has been outstandingly successful at, particularly during the period of industrialisation. It seems reasonable therefore, to regard the health services as being also provided to meet health needs (regardless of whether they return a worker to productive activity), or even desirable consumer goods in their own right producing nothing but intrinsic satisfaction. There is no doubt that the development of health care in the 1920s was based on such notions. For example, the rapid expansion of the number of doctors after the Revolution provided for many rural peasants their first experience of medical care. Today the continued expansion in the production of doctors and the growing proportion of the population which is regularly screened can only be explained as an attempt to meet health needs, since an ageing population cannot promise much in the way of economic returns on human capital investment. Similarly the small but vigorous appearance of a private market in health care indicates, in the face of a relatively successful public service, that there is considerable consumer demand for health-care goods.

Finally, we can suggest that certain aspects of the health service are a necessary expense through which the state can purchase legitimation and control and can reproduce those inequalities which have developed in twentieth-century Soviet society. In common with other social services, the health service is today presented as an important indication of the Soviet state's generosity to Soviet workers. Free health care is represented as a gift, rather than redistributed surplus, which itself is held to be a result of the identity of interests of the state and the people. In comparison with the USA, where medical indigence is a nagging worry for many,[80] such a view is justifiable. However, the Soviet people are asked in return to accept other less generous aspects of Soviet society, such as the political use of psychiatric hospitals, the provision of private health care for the privileged and the academic production of high technology medicine with little public participation in policy decisions.

In this respect, while the Soviet health service must be commended

5

Housing in the Soviet Union

The development of housing under socialism involves issues which touch
on the very core of the new society: the nature of the city and the
country, and the relationship between them; the nature of the family,
property relations, architecture and the creative arts; and the pattern of
economic investment.

Marxism and housing

In common with the other services, ideals expressed by Marx, Engels and
Lenin about housing were tantalisingly brief. As a result ideas developed
since the 1917 Revolution have fluctuated between the utopian and the
severely realist, and have exhibited clearly the continuing struggle for
both economic growth and a socialist way of life.

Engels associated the appalling Manchester housing conditions he
described in *The Condition of the Working Class in England* with the
development of capitalism:

> Everything which here arouses horror and indignation is of recent
> origin, belongs to the industrial epoch.[1]

The earliest comment on the solution to these problems comes in *The
German Ideology*, where Marx and Engels link the division of labour and
private property (including land and housing) as 'identical expressions',
which would disappear under communism. The ultimate division of
labour was 'the antagonism between town and country', the abolition of

which thus became 'one of the first conditions of communal life', since it was

> the most crass expression of the subject of the individual under the division of labour, under a definite activity forced upon him which makes one man into a restricted town-animal, the other into a restricted country-animal, and daily creates anew the conflict between their interests.[2]

This general problem is explored in more detail in *The Housing Question*, where Engels argues that

> the peculiar intensification of the bad housing conditions of the workers as the result of the sudden rush of population to the big towns . . . can only be solved when society has been sufficiently transformed for a start to be made towards abolishing the antithesis between town and country.[3]

In contrast to the bourgeois solution in which

> the infamous holes and cellars in which the capitalist mode of production confines our workers . . . are merely shifted elsewhere

Engels envisaged that 'the housing shortage can be remedied immediately by expropriating a part of the luxury dwellings belonging to the propertied classes'.

In the long term 'the modern big cities . . . will be abolished' and

> as uniform a distribution as possible of the population over the whole country, . . . an integral connection between industrial and agricultural production together with the thereby necessary extension of the means of communication, would be able to save the rural population from the isolation and stupor in which it has vegetated almost unchanged for thousands of years.[4]

However, he is careful to qualify this image further on:

> To speculate as to how a future society would organise the distribution of food and dwellings leads directly to utopia. Even the transitional measures will everywhere have to be in accordance with the conditions in existence at the moment.[5]

In fact Engels's policy for the immediate redistribution of luxury dwellings was 'the cornerstone of Soviet housing policy' during the post-revolutionary period of war communism,[6] when there was little possibility of any more constructive activity. Lenin had promised 'peace, bread and land' and the day after the seizure of power land was nationalised, followed by the requisition of apartments in November and the abolition of private ownership on 20 August 1918. Otherwise Lenin said nothing specific about post-revolutionary housing, save for general comments on utopian tendencies in architecture (as in other areas).[7]

The nature of housing to be built after the initial reallocations of existing buildings depended on the resolution of several problems. To what extent was Czarist Russia pre-capitalist and hence needed investment in industry rather than houses? How far should social life, including the family, be purged of individualism in favour of communal arrangements? Thus, what should the new urban environment look like, and what was a socialist architecture? 'The Bolshevik Party had no predetermined model' in these areas and many issues were developed amongst the 'so-called Left Front' searching for 'new architectural and urban forms ideologically appropriate to socialism'.[8]

It is therefore difficult to isolate one set of ideals, and we shall first have to review the contending ideas which developed in the 1920s. The development of housing itself was closely linked to the question of whether family life should move away from bourgeois individualism towards some kind of communalism. Engels had argued in *The Origin of the Family, Private Property and the State* that the form of the family was historically determined. The bourgeois family merely reflected capitalist relations. The woman was exploited and in effect sold herself into permanent slavery on marriage; and the proletarian family was torn apart by industrialisation. After 1917 many new views about the family were put forward, varying from notions of 'pure' relations and sexual abstinence, to the more notorious ideas of Kollontai[9] who advocated the divorce of love and sex relations, demoting the latter to mere physical need. However, Engels had also argued that 'the first division of labour is that between man and woman for the propagation of children.'[10] Hence inequalities of biology, sexual relations and age were not necessarily due to particular modes of production. A parallel drawn between the withering away of the state and the withering away of the family was therefore too simple. In any case, Lenin had argued in *State and Revolution* that the state would not wither away until the arrival of the higher phase of communism in the distant future, and hence any radical reconstruction of the family was premature.

This uncertainty about the family was reflected in the design of housing. As in other areas of social policy, the Bolsheviks were not averse to borrowing ideas from Europe. One powerful influence was the English 'garden city' concept of Ebenezer Howard, which could surround large cities and relieve congestion. These 'Red garden cities' were to consist of practical, individualistic 'English' cottages and surprisingly found favour with many Bolsheviks.[11] Perhaps more typical of this period were the proponents of a 'left tendency' in social planning which envisaged the collectivisation of most social life. Echoing Kollontai's views on the family these planners proposed the development of house-communes, which were not at all designed for traditional family living. The most extreme example was a design by Ivan Leonidov for a

> high rise structure with the ground floor and the roof terrace allocated to sport and recreation and with an intermediate floor for common dining. All other floors were identical glass-enclosed spaces without any interior partitions. About two-thirds of each floor was divided by planting boxes and by carpeting into 120 equal squares of 55 square feet each. Every worker was allotted one such square with only a bed in it for sleeping. The remaining third of the floor area was common space for relaxation, reading, games and exercises. Even a running track and a swimming pool were provided within the same floor space.[12]

In fact communal living during the 1920s was only realised in urban communes using existing housing and the construction of barracks to accommodate workers in new industrial areas, the real motivation being more practical than utopian. Desirable though new living arrangements might be, ideally the need to free women for employment[13] and the acute housing shortage[14] were more pressing realities.

These ideas for housing were closely linked with large-scale plans for the city. Although city planning was not well developed at this time beyond such formal plans as had been developed for pre-revolutionary St Petersburg, the Revolution released a powerful new interest in reconstructing cities. Out of a mixture of European ideas and the comments of Marx and Engels, several new approaches appeared. The main alternatives, in the effort to reduce urban-rural differences, were either to concentrate rural populations into small towns spread across the countryside or to disperse the whole population, including present city dwellers, evenly over the whole country. Various solutions were offered in between these two polar positions. 'Ribbon' cities spread along main transport routes and the 'Red garden cities', mentioned above, both combined elements of dispersal and limited urban concentration. Extreme concentration, for example in Le Corbusier's skyscraper city of efficient superblocks, was too 'capitalistic' and hence politically unacceptable.[15] Yet complete de-urbanisation, spreading the population uniformly across the entire territory, was rejected as economically unsound especially in terms of transport costs.[16] Perhaps the most famous and successful compromise was Miliutin's 'linear city', which could extend indefinitely in a series of parallel strips — industry, transport, green belt and residential zone as 'an artery along which the principles of Karl Marx could be pumped'.[17]

These ideals would require huge capital investment and thus implied certain economic priorities. However, as we pointed out in chapter 1, there was some uncertainty at this time as to the correct industrial path to follow. Most urban planners envisaged a convenient simultaneous and proximate construction of housing and industrial facilities, but they were not realistic about the difficulties of economic development, particularly in view of the failure of the expected world revolution. For example the most prominent urbanist, Sabsovich, believed that

> full collectivisation of agriculture would be completed in two to three years, that the country would be covered in a modern network of transportation and communication within three to four years, and that in ten years time the Soviet Union would surpass the United States in national industrial production. He assumed that all existing towns and villages could be rebuilt as new socialist towns within fifteen to twenty years.[18]

Where the capital for such an investment was to come from was not clear. Moreover the possibility that housing and industrial construction might be in competition for capital investment was not appreciated in the quest for harmonious development. However, just such competition is a major theme in the way housing, city planning and industrialisation have developed and influenced each other.

It is difficult, and potentially misleading, to summarise all these ideas in one general scheme. Since we are interested here in the development and impact of housing on individuals and families rather than the more general construction of urban forms, we can focus directly on the provision of housing in our summary, leaving the wider implications for discussion in the rest of the chapter. The early ideals for housing are thus as follows:

1 'A separate apartment with a total floor space of at least 50 square metres; the apartment shall consist of two habitable rooms, a vestibule, a kitchen, a bathroom, and . . . a separate storeroom or cellar' (Decree of the People's Commissariat of Labour, 1920).[19] This has more usually been expressed as 9 square metres per capita of living space (bedrooms and living rooms only), the 'sanitary housing norm', derived from nineteenth-century work by Pettenkofer, a German health specialist, on the adequacy of ventilation.[20]
2 This accommodation should be available to everyone.

3   All housing should be state owned (either nationalised by enterprises, or municipalised by Soviets).

4   Accommodation and utilities should be free.

5   Provision should be determined by need, and hence urban-rural differences eliminated by reducing problems (such as overcrowding and pollution) of the 'capitalist' city, and by raising the cultural and economic level of the countryside.

6   There should be workers' participation in the administration of housing through the soviets in accordance with central planning norms and regulations.

Historical developments

In order to understand the housing situation on the eve of the Bolshevik Revolution we must consider the following: the existing housing stock, its distribution in relation to the population, the nature and extent of urbanisation and local government arrangements.

Pre-revolutionary housing consisted in the main of small one-or two-storey wooden structures. These were universal in the countryside and in the towns still made up two-thirds of the stock; even in Moscow and Leningrad well over half was wooden.[21] Sewage, water and central-heating systems were the exception rather than the rule. In the country most families built their own wooden houses, and the necessary skills continued to be widespread at least up until the Second World War.[22] But in the city housing conditions were far worse. The availability of urban housing in comparison with the urban population was extremely meagre, and clearly the worst of any industrialising western country. Although no comprehensive pre-revolutionary data exist, Sosnovy estimates that the urban population had an average of 7 square metres of dwelling space per capita.[23] According to the 1912 census there was an average of eight people per apartment in Moscow and St Petersburg – twice as many as in Berlin and three times as many as in Paris at that time.[24] However, this average concealed a sharply unequal distribution, such that 2 square metres per person was not unusual.[25] As a result, in St Petersburg in 1908 70 per cent of single workers and nearly 50 per cent of married workers had only a corner of a room.[26]

This mismatch between urban housing stock and the urban population was a result of steady urbanisation throughout the late nineteenth century. Although some disagreement exists about the extent and causes of this change, we can suggest a general picture. In the early part of the nineteenth century, somewhere between 5 and 8 per cent of the population lived in urban areas. This proportion began to increase in the middle of the century as a result of mobility made possible by the end of serfdom in 1861, and the extension of the railway system in a country where distance and terrain were significant difficulties.[27] This potential mobility was more positively triggered by the expansion of domestic and foreign trade and especially factory industry late in the century. However, much of this industry was located outside cities, since the absence of an independent entrepreneurial class and the encouragement of a powerful central state had resulted in many land owners building factories on their estates. Thus the urban proportion of the population was still only 15 per cent by 1910, but since the total population, at 160 millions, was by this time four times its early nineteenth-century level, the absolute number of people now trying to find accommodation in the cities had created an acute housing shortage. Whether transport accessibility[28] or the growth of 'economic' cities[29] was responsible, while an important question for the nature of pre-revolutionary capitalism, the implications of this problem are clear. It was to make a significant contribution to the revolutionary tensions which the Bolsheviks, as we shall see, could dramatically ease by decreeing a radical redistribution of housing stock immediately after the Revolution.

To the extent that pre-revolutionary social policies shaped subsequent expectations, if only for something much better, the question arises here as to why this potentially explosive issue was not tackled by the Czarist government even in the limited way that it had tackled disease through zemstvo medicine and meagre social security. In fact such an attempt was made in the 1870 Municipal Statute which allowed city leaders some degree of self-government, particularly with regard to managing the local economy and raising taxes. However, this 'apex of statutory freedom for municipal self-rule in the history of the Russian empire'[30] was criticised locally for its transparent motive of 'avoiding the outflow of state funds for urban needs',[31] and centrally for the potential chaos which self-government might unleash. By 1892 local independence was restricted again, even more than it had been before 1870, by a new Municipal Statute. This effectively reduced local tax revenues such that the compulsory support of imperial troops in the absence of cheap state-provided credit exhausted city budgets. Since they were now not allowed deficits in city spending they could not cope with rapid urbanisation. Hamm concludes that this 'myopic perspective of the Tsarist government towards the whole complex of problems related to urbanisation'[32] should be reassessed as a vital factor in the ultimate demise of the Czarist empire.

Not surprisingly, then, very little urban building was in evidence prior to 1917, and planning and architecture remained for the most part un-realised paper exercises. However the February Revolution in 1917 gave new freedom and scope to the development of professional activities.

135

We have already seen how it encouraged the doctors to set about re-organising the health services. As far as housing is concerned, a similar professional revival began. The Revolution

> had the very positive function of destroying these bureaucratic regulatory bodies and thereby liberating architects and city planners from a major source of frustration. From that moment . . . the architects and planners had every reason to believe that they, the designers, would be free to make plans for whatever seemed necessary for the architecture and urban development of Russia and to present those plans to the government with every expectation that they would be adopted.[33]

After the October Revolution, in marked contrast to the doctors who were quickly suppressed as an independent profession, planners and architects gained even further opportunities to realise their ideas through the widespread state control of construction, land and property, and the encouragement given to city planning. These controls were put into effect very quickly. The day after the seizure of power (26 October) Lenin drafted a law 'On requisitioning the houses of the rich for alleviating the needs of the poor'. Twelve days later he issued the 'Fundamentals of the law on the confiscation of apartment houses'. However, in the chaotic aftermath of the Revolution, while the Bolsheviks were consolidating their power in the urban soviets, much of this redistribution of housing occurred spontaneously. 'Bourgeois, parasitic elements' often lost all their possessions, including their accommodation, rather than just their excess rooms. These changes were finally codified in the 1918 law, passed on 20 August, which was the foundation of all subsequent housing law: 'On the abolition of private ownership of urban real estate' (i.e. land and buildings). Significantly, sections two and four exempted buildings 'which are an essential part of industrial enterprises', small buildings and small settlements (less than 10,000 people).[34] In effect owner-occupied and factory housing was excused, which thus divided the housing stock into three types − privately owned, municipalised (by the local soviet), and nationalised (in the hands of industrial enterprises).

The impact of these early laws on the nature of the housing stock was severely distorted by two factors: first, the limited capability of the new local soviets to take over and effectively manage the housing stock; and second, the chaotic impact of war communism. As in other areas of post-revolutionary life it was still uncertain how the dictatorship of the proletariat envisaged by Lenin would actually be organised. 'All power' was not going to the soviets, since workers' committees and trade unions at factories (some of which owned housing) and various residence-based housing committees also represented workers' interests. In addition to spontaneous requisitions by tenants who 'behaved not like responsible owners, but like a licentious army of conquerors'[35] soviets were uncertain about which properties should be municipalised. Furthermore, the shortage of food and fuel and the decline in industrial production during this period encouraged many urban dwellers to leave for the country. Those who stayed actually destroyed many buildings by taking the wood for fuel with little regard for the efforts of the 'Commission for the Demolition of Houses and Country Homes for Fuel' set up to co-ordinate this activity in 1918.[36] Much of the legislation of this period, then, merely rationalised existing practice. For example, rents were abolished in 1921 not least because a combination of a rent freeze and inflation since 1917 had reduced them to insignificant levels.[37]

At the end of the period of war communism, we find a substantial reduction in urban housing stock (Moscow 30 per cent; Leningrad 17 per cent; Kharkov and Odessa 28 per cent), and in addition an even greater reduction in urban population, for example by 75 per cent in Leningrad.[38] The quality of existing accommodation had also deteriorated. A survey in Moscow in 1920 revealed that in nearly three-quarters of apartments both heating, plumbing and roofs were damaged, and hence only one-quarter were deemed fit to live in.[39] However a great deal of property had been municipalised (about 50 per cent of the total volume of urban housing, containing about 40 per cent of the urban population),[40] and the redistribution of housing had made substantial improvements for millions of urban dwellers. Although to the extent that this was a result of de-urbanisation, demographic trouble was being stored up for the future.

These housing difficulties, along with others which threatened to swamp the new Soviet state, played their part in bringing about the New Economic Policy of 1921. During the previous four years it can be argued that limited efforts were made to fulfil some of the original ideals that we outlined: free rent, Soviet administration, state ownership and a fairer distribution. After 1921 there was a clear change of policy with regard to housing. The deterioration of existing housing and lack of new construction were the focus of new measures. One of the first acts was 'On the correct distribution of dwellings among the toiling classes' (25 May 1920) which aimed to encourage repairs by reducing the insecurity of tenants liable to sudden eviction, or 'compression', of their housing space. This was followed in 1921 by a decree 'On inducing the inhabitants of municipal houses to repair installations for the supply of water, central heating and sewage'. This required payment for current repairs and offered three years security of tenure in return. In effect it opened up the return of rents, at first locally determined (1922) and then nationally (1926). Rents were steeply graduated in accordance with the quality of accommodation, the income of the tenant, and his status — in

1928 'non-working elements' were paying eighty times the minimum worker's rate.[41]

In order to try to balance the housing economy rents were gradually increased throughout the 1920s from 2.8 per cent of average income in 1922 to 10.4 per cent in 1929 (it was 20-25 per cent before 1917). As a result, rental income met about two-thirds of the costs of the housing economy (including replacement) in the early 1920s, and the total cost by the late 1920s. However, this could not provide for expanding the stock and further measures were taken to increase investment. In 1921 a decree calling for de-municipalisation where not essential returned buildings to former owners in return for an undertaking to do repairs and the retention of 10 per cent of space for the local soviet. In 1922 private individuals were given the right to build and land could be made available without charge. 1924 saw the first appearance of housing co-operatives, both in terms of managing municipal accommodation (house-renting societies − the 'Zhakty' − which rapidly took over 50 per cent of municipalised dwellings), and in terms of new building. This was the most constructive development of this period, stimulating investment and improving management.

By 1926 house building had revived quite strongly taking 17 per cent of the total investment in the economy of which two-thirds was privately built. However, the return of city-dwellers and first-time migrants outstripped this expansion and by 1926 dwelling space had fallen to 5.85 square metres per capita. In response, new incentives to private builders were introduced in 1927, for example extending the length of leases; and in 1928, in the pursuit of 'big private capital' for housing, a variety of extremely generous measures were introduced such as freedom to set up private joint-stock companies, tax exemption, and so on. Block describes this last act as 'the biggest 'retreat', if there ever was one, on the housing front. It was passed six years after Lenin declared that the 'retreat' had ended, and was in force more than ten years.'[42] However, the war against 'capitalists' in other areas effectively undermined the 1928 act. It was decided to nullify all private leases by the end of the first Five Year Plan (1933), building credits were discontinued in 1930, and materials and plans were denied private builders. Between 1929 and 1932 individual housing construction dropped from 40 per cent of the total to less than 1 per cent.[43] But these changes, signalling the end of NEP, were not all as uniform as appears at first. The drive to collectivise agriculture and industrialise set in motion a cultural revolution bent on 'a wild orgy of negation'[44] which looked forward to the withering away not only of bureaucracy, but academies, schools, and even the city itself. This crescendo to the utopianism released by the October Revolution produced the most far-reaching ideas for modelling a new Soviet man through a new-built environment. The gap between ideals and reality was enormous at this time, for in fact unplanned urbanisation between 1926 and 1939 set a world record. Rural-to-urban migration totalled 40 million: equivalent to the total for Europe between 1800 and 1940.[45] Indeed it may be that this utopianism was an important vision with which to soften the realities of the early 1930s.

Many elements of the NEP such as the 'Zhakty' and the 1928 act existed well into the mid 1930s, while there was considerable confusion in architecture over whether reformulated classicism (the formalists) or avant-garde functionalism (the constructivists) was appropriate to meet Stalin's pressures for 'socialist realism', long after other arts such as literature had settled on a uniform interpretation.[46] The first major bridge to be built between these ideals and the realities of urban life was the preparation of a general plan for the reconstruction of Moscow in the early 1930s to celebrate the industrial success of the first Five Year Plan. The government rejected the usual crop of avant-garde proposals, and 'by themselves, set out to rejuvenate and beautify Moscow on more practical and economic lines'.[47] The plan became in fact a model for urban development and hence the problems surrounding its implementation are a useful guide to the general difficulties of city planning in the 1930s.

The major elements of the plan included limiting population growth, removing differences between the rich centre and poor outskirts, an even distribution of public buildings, limiting industrial sprawl through zoning and green belts, and constructing sufficient housing organised into residential districts with all facilities.[48] However not all elements succeeded. Population growth continued rapidly, many buildings were not completed according to plan, or were designed without the general plan in mind, and the quality of construction was poor. Zoning rules were ignored: for example tall buildings were erected in the suburbs and the Moscow soviet itself allowed industries to develop in residential zones. The greatest failure was in not building sufficient housing. Not only was the unexpected increase in population not housed adequately, but even the original schedules were 80 per cent unfulfilled in the first five years.[49]

To understand these shortcomings we must turn, as in other chapters, to the influence of rapid industrialisation as a fundamental policy object-ive from the 1930s onwards. This was formally reflected, as we saw in the health services, in a division of labour between service planning and economic planning: in September 1933 urban planning projects were separated into one agency and industrial development into another, both subordinate to the Commissariat of Heavy Industry.[50] Industrialisation affected four aspects of housing: planning; the distribution of invest-ment; ownership and management; access and security of tenure.

As a result of the experience gained in Moscow, city planning expanded rapidly. During the third Five Year Plan (1938-42), plans for reconstructing 225 cities in the RSFSR alone were drawn up. However it was clear that earlier ideals were now to be subordinated to economic goals. Molotov stressed that

'new construction in regions of the U.S.S.R. should be based on the principle of centering industries in locations most accessible to sources of raw materials and to regions of greatest demand, with the aim of liquidating irrational and lengthy transport.' Planners were told 'to develop further express methods of construction of multi-storey apartments' and 'to pay more attention to problems of economy'. (Speech to the 18th Party Congress, 1939)[51]

In addition there was renewed effort in principle to integrate these practical concerns with careful aesthetic design, cultural facilities and full services; and to avoid repeating mistakes such as Magnitogorsk — 'a city without a centre, without squares, without streets, with endless monotonous rows of buildings'.[52]

In fact investment in housing suffered particularly as a result of the concentration on industry after the early 1930s. As a proportion of total investment in the economy it fell from an all-time high of 17 per cent in the 1920s to 9 per cent in the first Five Year Plan and 8 per cent on the eve of the Second World War. However this was not simply a result of competition over public investment funds. The average rate of plan fulfilment over this period was only around 50 per cent. Moreover the proportion of housing construction in the private sector fell from 84 per cent in the mid-1920s to 16 per cent in the 1930s and early 1940s.[53] The obvious economic solution, to encourage individual house building, was discouraged for its political implications — the possible revival of private entrepreneurial activity. Balinsky has even argued that publicly-controlled and scarce housing was a deliberate policy designed to give greater control over the labour force.[54] Within the public sector industrial enterprises became the main builders. Their share of public-housing investment rose from 50 per cent in the mid-20s to 85 per cent (73 per cent of all housing investment) in the late 1930s. Much of this investment was in the form of new towns in areas of expanding industry, such as coal, iron and oil, where an enterprise often came to dominate the 'company town' with up to 95 per cent of housing under its control. By the beginning of the war this kind of housing amounted to one-third of the total public stock.[55]

Thus by the late 1930s the housing stock was broadly divided between individuals (40 per cent), local soviets (40 per cent) and state industries and institutions (20 per cent). These categories were concentrated in certain areas with significant consequences for their management. Individual owners were located chiefly in rural areas. They had always been allowed to own a house, though only one, and this right was written into the 1936 constitution, article 10.[56] Housing owned by soviets was concentrated chiefly in older administrative centres and had been mainly delegated to the 'Zhakty' since 1924. But in 1937 a new act 'On the preservation of the housing fund and the improvement of housing in towns' ushered in a major change. It scrapped the co-operative 'Zhakty' and returned all municipal housing to the soviets for direct management. The reasons for this included a strong desire to reassert the soviet as the central administrative body, and to undermine the independence of co-operatives. In addition, co-operatives had not channelled as much private money into housing as had been hoped, but had relied mainly on government credit. Furthermore, this law finally abolished the remaining vestiges of the NEP, particularly the 1928 act. The strengthening of the soviet not only provided more direct control over housing (including the infamously close liaison between house managers and the police), but also more resistance to the growing power of various state enterprises: since the early days of Revolution, factory committees and trade unions had competed with the soviets for factory-owned housing, and in the 1920s the institutional (i.e. office) use of urban dwelling space had expanded to over 30 per cent and by the 1930s industrial enterprises were expanding their control of housing through new construction.

State enterprise housing was concentrated in the newer industrial areas, where it was managed independently and in a fairly manipulative fashion. In particular under Section 31 of the 1937 act:

It is established that the occupant may be evicted . . . without the provision of dwelling space . . . if the occupant . . . to whom dwelling space has been provided in a building of a state enterprise, . . . state office, or of a social organisation is dismissed at his own request or for violation of labour discipline or for the commission of a crime.[57]

But not only was housing used as a means of attracting and keeping labour, it was built at the minimum cost: 'We all remember those not so distant years when ministries and factories literally tore cities apart, each trying by fair means or foul, to build "its" houses.'[58] For example, in Magnitogorsk the Metallurgical Combine and Construction Trust owned 76 per cent of the housing between them, but planned for insufficient services: 'The city's heating, water, and sewage systems were painfully inadequate.'[59] Even in 1965, when the Magnitogorsk city soviet complained to the Ministry of Municipal Services, 'why haven't you helped our city?', the minister replied, 'But there is no such city, your city is not a city. It is the property of the metallurgical combine'.[60]

Finally, of course, these aspects of industrialisation in the 1930s had their impact on the tenants. Access to urban housing in principle was on the basis of need (including illness), once management had settled down in the mid-1920s. However certain exceptions developed. Enterprise housing was allocated preferentially to enterprise employees, and from 1930 privileged people, important for industrialisation, could be both advanced along the waiting list and receive additional space: these included creative artists, academics and technicians, the military and party members. Unfortunately there was also a noticeable level of corruption, admitted within Soviet publications in the 1930s, as a result of the acute shortage of housing.[61] The effects of this allocation system can be seen in the availability of urban housing space. Overall this had increased from 7 to 9 square metres per capita by 1920 as a result of redistribution and de-urbanisation. But by 1940 it had dropped to 4 square metres because of the doubling of the urban population (two-thirds as a result of rural migration). However this low average level concealed sharp inequalities. Although data are difficult to find, Sosnovy estimates that by 1940 scientific workers averaged 50 per cent more dwelling space than industrial workers and that members of the bureaucracy averaged over 100 per cent more.[62] In contrast to this pattern, inequalities between cities and between Republics declined markedly after the early 1920s up to the Second World War.[63]

Security of tenure in municipal housing was officially guaranteed in law, preference in renewing leases being given to existing occupants. However, compulsory and not infrequently illegal usurpation of rooms and 'compression' occurred through personal connections ('blat'), patronage and inefficient administration. Consequently, housing cases have become the most common category dealt with by the USSR supreme court of which eviction and the division of apartments are the most frequent concerns.[64] But once secured the accommodation was now very cheap again, rent having fallen back to the early 1920s level of less than 5 per cent of income by the late 1930s, where it is still.

If this pre-war situation looked difficult enough, the war visited upon the USSR a massive additional burden: 1,710 cities and towns were destroyed, amounting to more than 6 million dwellings which had housed 25 million people.[65] Reconstruction began where possible during the war, and the fourth Five Year Plan (1946-50) aimed not only to make good the loss, but also to expand on the total pre-war stock. In fact the plan was 77 per cent fulfilled, improving the overall average per capita dwelling space by half a square metre over the 1940 level,[66] although continued migration had made specifically urban space even scarcer, reaching an all-time low, for example, of 3.65 square metres in Moscow.[67]

In order to stimulate the greatest possible construction effort the decree of 1948 'Concerning the right of a citizen to buy and construct individual dwellings' offered the individual builder the use of house and land in perpetuity, and even the right to bequeath it to an heir. This 'new NEP in housing' was the first time the USSR had 'come close to reinstituting private ownership of real estate'.[68] However, state industries and institutions continued to be the main builders, providing more than three-quarters of all new housing in this period and hence reinforcing their already dominant position.[69]

The early 1950s gave planners a new chance after the disruption of Stalin's 1930s policies and the war to think about future developments. One of the new ideas was the agricultural city (agro-gorod), aimed at a further concentration of collective farms. Interestingly, this idea was one of the first launched by Khrushchev in 1950 just after he had become secretary to the Moscow branch of the CPSU.[70] As far as urban planning was concerned, the microrayon became the basic planning unit. It was larger than the original communal housing complexes suggested in the 1920s, catering for between 5 and 20 thousand people. Essentially it was to consist of apartment blocks grouped round shops, services and amenities in a style common to many notions of the urban neighbourhood around the world. The planning norms for these districts were laid down in 1958 and reflected more a concern for convenience than the construction of a communist way of life, the central concern of the early 1920s.

Stalin's death in 1953 opened up the 'new course' of Malenkov, of which a first step was to try and reorganise many scattered housing construction units on a more rational basis and to restrict the rights of eviction to certain key enterprises. However, these ideas were soon to be overshadowed by Khrushchev's whirlwind attempt to propel the USSR into communism.

In 1957 Khrushchev not only set up regional economic councils, but also decreed that local soviets were to become the sole customers for new housing and were to take over existing enterprise-operated housing and utilities, and certain local industries.[71] These dramatic reforms were resisted locally by the industrial ministries and were at first even ignored in the national economic plan. The 1957 'Decree and Programme on Housing' further set out to reorganise housing construction along industrial prefabrication lines, based on earlier experiments ranging from standard components to totally prefabricated rooms,[72] although prefabrication itself had much longer historical roots back into the seventeenth century.[73]

During the 1950s housing construction in fact exceeded planned levels for the first and only time in Soviet history.[74] By 1959 the USSR was building annually 12.8 apartments per 1,000 population, the highest rate in the world[75] and this improved the average per capita living space to nearly 6 square metres. Yet this was still too little, and the search for a 'final solution' to the housing problem stimulated the resurrection of co-operatives at the expense of individual builders. Restrictions on the size of private houses were introduced in 1958, and the 'anti-private housing attitude was to become manifest in 1961-62 in a wave of confiscations of privately owned housing'.[76] In 1964 all private house construction was banned in big cities. At the same time Khrushchev rehabilitated the co-operative idea, and the 1962 decree 'On individual and co-operative housing construction' made credit available for up to 60 per cent of co-operative construction costs over fifteen years. In effect Khrushchev was attempting through all these measures to double the amount of urban housing stock during the period of the Seven Year Plan (1959-65).

This drive to expand the housing stock meant that once again planning norms, in particular the microrayon concept, were sacrificed and 'construction organisations reckoned their output largely in terms of square metres of housing space'.[77] Hence prefabricated five-storey walk-up 'Khrushchev' apartments sprouted everywhere, while meagre funds for services were often reallocated for more housing. However, by the early 1960s the initial rush to expand space slackened enough for planning ideals to find some concrete realisation. Ever lurking just beneath the surface of practical austerity they emerged again in a famous article by Strumilin: 'Family and community in the society of the future.'[78] This vision was clearly in the spirit of the 1920s, including extensive communal services and the removal of children from their parents. But in this case the design was actually realised in the construction of an experimental housing complex in Moscow for over two thousand people: the 'House of the New Way of Life.'[79]

Many of these ideas were debated in public at an all-union conference on urban development in June 1960, attended by Politburo members and other senior officials. In reviewing forty-three years of urban development it became clear that the major failing had been in regional planning – the co-ordination of industrial and urban growth. The Chairman of the USSR State Construction Committee (the most senior post in urban affairs), Kucherenko, declared 'Unfortunately we still make inadequate use of the basic advantages of socialist society'.[80] The basic dilemma was that industry favoured the economies of scale available in large cities, which overburdened the urban infrastructure, while small towns stagnated for want of investment. However, since the majority of new housing construction was undertaken by industry, Khrushchev's rapid housing expansion was exacerbating this problem by undermining still further the control of city soviets, notwithstanding the 1957 decree in their favour. The declared intentions of limiting large city growth and the expansion of housing had proved incompatible.

Khrushchev had 'sacrificed quality for quantity'.[81] Workmanship was extremely shoddy and gave rise to numerous complaints in the press. In addition, his pursuit of the 'final solution' led him to make several major administrative reorganisations which were strongly resisted and resulted in considerable confusion. After his fall from power, industrial enterprises were returned to the control of central ministries in 1965 and housing construction levelled off at the rate of the early 1960s where it has stayed well into the 1970s.

Despite a period of relative stability in the housing field since the 1960s the effectiveness of planning continues to be weak. The problem continues to be 'that planning and financing spring primarily from different sources'.[82] In March 1971 further efforts were made, as in 1957 to tackle this issue: a party resolution 'On measures to further improve the work of city Soviets'; the supreme soviet's declaration on 'The basic rights and duties of city Soviets'; and the Council of Ministers' 'Measures for strengthening the material and financial base of city Soviet executive committees.'[83] Whether these will prove more effective than those of 1957 is unclear as yet and will be explored further in the next section. Suffice it to say that 'the basic problem of a departmentalist mentality has not been resolved.'[84] Thus services like education and health by way of comparison are noticeably free of 'restricted resources and confined management' since 'they were important either to the output of basic industries or to the maintenance of control' and hence 'central authorities maintained direct control over their expansion'.[85] But this solution is not available to housing since, as in all industrial societies, the whole range of local services involved requires local co-ordination; indeed central control in the form of industrial ministries has itself contributed to these very difficulties.

Housing today

Housing today is mainly state-provided with very low rents, although owner-occupation is the dominant rural tenure. Living space is meagre by western standards but great improvements have been made since the 1950s. However, this expansion has not been satisfactorily planned, particularly as a result of conflicts between economic and social priorities. As a result, the supply of and access to housing is determined by two competing criteria — need and economic incentive. In this section we shall examine three aspects of housing: demand, supply and finance.

Demand

To the extent that housing is operated as a social service, allocation
should be on the basis of legitimate need. However, as is apparent from
the previous historical section, the development of housing has been and
continues to be influenced by many other factors. In comparison with
some of the other social services the mediating profession for housing,
the city planner, has been extremely weak in the face of competing
government (especially economic) priorities. Hence it is more accurate
to talk of demand rather than need as the general determinant of
supply. We can divide demand factors conveniently into two types:
objective and subjective. The first type includes demography and the
current shortfall in housing provision in terms of space per capita,
availability of self-contained units, provision of utilities and services and
location. The major demographic characteristic which affects housing
has been the massive migration to the cities (now 60 per cent of the
population is urban). This was stimulated initially by the collectivisation
of agriculture and then the development of industry, but now preference for the higher cultural and material standards available in cities
attracts people. This relieves pressure in rural areas, to the extent that
the western Republics are experiencing rural depopulation, but creates
acute urban pressure.[86] Large cities suffer particularly since they also
attract migrants from small cities and are hence growing both absolutely
and proportionately faster than anywhere else. Despite this, as many as
17 per cent of jobs in major cities are occupied by commuters since
internal passports prevent migrants living closer to work.[87] Large cities
are consequently suffering both from rapid growth and an acute shortage of labour, partly as a result of trying administratively to restrict
their size, but also because pressure on housing has depressed the birth
rate and hence artificially aged the population.[88]

The availability of housing space in comparison with the 'sanitary'
norm is the most direct measure of objective demand. Since this was laid
down as 9 square metres of living space (bedrooms and living rooms
only) in the early 20s it has become as basic a guide to living standards, and with similar qualifications, as mortality rates are for health
standards. Unfortunately data are not available, and would probably be
difficult to collect, on rural housing space, although informal observation suggests that average space per capita (often owner-occupied
wooden houses) is higher than in urban areas. Urban living space itself,
after dropping below 4 square metres per capita in the early 1950s, has
recovered steadily to a current average of very nearly the sanitary norm
exceeded in certain cities (Moscow, Donetsk) and Republics (Latvia,
Estonia).[89] To set this in context it can be pointed out that western
cities average well over twice this provision; and that this level is not
maintained for eastern Republics and cities, such that 'the U.S.S.R. can

be divided into developed and undeveloped republics in terms of urban housing'[90] (this variation will be discussed further in the next section). Furthermore, a family with less than this space does not thereby establish a right to housing; rather the level of official housing need (which gives eligibility for admission to the waiting list for new housing) is much lower — 4.5 square metres in Leningrad, for example.[91]

In addition to amount of space we must also consider the services available with it. For example, although rural housing space may be more generous the availability of services such as water, heating, drainage, transport and so on is markedly inferior. Data are again only specific about urban areas where, although electricity is universally available, still a small proportion of dwellings — 20 per cent — have no running water and half have no piped gas or central heating. In large cities transport demand also becomes significant. For example, in Moscow the overall average time spent travelling to work is 53 minutes each way.[92] Finally, overall available space conceals the proportion of urban families without self-contained flats. Recent surveys suggest that this reached 50 per cent only in the early 1970s, and that almost all recently married couples have to share, usually with their families.[93]

We can summarise these fairly objective determinants of demand as more typical of a developing than an advanced industrial society. Despite extensive rural-urban migration a large proportion of the population still lives in the country with markedly inferior housing in terms of construction and available services; and in the cities although services are far better, space and particularly self-contained apartments remain relatively scarce. However, demand for housing is also determined by more subjective factors, particularly the relative strength of economic and social planners, unplanned industrial activity, and the impact of popular expectations.

Ever since housing owned by industries was nationalised rather than municipalised after the Revolution, there has been conflict between industries and soviets over the provision and control of housing and associated services. The framework of Appendix 1.4 illustrates the source of this conflict. First, city and non-city enterprises are only co-ordinated at a very high level. Second, at that level state planning responsible for city affairs continues to be divided between the State Planning Commission (Gosplan) for industrial production and the State Construction Committee (Gosstroi) for housing construction. Third, since industrial growth has been a major aim this arrangement has enabled industrial ministries to dominate urban development, particularly in newer industrial or smaller cities where soviets are dependent on one industry, or are administratively remote from the Republic level where major decisions can be made. In effect the demand for housing space where industries need workers tends to be met by industries themselves. However, the proper standard of such housing in terms of adequate space, services, location (particularly with respect to pollution) and maintenance cannot be easily enforced by the soviets. They are by comparison to industry financially weak, do not own the houses, and are politically weak with respect to controlling location.[94]

This imbalance of power between economic and social planners and the resulting unplanned industrial activity has been periodically redressed, notably in 1957 and 1971 as mentioned in the previous section. However, housing demand continues to be influenced by powerful ministries as a result of a political and bureaucratic system laid down in the 1930s which is now resistant to change. The most significant result has been for the pattern of location of housing and in particular the growth of large cities. Although the exact mechanisms of growth are disputed it is quite clear that the larger the city, the greater is the return on economic investment: the infrastructure already exists, labour is more skilled, supply routes are shorter, and so on. Indeed it has been estimated that in cities of more than 1 million, production per inhabitant is 20 per cent above the urban average, production per worker 38 per cent above, and return on investment 111 per cent above.[95] These advantages together with weak controls on industry have combined to upset all attempts to control and predict the growth of large cities begun in the 1930s, re-emphasised by Khrushchev, and still official policy today. Although the current (1976-80) Five Year Plan calls for investment in small-(up to 50,000) and medium-(50-100,000) sized cities, we can see in Table 5.1 that they contain a shrinking proportion of the population:

TABLE 5.1
Percentage of urban population in towns by size category[96]

Population	1926	1939	1959	1970	1974	1977
Less than 3,000	4.6	1.5	1.6	1.5	1.4	
3,000-5,000	4.8	3.5	3.7	3.0	2.7	
5,000-10,000	10.2	8.9	9.2	7.4	7.1	30.5
10,000-20,000	13.4	11.4	11.2	9.4	9.1	
20,000-50,000	15.1	16.0	14.8	13.6	12.8	
50,000-100,000	15.6	11.6	10.9	9.6	9.8	9.6
100,000-250,000	12.1	14.8	13.0	15.7	15.6	15.4
250,000-500,000	8.4	11.1	11.4	12.4	13.6	13.8
500,000-1,000,000	2.0	8.6	13.7	12.0	12.0	12.3
Over 1 million	13.8	12.5	10.5	15.4	15.9	18.3

A final subjective factor affecting demand is the general level of expectation of what reasonable housing should be. It is a commonplace observation in the west to note that expectations for housing are fundamentally affected by supply. What was in the past a luxury comes to be seen as a basic necessity, for example central heating. In the Soviet Union, as a result of the acute shortage of housing in the past, expectations are generally low. The major hope is for a self-contained apartment, even if only two rooms. Much of the housing built since the late 1950s is of this type, and more than half of the urban population now have their own flats. There is some evidence that expectations are now rising, in that public criticism concentrates on quality rather than the mere availability of space. This rise in expectations may well become a problem in the future, when separate flats are available for all families but are felt to be too small. However, in the past consumer expectations have had little effect on priorities for housing.

Supply

The growth in provision of housing since the 1950s has been as remarkable as the limited level of investment before this time. By 1960, units built annually per 1,000 people reached a world record of 12.8; and although this rate has now slipped back to around 9 since the mid-1960s, the overall average per capita available space is at last approaching 9 square metres — the historic sanitary norm. However, this level of supply must be qualified in several ways. First, the distribution between cities and Republics has not been even. As was apparent from table 5.1, despite official policy large cities continue to grow fastest with the result that 60 per cent of the population are now urban dwellers. This urbanisation has not been uniform, occurring more rapidly in the European Republics than in the east. By 1970, 54 per cent of the population in the European Republics were urbanised, compared with 42 per cent in the east. Moreover, per capita urban living space in the east at this time was only 6.4 square metres, 20 per cent less than in the European Republics. Table 5.2 presents in more detail the change in per capita urban living space for the best and worst provided Republics over the period of greatest housing construction — 1958-74. It can be seen that the gap has grown, increasing the standard deviation of distribution of average living space between Republics from 0.93 in 1958 to 1.21 in 1974.[97] However, if the increase in overall average space is taken into account, we find that the coefficient of variation has only increased marginally from 0.155 in 1958 to 0.158 in 1974. Nevertheless this indicates that the massive overall development of housing has not decreased geographical inequalities.

149

TABLE 5.2
Highest and lowest square metres of urban living space per capita
in Union Republics, 1958 and 1974[98]

1958		1974*	
Latvia	8.4	Estonia	9.9
[Estonia	7.6]	Latvia	9.8]
[Uzbekistan	5.2]	[Kirgizia	6.5]
Kirgizia	4.9	Uzbekistan	5.8

*Average urban per capita living space, USSR = 8.0

Housing is not only distributed unevenly between Republics and cities but also between different groups in the population. The vast bulk of housing is allocated according to a common system, rather like British council-housing. An applicant to get on the waiting list must demonstrate sufficient need in terms of existing space, amenities, state of health and so on. Subsequently people are actually housed from the waiting list in order of original acceptance. However this system is modified in several important ways. First, the waiting list can be circumvented either by someone being housed directly, or by being placed at the top of the waiting list, or by being given preference 'other things being equal'.[99] Second, extra space may be allocated to certain preferred groups. Third, rents are low for certain favoured groups, but higher for others (such as the 'free professions'). In general these advantaged groups include either those with exceptional needs (the ill, large families, and so on) or those politically favoured (specialists, the military, those who do 'socially useful activity'), but Dimaio argues 'too much should not be made of these housing privileges. In many cases they are small'.[100] But for the really privileged, 6 per cent of new stock is co-operatively built which is self-financed and offers a means of circumventing the waiting list. In the early 1970s a typical co-operative flat cost about six times the average wage to buy, for which a 40 per cent deposit was required. However, Matthews argues that for the upper elite even this opportunity is unnecessary. An official flat or 'dacha' (country house) will be available at low rent from a small category of housing called the 'official-service fund'.[101] This is linked to certain jobs from caretakers to ministers in much the same way as the police or farm workers receive houses in Britain. In general much of this housing privilege, large or small, is fairly informally negotiated, lying in the murky boundary between housing law and political process.

A second qualification to consider is the quality of this new housing stock. The quality of new housing in the boom of the late 1950s was very poor, partly because of the poor materials supplied by the construction industry, but mainly because of the rush to finish on or before schedule. The relative calm in housing construction since the 1960s and the steady increase in the proportion of prefabricated housing (from 2 per cent in 1959 to 60 per cent in 1980) has helped to improve quality, but 40 per cent of investment in housing construction still goes on maintenance and (mostly) repairs.[102] Recently, efforts to improve quality include measuring output in wider terms than just living space, the redesigning of bonus schemes, and the allocation since 1967 of 10 per cent of new housing for construction workers themselves.[103] This use of economic incentive in addition to administrative control has proved effective, although as mentioned earlier public expectations seem to be rising fast, stimulated perhaps by the very improvements apparent in the newest microrayons.

Finally we must consider the general organisation and philosophy of housing as a qualification to overall supply. It is clear at this point that in both the production and distribution of housing the Soviet Union has unsuccessfully tried to meet irreconcilable goals. Public construction and control of housing as a social service through the soviets has been constantly undermined on two fronts. First, Table 5.3 shows that construction by the private and co-operative sectors remains significant.

TABLE 5.3
Estimated current ownership of new and existing housing stock in urban and rural areas (%)

			New construction	Existing stock
	State	Industry	35	30
		Soviet	45	35
URBAN	Private		9	30
	Co-operative		11	5
			100 (75% of all construction)	100 (66% of all stock)
	State		60	10
RURAL	Private		40	90
			100 (25% of all construction)	100 (33% of all stock)

Second, allocation according to need continues to be modified by criteria of economic incentive: 'Brezhnev has reiterated more than once the importance of linking the assignment of good housing with a record of good labour discipline and productivity.'[104]

At the level of the individual tenant we can see these general conflicts acted out in a specific administrative framework. The establishment and use of the waiting list (discussed above) by the housing office takes place under the scrutiny of several interested organisations, as can be seen in Appendix 1.5. The key body is the housing office for either soviet or enterprise housing (the two systems operate similarly in many respects). Within this office, broadly responsible for managing the housing stock, access and so on, the technical inspector is the 'central pillar of the urban housing economy'.[105] However, the general level of training and efficiency at this level is poor, and since Khrushchev's time new voluntary administrative bodies have been encouraged both to improve housing management and to generate greater public participation in government in pursuit of Khrushchev's concept of the 'State of the whole people'. The house committee (Domkom) is the most important of these voluntary bodies. In contrast to its earlier post-revolutionary version, this body is no longer spontaneously formed or has prime responsibility for housing. Rather its function is to advise, supervise and act as a complaints channel to the housing office. Its main contact in that office is through certain interested deputies in the soviet who have also been encouraged since the 1960s to help sustain public participation.

Since 'manipulating and changing the administrative structure for improved efficiency is a favourite device of Soviet leaders at all levels'[106] many of the links between these different bodies are unclear, with the result that their relative strength varies considerably from one area to another and confused jurisdiction is common: a decision may have to meet the interests of the local soviet, the housing office, the house committee, the party, a trade union, and so on. There is 'widespread dependence on personal relations'[107] and in many respects the outcome is the same as for the higher level conflicts between soviets and enterprises — political ideals are compromised. In this case public participation through the House Committee is in effect weak and hence subject to periodic central campaigns to reassert its strength. The last one, in 1968, suggested that House Committees should indeed control the housing office, but like attempts to strengthen the soviet itself, little change has occurred.

Security of tenure, once access has been gained, illustrates further organisational constraints on the overall supply of housing. In general Dimaio argues that 'the most outstanding feature of Soviet housing law is the great protection it affords those persons who are evicted from their apartments through no fault of thier own'.[108] In Soviet housing only extreme cases such as systematic property destruction or lengthy absence leads to eviction without rehousing. However, in enterprise housing, less security of tenure represents one of the most significant differences from other housing. Ministries may establish lists of enterprises entitled to evict without compensation when tenants have voluntarily left their job, been sacked, or committed a crime. Since the criteria for putting enterprises on the list and for sacking workers can vary (indeed the list is currently growing),[109] this law 'offers an excellent example of housing law employed to stabilise the labour force, and of housing as an incentive'.[110] In fact a survey in 1974 found that in the main, voluntarily leaving work was the principle reason for eviction (89 per cent), while being sacked (10 per cent) and committing a crime (1 per cent) were less important.[111]

If we look wider than the mere production and allocation of housing similar conflicts appear. Relations between town and country continue to frustrate the efforts of planners. Early ideals about eliminating urban-rural differences centred on controlling city size as a major practical goal, but the ideal size has constantly risen in line with actual urban growth: from 50,000 in the 1930s to 150,000 in the 1950s, and 300,000 in the 1970s. Since the late 1960s the concept of controlling growth has been increasingly challenged, and Bater comments bluntly: 'Events since have put paid to its utility in town planning theory and practice.'[112] Rather than trying merely to stop growth, recent efforts have re-emphasised more rational land-use, in particular through the calculation of surrogate market-produced land prices.[113] A second development has been a more or less orchestrated grassroots movement for urban 'social planning'.[114] While one might expect this to be concerned with improving the urban living environment, or even developing a 'socialist way of life', it turns out in fact to be an attempt to offset flagging productivity and reduce labour turnover through greater provision of work-related welfare and more participation at work.

We can conclude that the determinants of the supply of housing are divided amongst different (and in some respects, competing) bodies. In general there has been a close shaping of housing policy by economic policy, although the detailed realisation of this is in fact a quite complex political process. Consequently, political initiatives to affect the organisation and supply of housing have often been frustrated, or at least distorted in their implementation.

Finance

Housing in the Soviet Union stands apart from the other social services in that around 50 per cent of existing stock is privately owned (including a small proportion of co-operative flats which are effectively owned on mortgage from the state), and one-third of new housing built is private or co-operative.[115] There are three major points to be made in connection with this. First, the reason for this private sector is that the state cannot by itself provide enough housing construction. It needs to rely on rural inhabitants to provide much of their own housing in traditional materials. It also needs to claim back some of the money available to urban higher-income earners as housing investment through co-operative state loans. This has the added advantage of dampening potential consumer goods' demand which would divert economic investment away from heavy industry.

Second, the existence of the two major tenure categories, state and private, necessarily generates inequalities since state housing is of better quality and more heavily subsidised than any other. Since 50 per cent of it is currently built by industry and almost all of it is in cities, managers, technicians, and skilled workers favoured by industry receive large housing subsidies compared with rural inhabitants. This may be a transitional problem for any urbanising society until sufficient housing is built. Certainly the current rate of construction in the Soviet Union, if maintained, will gradually eliminate these inequalities by providing state housing for all.

Third, the existence of a private market gives a measure of the shortfall of supply in urban areas. For example in Moscow unofficial (though legal) subletting rates have doubled since the mid-1970s, amounting now to around 100 roubles a month for a two-room flat. This compares with 40 roubles a month loan repayment on a similarly-sized co-operative flat, or 7 roubles a month rent on a state-owned flat.[116] Matthews estimates that this privately rented sector of the housing market provides for 5-10 per cent of the urban population.[117]

The rate of housing investment, both public and private, has remained steady since the early 1960s at around 17 per cent of all investment, or 5 per cent of the national income.[118] Only a small proportion of this comes from rents which since the 1930s, though rising, have never amounted to more than 4-5 per cent of income. An additional source of finance comes from the 'profits' of enterprises providing nearly 10 per cent of total housing investment.[119] However the vast bulk comes from the national budget, and hence the favourable position of enterprises is not a result of their own productivity, but financial allocation policies.

The provision of services associated with housing has, it is generally recognised, suffered from chronic under-investment. This is a result both of shortage of money and organisational confusion. Overall, city soviet local income has been falling since the war compared with central finance. In 1946 locally-raised revenue constituted two-thirds of the total, but by the mid-1960s this had dropped to one-third. A major reason was the abolition in 1959 of a tax on enterprise buildings, payable to the city soviet. In effect the equivalent of the British local rating was lost. Other continuing sources of local income are taxes on municipal enterprise profits, transport, collective farm markets, trade unions and clubs, and some legal services.[120] However, these do not generate the kind of large sums that central government gets from the turnover tax and personal income tax, the basis for central reallocation to the cities.

Organisational confusion is chiefly a product of the principle of 'dual subordination' whereby administrative departments are responsible both to the soviet and to their respective ministries (see Appendix 1.4). Some areas are more under the influence of central direction than others. For example education and health services are highly centrally directed, but social security is also answerable to the local soviet executive, while housing is entirely controlled locally.[121] Very broadly this means that the closer a service is controlled centrally the more evenly it is provided and the less it is subject to local political manoeuvre. Hence investment in sewage, water, transport, gas, repairs and so on is more likely to be delayed or diverted than investment in health and educational services to match new housing.

Generally the finance of housing and associated services is a very complicated affair influenced broadly by several interlocking 'markets' for housing, and several interlocking 'interest groups' for local services.

Soviet housing – an assessment

In the light of the foregoing discussion we can now return to the original ideals to see how far they have been fulfilled. It is important to remember that apart from immediate post-revolutionary housing redistribution, neither Marx, Engels nor Lenin were very clear about future housing policy, since such speculation was theoretically incorrect. However others did speculate, and during the 1920s utopian plans for the future city on occasions reached fantastic proportions. But since there is some evidence that Lenin and the government did not support these excesses we chose more modest ideals, such as those of the Commissariat of Labour, as representative of mainstream Bolshevik ideas at the time.

The first was the aim that each family should have a separate apartment with a total floor space of around 50 square metres. As we have pointed out this goal became more and more remote during the 1930s and 1940s. However, with the new era of expanded construction started in the late 1950s and continued ever since, this aim is now well within sight for the 50 per cent of the population in state-owned housing. Given the short space of time that construction has been emphasised this is a considerable achievement. However, there is still a long way to go to provide modern flats for the other half of the population in private (and mostly rural) housing. The second aim of making such self-contained flats available to all is therefore far from realised. Indeed a current snap-shot view of Soviet housing stock shows great parallel inequality on two dimensions: the urban dweller's advantage over rural inhabitants, and managers, technicians and skilled workers' advantage over unskilled and farm workers. By comparison the privileges of certain minority groups in terms of more space and so on are insignificant; indeed relative equality within the state-owned sector is impressive. It seems reasonable to expect therefore that as more and more of the population gain access to the third original ideal (state-owned flats), housing inequality will steadily decline, as long as expectations do not expand to outstrip current provision.

In terms of the design of housing this precludes any wide-scale development of communalism in domestic life. Indeed with the growing availability of self-contained flats the degree of communalism enforced in the past by overcrowding will diminish. The current prospect for a 'socialist way of life' is thus as much centred on the house as the community and as more domestic facilities become available this focus will intensify.[122] Whether this is a retreat from socialism is debatable. The nuclear family has not only become acceptable within Soviet think-ing but is now praised as a major and desirable social institution. Accord-ing to Stretton the family now has the greatest potential for the practical realisation of socialism, since 'a third of rich countries' capital is now in their housing and domestic equipment; at least a third of their work is done there, and a third or more of economic goods . . . is produced there'.[123] However, this point is not generally appreciated by eastern and western Marxists alike who continue to over-emphasise the institutional economy and under-emphasise the domestic economy. Consequently, investment in and design of housing as *productive* items has been under-emphasised:

> Communist governments do their best to confine productive work to the institutional economy, and to prohibit production outside it . . .
> In that and other ways they do their best to build for twenty-first century Russia the urban fabric of nineteenth century Manchester . . .
> The hard left — marxist and technocratic — thus works as hard as any capitalist to kill the most promising of all socialist opportunities, and to perpetrate the alienation which Marx condemned as the worst effect of primitive industrial capitalism.[124]

This is not a plea for communalism, but rather the opposite — that Soviet housing is not doing enough to allow the nuclear family its proper place as a production unit in the economy. In practical terms it would mean abandoning small multi-storey flats, for low-rise housing with large gardens and personal workshops more in the style of the 'Red garden cities' designed in the early 1920s — a 'hearth-and-home, do-it-yourself' socialism.[125]

The fourth ideal was that accommodation and utilities should be free. Apart from the sharp rise in rents in the 1920s, rent and the price of utilities have remained very low, though growing in line with incomes. In so far as state-owned housing expands this subsidy will spread eventually to most people and relieve them of the cost of private building. At that stage co-operative flat owners may come to be seen as disadvantaged in that their housing subsidies are far lower but currently off-set by the benefit of jumping the housing queue. The Soviet government is committed to abolishing rents eventually, but it must be remembered of course that housing still has to be paid for out of surplus generated in the economy. In terms of opportunity cost tenants thus pay for housing through either the unavailability of other goods (e.g. cars) or higher prices (e.g. clothes, which are very expensive by western standards).

The achievement of an egalitarian housing distribution outside the market requires very careful administration to avoid the kind of accumulated inequalities which are appearing in the field of education. This fifth ideal was originally to be safeguarded by extensive public participation (as in other areas of social welfare) and the control of housing by soviets. This would ensure the local co-ordination of centrally-planned services. After declining to a very low level in the 1930s and 1940s popular participation in local government, including housing, was strongly revived by Khrushchev. In the early 1960s literally thousands of volunteer organisations (including house committees) were set up in all cities. These were to function both as controls on official representatives, such as the soviet of deputies, and to provide direct administrative labour. In the event they came to be used far more as free labour than as a form of political representation.[126] Other channels for participation, such as the permanent commissions and the trade unions for monitoring and helping to organise housing allocation, operated much as they did for other social services — very much in line with central government policy. Perhaps the most effective channel for influence and complaints has been the exposure of housing inadequacy in the press — a useful source of qualitative information about housing. Finally, the very existence of a private sector in housing including individual, collective farm and co-operative building, and a small market in sub-letting, has provided the most direct form of 'participation' in housing for many Soviet citizens.

The final ideal was the more tenuous one of eliminating urban-rural differences by eradicating the evils of the capitalist city and overcoming the general idiocy of rural life. This notion has a very deep root in socialist thought, stemming from Engels's observations of life in Manchester and the earlier utopian socialists. Its romantic appeal is strong and gave rise, as we have seen, to much utopian speculation in the 1920s about a future environment suitable for the new society. In many respects rural life has been changed by the extension of services such as health and education. However, in terms of housing it still represents the least socialised sector, containing the bulk of private stock. In addition new investment is disproportionately channelled to the larger cities despite policy attempts to reverse this trend. Perhaps the most successful, though unintended, transformation of rural life has been achieved through massive rural-urban migration, currently around two million a year. This has raised the material and cultural level of the migrant but, as can be observed throughout the world, those left behind — the old, female, least skilled, least productive, and poorest — are concentrated in the 'centuries-old economic and cultural backwardness' of village life.[127]

By contrast the problems of urban life are more dynamic. City planning has been to slow development and is regarded in many respects as a luxury. For years it has been reduced to such crude activities as trying to enforce administrative restrictions on city growth, but with very little success. However, such growth has not been well serviced with an adequate infrastructure. This, we have argued, is because a fundamental error has been to regard only the institutional economy as productive. If Soviet planners were to acknowledge the household as an important unit of production as well as consumption there would be less need to restrict urban growth in favour of industrial development, most dramatically illustrated by the decline in per capita housing space during Stalin's era.

The essential imbalance has been a shortage of houses and people in comparison with jobs in the cities. This 'under-urbanisation', though arguably preferable to the more common world-wide development pattern of a shortage of houses and jobs in comparison with people, has generated an unplanned response from ordinary people. The typical reaction is excessive commuting and, as a result of guaranteed employment, a competition for scarce labour and hence a type of unorganised labour bargaining which plays off agricultural and industrial employers.[128] Indeed, Kansky argues that this response is not merely derivative, but that

In every socialist city, there exists a contradiction between governmental developmental policies and the private goal-oriented behaviour of residents. The unresolved contradictory and competing interests are the cause forming future urban physical and social landscapes and are the primary factor of socialist urbanisation.[129]

In comparison with all the other ideals which have survived more or less intact as current policy goals, though to a greater or lesser extent fulfilled, the elimination of urban-rural differences is no longer seriously upheld as attainable in the foreseeable future, surviving merely as a rather vague long-term hope.

In concluding this chapter we may speculate more generally on the reasons for deviations from the original ideals. In contrast to the education and health services which have been centrally controlled and steadily expanded as an investment in human capital, housing was clearly regarded up to the early 1950s as an unfortunately necessary consumption good which of itself generated little economic return. However, as a method for encouraging good labour discipline it was seen as an important secondary device, useful for the control and direction of human capital investment. If this is so we must consider additional explanations for the scarcity and poor planning of Soviet housing. There is no doubt that the inheritance of an inadequate and largely wooden housing stock, plus the physical destruction which occurred under war communism and particularly the Second World War, must be acknowledged. Even without the severe priorities set by rapid industrialisation this backlog would have been difficult to eliminate. In addition, large-scale urbanisation quickly overwhelmed such efforts as were made to expand urban stock where the shortage was most acute.

Since the late 1950s investment in housing has been sustained at a relatively high level, and despite difficulties over co-ordinating associated services at the local level this indicates a radically changed view of housing. Is this because housing is now regarded as a useful productive investment? There is no evidence to this effect, and it seems more likely that it is still felt to be, indeed being expanded deliberately as, a consumption good. This is partly as a genuine benefit from earlier years of industrial growth, since production without eventual consumption seems rather pointless. But housing, particularly at the low rents charged for state-owned stock, is presented as an important manifestation of government goodwill towards the people, and hence helps to legitimate the post-Stalin era. It also serves justifiably to increase or at least reproduce inequalities, and thus continues to be used as an incentive to various groups such as key workers and party members.

In this respect Soviet housing, while rapidly expanding in the last twenty years, continues to be a divisive and scarce good which has been diverted from the original ideals both by conscious policy, but also as a victim of rapid industrialisation and unplanned urban growth.

6

The political economy and social policy of the USSR

The primary concern of this chapter is the inter-relationship between social policy and the political economy of the Soviet Union. It is an examination both of the constraints and opportunities through which the political and economic system affects social policy and of the influences of social policy on that system in its professed attempt to industrialise and create a fully socialist, i.e. communist, society.

We need to discuss first, however, the nature of the political economy and of social policy. Some repetition of points made in passing in previous chapters is inevitable but it is necessary in order to prepare the ground for the main discussion of this chapter.

The political economy of the Soviet Union*

Unlike the relatively clear distinction which can be drawn between economic and political systems in capitalist societies, we shall have to consider the political economy of the Soviet Union as an interlocking whole. The economy is shaped by two key principles: the public ownership of the means of production, and the centralised planning of major production and distribution decisions.[1] We characterise it as centralised state socialism. It aims to generate surplus (as must all economic systems) but the accumulation and distribution of this surplus is determined primarily according to the political aims of the Communist party acting through the central government administrators rather than by the

*Appendix 2 is an attempt to relate the logic of the Marxist theory of the state in capitalist societies to the nature of the Soviet state.

profit-maximisation typically pursued by private owners of capital in capitalist societies.

The political determination of priorities occurs at the top of the hierarchy of power in the central committee of the party. Decisions reached here are transmitted down according to the principle of democratic centralism. This has resulted in a very centralised hierarchical system whereby all levels, from enterprises or small city soviets upwards, are accountable to those above. In terms of economic and social activity this can often mean subordination to three authority systems: the soviet, the relevant ministry and the party, not all of which necessarily agree on all policy issues. However the party has become the dominant authority:

> It controls all the functionaries throughout the hierarchy in two ways: as subjects of particular institutional roles via the system of dependence between party and functional management, and as party members — regardless of their official duties and interests — via its own organisation. This double mechanism provides a guarantee that no section of the hierarchy can become the direct instrument of special interests.[2]

The official view is that the Soviet Union, having transcended capitalism, is not now, as Khrushchev had hoped, moving into communism but has only reached the stage of 'developed socialism', 'a natural, logical stage on the road to communism'.[3] Consequently although antagonistic social classes disappeared officially with the abolition of private ownership of the means of production, two harmonious classes (workers and peasants) and a stratum (the intelligentsia) are acknowledged to exist. Divisions of interest between and within these groups exist but they can be reconciled without a change of the political and economic system of the country. At the stage of developed socialism, political priorities remain those of economic growth, distribution primarily according to work, and the 'scientific-technological revolution'.[4] Gradualism and caution make up the political style of the present leadership, anxious of the heightened expectations and conflicts of interest made public by Khrushchev's flamboyant reorganisations. There is a far greater awareness of the problems and hazards in attempting to move quickly towards communism. The result is, in McAuley's words, that 'the ruling group hesitates, tries to avoid making choices, and continues where possible with existing policies'.[5]

However, many observers have suspected that this relative defence of the *status quo* is actually intended to conceal and preserve privilege and they have looked for alternative explanations to the official version of the nature of Soviet society. The question 'Is there a ruling class in the Soviet Union?' has been raised by many and answered in the affirmative by most. The affirmative answers vary from the simplistic which confuse group with class, to the sophisticated which first define the nature of class and find evidence to substantiate its existence. Those who refute the existence of a ruling class are divided between those who follow the official view and those, including ourselves, who maintain that there is a ruling elite but it is different in nature from a ruling class found in capitalist societies.

Before considering the evidence and arguments about the nature of the ruling group we must first define it. There is abundant evidence that there is a ruling group which controls the political and economic system. It consists of 'those who from regional level and above sit on the committees, praesidia, or bureaux and those who head ministries, state committees, and secretariat departments and sections'.[6] Or, using Matthews' definition of the membership of this group, we are talking of about 140,000 people. This group must be distinguished from the larger group of the intelligentsia consisting of scientists, engineers, academics, teachers, doctors, agronomists, low-level civil servants, and so on – about 36 millions in all.[7]

We accept the argument that a ruling class can theoretically exist even if it does not own the means of production. For such a class to exist, however, it must satisfy the three criteria advanced by Wesolowski: first, this group appropriates a disproportionate amount of material goods, political power and cultural (especially educational) privileges; second, the members of this group can pass on all these privileges safely to their children; and third, that they have developed a common consciousness, partly because of family background, intermarriage, attendance of same schools, and the like, as well as because they subscribe to the same dominant ideology.[8]

Members of the ruling group have incomes which are higher than those of the rest of the population. But these inequalities are not of the same dimension as those between the top 1 per cent of wealth owners and the rest of the population in advanced capitalist societies. With regard to political power, the ruling group of the Soviet Union is as powerful and perhaps even more so than a ruling class in capitalist societies, though direct comparisons can be misleading because of the more concealed ways in which a ruling class exercises political power. The educational advantages of the ruling group have been discussed in an earlier chapter but they are not greater than those of a large section of the intelligentsia. Nor does the ruling group send its children to a small number of exclusive private schools as is the case in capitalist societies.

Clearly the children of the ruling group inherit some of the privileges of their parents. But in terms of education their privileged position is no greater than that of many children of the intelligentsia. There is no evidence either that all or most of the children of the ruling group inherit political or economic power. If we view class not only in static terms but also 'as a process', then there has, so far, been substantial movement into the ruling group from below.[9] This high-level upward mobility has militated against the crystallisation of a separate ruling class, even though there has been no significant downward mobility among the children of the ruling group either in terms of numbers or in terms of extent of fall down the social ladder.[10] Most of the data we have, however, relate to such groups as 'specialists' or 'intelligentsia' which are bigger than the ruling group, as defined here.

The criteria of class-consciousness are difficult to assess. Sociological research into the ruling group's attitudes is non-existent. The dominant ideology of the Soviet Union, however, has always been that the present social system is of a temporary nature to be followed eventually by communism when distribution will be primarily according to need. This ideology has been urgently and consistently propagated by the ruling group since the Revolution though the time-scale for the arrival of communism has been changed several times. This dominant ideology cannot but have some unifying effect on the different strata of Soviet society. This, combined with the high degree of upward social mobility and the comparatively modest acquisition of privileges by the ruling group, militates against the development of a consciousness of distinct class interests. This is not to deny the existence of different attitudes among the various socio-economic groups with regard to education, child-rearing practices, marriage and divorce, etc., but these are not the same as class-consciousness which questions or defends the existing socio-economic order.

We can conclude that the nationalisation of the means of production and distribution has abolished social classes in the Soviet Union but it has created a number of socio-economic groups and a ruling elite. The main differences between the ruling class, in Marxist terms, of advanced capitalist societies and of the ruling elite of the Soviet Union are these: first, the ruling class is more secure than the Soviet elite in transmitting its privileges to its children and is thus a more homogeneous and crystallised social formation. Second, the parliamentary form of government enables the ruling class to rule without having to govern. The Soviet elite has to govern and it is thus more vulnerable to public criticism when things go wrong. A ruling class cannot be blamed by the public for the economic crises of capitalism but the Soviet elite can be so blamed for bad harvests, inadequate industrial production, and so on. Third, the dominant ideology of the ruling class aims at its preservation while the dominant ideology of the Soviet elite aims at its liquidation — the withering away of the state under communism. These differences have implications for social policy which are discussed later in this chapter.

The ruling elite dominates but does not necessarily determine economic and social policies. Interest groups influence government policies both openly and in more discreet ways. The view of the Soviet elite as a totalitarian dictatorship that was very popular in the 1950s has lost ground, partly because of the economic, political and social changes introduced after Stalin's death, partly because of the realisation that no country of the size of the Soviet Union could be governed against its will by a small group residing in the Kremlin and partly because of the accumulated evidence that interest groups exert influence on the shaping of government policies, both before their formulation and after during their administration.[11] There has also been an increasing awareness of the divisions of opinion and of interests among the different groupings of the government bureaucracy, particularly at the local level — between the industrial lobby, the local soviets, the local ministry office, etc. For example, both in 1957 and 1971 attempts by the central government to transfer housing from industrial enterprises to local soviets have been frustrated by local industrial lobbies.[12]

The nature of socialist social policy

In spite of the numerous inter-relationships that one finds between social policy and the economic system in different countries, they can be grouped under three headings. These are ideal types, stages on a continuum. Firstly, in those capitalist societies where the private market is considered a perfect, well-functioning mechanism for the production and distribution of goods, social policy plays a residual role. It is confined to providing minimum assistance in kind, in cash or in services to those few people who, for a variety of mainly personal reasons, find themselves unable to cope or to benefit sufficiently from the operation of the private market. Such countries do not exist today among advanced industrial societies despite the protestations of liberal economists and politicians. Whether such societies can exist among advanced industrial societies is a moot point. Our view of the functions of social policy leads us to the conclusion that advanced capitalist societies are inextricably linked to social policy. Without substantial social policy provision there will be not only intolerable social and political tensions but economic growth itself could suffer.

Secondly, the general feature of advanced industrial societies today is their recognition of the inadequacies and severe limitations of the private market. If left to itself the private market oscillates between economic stagnation and expansion, creating serious problems of unemployment and inflation. Though the private market is accepted as the best way of organising the economic affairs of the country, it is recognised that it needs government intervention and regulation in order to enable it to function more effectively and more humanely. All advanced industrial capitalist societies are welfare states of a sort. Clearly this, the welfarist model of social policy, implies much more government provision, both in terms of aspects of life, people covered and standard of services provided. Clearly, too, the welfarist model of social policy contains too many strands of thought and actual practice. Nevertheless it is based on the Keynesian model of economics and, as such, it has one basic common element. In the words of Heilbroner:

> This common element lies in the relation of the welfare apparatus to its underlying socio-economic formation which is, of course, capitalism. Welfare institutions, I think all will concur, arise mainly to cope with the difficulties and damages that are brought about by the workings of a capitalist system. The welfare state, in a word, is a kind of apotheosis of capitalism — the form that capitalism takes in seeking its own salvation.[13]

Countries such as Sweden or West Germany where welfare provision is accepted and promoted by all governments, as well as the United States and Japan where social policy is reluctantly used, fall into this same category. Social policy will range from the universalist to the semi-residual type and it will take various forms but its costs will amount to a substantial proportion of the GDP. Thus the proportion of GDP taken up by public expenditure amounted to 22.4 per cent in Japan; 33.2 per cent in the USA; 39.4 per cent in West Germany; 43.3 per cent in the United Kingdom and the highest figure of 49.8 per cent in the Netherlands in 1975.

Thirdly, there is the socialist form of social policy which rests on the assumption that the private market has been largely or wholly abolished. The means of production and distribution are vested in the hands of the government — the Soviet type of economic system. Theoretically it is argued that social policy in a socialist society plays a more ambitious role than it does in welfare states, for theoretically there is no fundamental and unresolvable conflict of economic interests between the various sections of the community.

As an integral part of this transformation of the social relations of production, the dominant ideology favours the use of economic resources for the satisfaction of human needs. Zsuzsa Ferge, writing from the experience of Hungary, describes this as societal policy in preference to the term social policy which is ingrained with the paternalistic traditions and values of capitalism. Indeed, societal policy becomes as important as economic policy rather than being subordinate to it, as was the case with social policy. Thus 'the main task of societal policy is to create conditions for the emergence of relations of production of a socialist type'.[14] It does this either directly by influencing the transformation of the social division of labour or indirectly by influencing the distribution and consumption of education, health services, and so on. It is a far more ambitious role than that of social policy in capitalist societies where it serves or humanises the economic system that benefits most the ruling class.

Writing from a similar perspective, Roos sees six important differences between socialist and capitalist social policies. First, 'socialist social policy has a more comprehensive and homogeneous goal-value system than capitalist social policy'. Second, and as a result, 'for socialist social policy the basic course for social development is given, whereas in capitalism the course of social policy is a question of social and political struggle between antagonistic interests'. Third, 'socialist social policy operates both on the level of social structure and the level of the individual and family situation, whereas capitalist social policy attempts primarily to affect the individual and family living conditions'. Fourth, and following from its third characteristic, 'socialist social policy implies basically an attempt at comprehensive and conscious direction of social processes, whereas capitalist social policy is oriented towards partial, isolated changes in response to perceived social ills'. Fifth, because of this harmony of goals, 'socialist social policy has more means and more effective means at its disposal than capitalist social policy'. Sixth, 'perhaps . . . there is less contradiction between economic and social policy in a socialist society, whereas in capitalism, social policy is either strictly subordinate or in conflict with economic policies'.[15]

Like Ferge, Roos sees social policy under capitalism as being essentially subordinate and supportive of the system, while under socialism it is a medium for change towards the communist society. His definition of socialist social policy is as follows:

> social policy is the totality of those collective activities through which social relations, processes and structures are managed and developed in that field of social life which is related to the needs of the population and their way of life and which is directed towards eliminating of social inequalities and creation of classless society.[16]

Social policy is thus seen in very broad terms — to help satisfy the needs of the population, to eliminate social inequalities and to help create a classless society. Socialist social policies, like welfarist social policies, will vary from one socialist country to another according to the country's economic development and its cultural traditions. In the same way that welfare states under advanced capitalism differ in a variety of ways, though their fundamental relationship to the economic system is the same, so will socialist social policies differ even though their main aim is to assist in the country's transformation to a classless communist society.

Political economy and social policy

What needs to be ascertained is the extent to which this ideal type of socialist social policy has become or is likely to become a reality in the Soviet Union. We will examine the main features claimed for socialist social policy under three headings: structural, ideological and redistributional. First, by the very nature of the economic system, universal and comprehensive social policies are structurally more possible in socialist than in capitalist societies. It is not simply that the ideology of a socialist society supports such policies but also because a centrally-planned economic system can function better alongside centrally-planned universal social services.

Social policy is in its intentions more comprehensive and universal in the Soviet Union than in any welfare capitalist society. It is not only more broadly defined but also more government-provided than in any capitalist country. It covers not only education, health and social security but housing and subsidies for holidays, transport and food. The responsibility for providing these services rests primarily with the government and it is not shared with private enterprise as is the case in capitalist societies. There is no private education or private health services or privately rented housing of any substance or occupational pensions, and so on. Social policy is a government responsibility to a far greater extent than in capitalist society. This is not a point of mere theoretical interest but potentially of substantial practical importance. The existence of private social services for the use of the wealthy groups in welfare capitalist societies means that the pressure on governments to improve social services is reduced. It can result in a division of social services where the private sector is superior to the government sector in terms of both quality and availability of services.

Though the intentions of social policy in the Soviet Union are more universalistic than those of social policy under welfare capitalism, it does not necessarily mean that its achievements are necessarily more universalistic too. Intent does not always match achievement. We have already pointed out that the gaps and deficiencies of the Soviet social security system are greater than those of some welfare capitalist societies. Similarly, the coverage of its education system is very similar to that of welfare capitalist societies, and so on. We do not wish to repeat all the evidence produced in previous chapters relating to this issue. Rather we want to point out that though social policy is more ambitious in its aims in the Soviet Union than in welfare capitalist societies, it is not always more comprehensive in its achievements. Whether it will become so with increasing economic growth, as is claimed by Soviet and other east European writers, remains to be seen. Argument is on their side but only history can prove them right.

The relationship between the economic system and the social service system is a two-way process. Thus not only does a centrally-planned society make the provision of universal social services more possible but vice versa, too, such services can be used more easily to promote economic growth. Thus higher education is more closely connected to the country's economic system, both in terms of courses provided and in terms of the employment of graduates than is the case in welfare capitalist societies. Similarly, social security benefits are partially shaped to encourage employment in certain parts of the country and in certain occupations; the health service is closely connected with work in industries, and so on. Social policy not only benefits from economic development but it also helps to promote economic growth. The relationship between the two is at times too close, with the result that economic policy becomes the dominant partner and the 'social' aspects of social policy suffer. The absence of a national assistance scheme and the dominance of science subjects in universities are examples of this type of relationship. The literature, however, on the influence of social policy on economic growth is of the general type. Thus Strumilin claims that the educational system 'promotes the achievement of the country's economic tasks', but provides no hard evidence apart from showing that the number of people registered in education has increased over the years.[17] Similarly, Lantzev claims that social security is important in such areas as work incentives, labour renewal, etc., all of which affect economic growth favourably.[18] The contribution of social policy to economic development is not only difficult to measure scientifically but it can also be both positive and negative.

A second and related difference between social policy in the Soviet Union and in welfare capitalist societies is that it is more in line with the dominant collectivist ideology of socialism than with the mixture of individualistic-collectivist ideology of welfare capitalism. As we pointed out earlier in this chapter, social policy in capitalist societies is reconciled to the private ownership of the means of production while in east European societies social policy is based on the nationalisation of the means of production and distribution. As a result, in welfare capitalist societies the right to private profit has been left largely unchallenged and thus when the operations of the welfare state undermine private profit the justification and usefulness of public expenditure is questioned. This is a fact, irrespective of whether it is explained in Marxist terms of the fiscal crisis of the state or in liberal economic terms of public expenditure undermining work incentives. In east European societies, however, no such threat to social policy exists. Moreover, the expressed hope of the Soviet Union is that one day it will reach the communist stage where distribution of goods and services will be according to officially-defined individual needs. It is true that this may prove an unattainable dream but it does not detract from the point made here, i.e. that the dominant ideology of the Soviet Union provides a more secure environment for the growth of social policy. Moreover, as the previous chapters have shown, hard economic facts have often made impossible the aspirations of collectivist ideology. In Marxist terms the structure of society was, at times, more influential on the development of social policy than the ideology of its superstructure. It is when structural and superstructural forces worked together that the development of social policy was at its best. Again, this does not detract from the claim that the dominant ideology of the Soviet Union is more favourable to the development of social policy than the ideology of welfare capitalist societies. What has been witnessed recently in several welfare capitalist societies — Britain, Canada, Australia, USA, etc., is an ideological orchestration against comprehensive social policy and a return of conservative governments, explicitly committed to substantially reducing social policy expenditure. It may well be that such attempts will come to very little but it does not negate the argument that the dominant ideology of welfare capitalist societies is more ambivalent and, at times, more hostile to the development of social policy than the dominant ideology of the Soviet Union. One might say that the Soviet Union is ideologically committed to improving its social services, broadly defined, but may not succeed completely because of its material base while affluent capitalist societies may not be always as committed but nevertheless may achieve high levels of social policy expenditure because of the pressure from labour and the needs of capital.

The relationship between dominant ideology and social policy is naturally a two-way process. If the dominant ideology provides a favourable social climate for the growth of social policy it is also valid to claim that social policy appears to contribute substantially to the legitimation of the country's political and economic system. In this respect social welfare provision performs the same function that it does under welfare capitalism. We referred earlier in this book to the effectiveness of the school system in transmitting dominant social values. The most direct evidence in support of this claim, however, has been provided by an American study of 3,000 emigres from the Soviet Union in 1950, who we might expect to be, if anything, critical:

It is evident from both the quantitative data and the qualitative impressions gathered from the personal interviews, that the refugees most favour those aspects of the Soviet system which cater to their desire for welfare benefits. Such institutions form the corner-stone of the type of society they would like to live in.[19]

Moreover, after the emigres had been in the United States and, to a lesser extent, in West Germany, they expressed even stronger support for the three main social services — social security, education and health. Writings by Soviet dissidents too show that their criticism is not of the welfare services but of certain aspects of the political system and of individual Soviet leaders. Social policy provision commands wide support, partly because of the benefits it confers to all and particularly because it is seen to embody the image of a socialist society.

Third, because of its ambitious intentions and relative ideological security, social policy is seen as a vehicle not only for the transformation of socialism from its early to its developed stages but also for the more qualitative change from socialism to communism. The well-known Soviet theoretician, Strumilin, thus sees social consumption as corresponding 'to the communist rule "to each according to his needs" '.[20] It acts as a catalyst because it reflects communist ideology and it also redistributes goods, cash and services according to need and hence it helps to reduce the inequalities that stem from the operation of the socialist principle 'to each according to his work'. We have already pointed out in previous chapters that the operation of Soviet social policy does not always achieve such egalitarian results. Indeed in many instances it achieves either the opposite or it simply reflects the inequalities of the labour market. Several east European authors, both inside and outside the Soviet Union, have acknowledged openly this discrepancy between the egalitarian aims and the not-so-egalitarian achievements of social policy. Mieczkowski summarises the relevant literature from Poland, which suggests that the overall effect of social consumption on income distribution is not as egalitarian as at first thought. He quotes the cautious conclusion of a Polish researcher, M. Winiewski, that social consumption decreases 'although inadequately and unevenly, the differentials existing between families at different levels of income and of different sizes'.[21]

Similarly the Hungarian writer, Z. Ferge, concludes her discussion of the redistributive effects of social consumption as follows:

social benefits in cash have a positive redistributive, i.e. levelling, effect, on the original income differentials both with regard to the overall income distribution and to different social groups. The redistributive effect of benefits in kind is more ambiguous. They reduce somewhat the dispersion of incomes though less effectively than cash benefits. But as far as differences between social groups are concerned, benefits in kind accentuate them, since they are even more unequally distributed than work related incomes.[22]

The Soviet author, N. Buzlyakov, indirectly admits to a similar situation in the Soviet Union. Having discussed the distribution of wages according to work done and the provision of social services on similar, but not identical lines, he concludes:

At the same time as the good things of life and cultural facilities become abundant and labour becomes a vital requirement, the distribution of the good things of life through social funds will gradually lose its connection with the work done by members of society and accord more and more with the communist principle of distribution according to needs, irrespective of the quantity and quality of the work done.[23]

These writers attribute the partially inegalitarian effects of social policy either to administrative faults or to the present stage of economic development and socialist consciousness. They therefore maintain that the partially inegalitarian effects of social policy are of a temporary transitional character. A different line is taken by Szelenyi, who puts forward the thesis that social policy in the centrally-planned east European societies is inherently and inevitably inegalitarian in its effects. In capitalist societies, wage distribution is decided largely by the economic power of private owners, while social policy is the outcome of pressures from labour. The result is that social policy reduces the inequalities created by the private market. In east European societies the political power of the government, the party and their officials largely decides both the distribution of wages and the nature of social policy. The inevitable result is that social policy compounds and accentuates the initial inequalities of the work situation. In his words

in state socialist societies social inequalities are basically created and structured by redistributive mechanisms. The east European experience seems to differ sharply from the experience of the market economies where the socio-economic inequalities are basically emerging from market situations and they might be restructured, or moderated by the redistributive intervention of the state.[24]

There are two errors to this argument: first, social policy is not in fact redistributive in welfare capitalist societies. Szelenyi's examples in support of his thesis in fact constitute clear evidence against it. He maintains that government housing provision in the UK for those who cannot buy or rent in the private sector is an example of the redistributive mechanism of social policy. He ignores the substantial and at times greater amounts granted by the government to house buyers in tax rebates. He also makes the erroneous assumption that the government covers the cost of council housing 'by taxing higher income groups, by redistributing real income generated in a labour market'.[25] Second, all types of social policy in east Europe are not inherently regressive in redistributional terms. The evidence produced here is that the situation is far more complex than he claims.

The conclusion on the redistributive aspects of socialist social policies must, however, remain gloomy. The accumulated evidence from all east European societies suggests very strongly that, whatever its aspirations and theoretical possibilities, socialist social policies are no more vertically redistributive than welfarist social policies. What is more, economic growth in the Soviet Union does not seem to have had the same positive effects on this feature of socialist social policy as on the other two. It can be empirically substantiated that economic development has enabled Soviet social policy to be more comprehensive; it is also correct to claim that the ideological base of social policy is more secure today than during the Stalinist years. What it is not possible to demonstrate is that economic development has had the same degree of effect on the egalitarian aspect of social policies. It is true that the 1960s and 1970s witnessed changes in social security which extended substantially the coverage of the service to more population groups and also made inequalities in benefits slightly less substantial. Extending the coverage of a service to lower-paid groups is a form of vertical redistribution but this is not the form we are concerned with here. Rather, we refer to the reduction of income inequalities after universal social services have been provided.

Economic growth and public expenditure growth by themselves do not reduce income inequalities. This is the broad conclusion that emerges from this study — a conclusion similar to that drawn from an examination of public expenditure in Common Market countries.[26] Social policy can only be vertically redistributive if it is so designed and this can only be done easily if it is in line with the way the economic and political systems are functioning. To have an egalitarian form of social policy in a country where the economic system functions in strongly inegalitarian ways and where political power is concentrated in the hands of those benefiting most from the operation of the economic system raises constant problems and conflicts.

Three main forces have shaped and are likely to continue shaping social policy in the Soviet Union: material factors, sectional interests, and the dominant ideology. The influence of economic development on social policy was illustrated in the first chapter. It was shown that the influence of this factor was both direct and indirect, explicit and implicit. Thus the ability of the country to provide social services improved with industrialisation and with the foundation of the country's industrial base. It was an austere policy that has been judged realistic or unduly penalising on the Soviet public, depending on the commentator's viewpoint. Increased industrialisation had also many indirect effects which were again discussed briefly in the first chapters. The growth of cities at the expense of rural areas was at times necessary to supply the necessary labour for expanding industries, but at times it was contrary to the government's policy of encouraging agricultural production. This was one of the reasons for the introduction of social security benefits for collective farmers in the mid-1960s. An indirect influence of industrialisation of a different nature is the effect that improved living standards are having on the quality of social services. Rising living standards generally mean rising expectations of social service standards. This is not always translated into government policy but it is a potent factor that will increasingly have to be taken into consideration.

Increased industrialisation and improved living standards usually lead to a growth of sectional interests. The country is no longer divided simply into workers, peasants and the intelligentsia but sub-groups with conflicting interests have developed within these large groups — a process similar to that in advanced capitalist societies. The ruling elite has to perform the intricate task of reconciling these conflicting interests as well as to fulfil its declared policy of steering the country towards communism where genuine egalitarianism will prevail. This is no easy task, for egalitarianism means redistribution of resources from the more powerful to the less powerful groups in society. One of the main lessons derived from social policy programmes in welfare capitalist societies is that programmes designed to help the poor, the deprived or the underprivileged usually fail if they involve taking away substantial resources from the more powerful groups. Why should expectations be different in the Soviet Union? Paradoxically, the denial of freedom to interest groups in the Soviet Union to pursue openly their objectives can theoretically make egalitarian policies more possible than they are in welfare capitalist societies where pressure groups can campaign freely for the satisfaction of their interests. It means that the Soviet government has much more power to pursue egalitarian policies if it so wishes than any reformist government in capitalist societies. There are, of course, limits to the power of the Soviet government because interest groups can negate or modify government policies by concealed pressure; because egalitarianism at this stage of the ideological consciousness of the country can undermine economic development; and because such policies will reduce the privileged position of the very same ruling elite that introduces them. Ideological factors thus become important even

173

when the material conditions are ripe for such changes — the willingness of the ruling elite to shed peacefully and preferably voluntarily its privileges for the professed greater ideal of egalitarianism.

The dominant ideology of the Soviet Union is maximum feasible egalitarianism in social policy and minimum feasible inegalitarianism in earnings from work. Payment according to work is seen as necessary at this stage of the country's economic and cultural development. Social service provision according to need as far as possible has met with opposition from vested interests and has, at times, been seen as being in conflict with the principle of payment according to work. At other times it is difficult to operationalise the concept of need in such a way that its implications are clear for policy makers. In brief, there appears to be a stalemate. Economic factors will, of course, be very important in resolving this contradiction between the expressed ideologies of social and economic policy. The attitude of the ruling elite will also be important and will, to some extent, be shaped by economic factors. The history of the Soviet Union suggests that the ruling elite acts neither in totally unselfish or selfish ways. It compromises in its policies but it retains the vision of a future communist Soviet Union intact. It is impossible to say how long it will continue to propagate successfully this tantalising ideology of inequality now and equality in the future. What one can say with some certainty is that the ruling elite will find it very difficult, if not impossible, to move towards greater inequality, or to introduce substantial reductions in public expenditure on the social services, as attempted recently in the west. The nationalisation of the means of production has not only assisted in the growth of the country's wealth but it has also helped to create a secure ideological environment for the development of social policy. A social service society, however, is not necessarily a socialist society and, as we concluded in the first chapter, the Soviet Union has a long way to go before fulfilling all the three basic criteria of socialism.

Appendix 1
Administrative structures of the social services

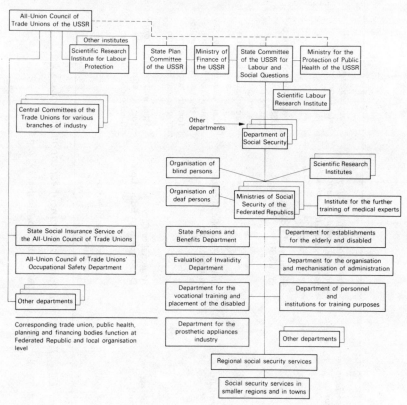

Appendix 1.1 – The administrative structure of social security in the USSR

Source: S. Lukianevko, 'Financing and Administration of Social Security in Socialist Countries', *International Social Security Review*, vol. XXXXI, no. 4, 1978.

Level of government administration	Pre-school establishments, primary and secondary general education schools	Vocational-technical establishments	Secondary specialised and higher-education establishments
Union	Ministry of Education of the USSR	State Committee of the USSR Council of Ministers for Vocational and Technical Education	Ministry of Higher and Secondary Specialised Education
Union Republic	Union Republic Ministry of Education	State Committee of the Council of Ministers of the Union Republic for Vocational and Technical Education	Union Republic Ministry of Higher and Secondary Specialised Education
Region (Oblast) or city (Gorod)	Regional or City Department of Education	Regional or City Committee for Vocational and Technical Education	—
District (Raion)	District Department of Education	—	—

Appendix 1.2 – The administrative structure of education in the USSR

Source: J.J. Tomiak, *The Soviet Union*, David & Charles, 1972, p.47.

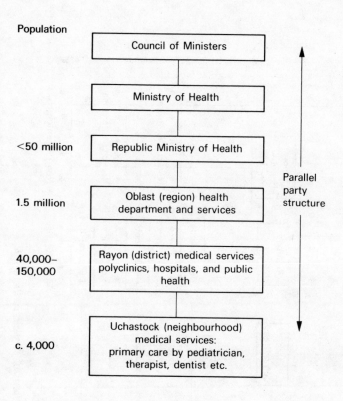

Appendix 1.3 – The administrative structure of the health service in the USSR

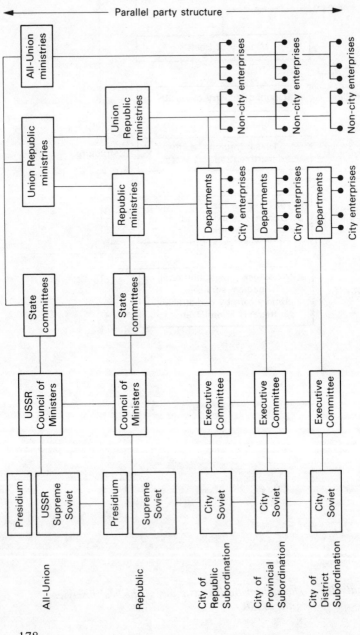

Appendix 1.4 – The administrative structure of housing services in the USSR

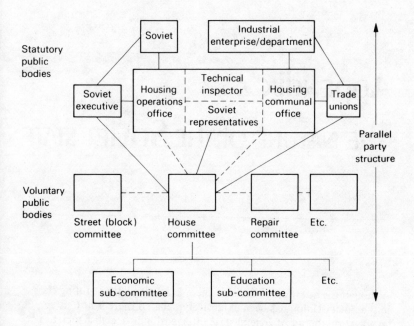

Appendix 1.5 – The administrative structure of local housing services in the USSR

Appendix 2
The nature of the Soviet state

Although the question of whether there is a ruling elite or ruling class in the Soviet Union has been extensively debated there is not, as yet, an adequate theory of general state intervention in socialist societies.[1] However, recent work on the nature of the state in capitalist societies may provide a basis for such work. Introducing a recent collection of papers on the derivation of the capitalist state, Holloway and Picciotto argue that the state neither represents simply the political interests of the ruling class, nor the economic demands of capitalist production, but

> the state is essentially restricted to reacting to the results of the process of production and reproduction; the state's activities and its individual functions (but not its form) thus develop through a process of mediated reaction to the development of the process of accumulation.[2]

A similar approach has been developed specifically in relation to social policy by Ian Gough.[3] He pinpoints the two key features of capitalism as first, the generation and accumulation of surplus value; and second, the dynamic nature of capitalist society which, while influenced by particular classes, is outside the complete control of any class.[4] In short, state intervention (including social policy) is a reaction to developments in capitalist society, aimed at maintaining and reproducing its fundamental dynamic: capital accumulation. This reaction is not automatically determined but is a matter for historical analysis of the form in which this function is manifested.

In this book we have reviewed in some detail such historical perspectives on the Soviet state's activities in the field of social policy. The question here is whether we can apply the logic of this recent analysis of the capitalist state to our historical analysis of Soviet social policy.

The key problem is, of course, to identify the essential similarities between capitalist and Soviet society, and hence the similarities in the role of the state in the field of social policy. This entails an analysis of those activities necessary in any industrial society (the production and distribution of surplus, the reproduction of labour, social relations and so on) and the way those activities are specified under capitalism or socialism. We can attempt this here by taking those features of the state identified by Gough and comparing them with our analysis of the development of Soviet social policy. Gough summarises the nature of the capitalist state in three parts: its form, the interests it represents (its 'constituency') and the specific constraints surrounding it.[5] First, it is formed of a set of institutions such as the repressive apparatus, administrative apparatus and local and regional government. In many respects these forms reappear in the Soviet Union — the central and local soviets, the ministries, the judiciary. But the administrative centralisation of power, the domination of a single party, and the curtailment of the market are notable differences.

The second aspect of the state, however, reveals more substantial differences between capitalist and Soviet society. There is no evidence for an equivalent to the capitalist ruling class in the Soviet Union, whose long-term interests the state represents. However there is a ruling elite, open to considerable mobility, which aims to represent through the state all interests in the long run, particularly with respect to industrial growth. Similarly, the Soviet state cannot represent the interests of all sections of the elite at once since they conflict from time to time, as do the interests of specific groups of the ruling class within capitalist societies.

The third aspect of the state is the most crucial. So far we have found some similarities between the capitalist and Soviet state in terms of their general form and the way in which they represent interests. The insignificance of these similarities is revealed when we look at the reasons that the Soviet state takes the particular form that it does, and hence pursues particular social policies. Gough identifies, after Miliband,[6] three kinds of reason. First, the personnel of the state in capitalist societies share a common ideology, common values and perspectives. For example, the British public-school system fosters ruling class solidarity in its children and supplies a disproportionate share of key state personnel.[7] Although higher education in the Soviet Union is similarly crucial for ruling elite membership there is no such system of special preparation as in Britain. Second, the capitalist

181

state is constrained by the power of property ownership of the ruling class. This is clearly not the case in the Soviet Union, since the elite cannot pursue the interests of private capital accumulation. Third, the capitalist state is constrained by the rationality of the capitalist economy. In terms of production, this means ensuring the preconditions for private capital accumulation for profit: in terms of distribution and consumption it means enabling supply to meet market demand expressed by the consumer. Once again this is not true of Soviet society, except in so far as it is increasingly constrained by world trade which is dominated by the capitalist mode. Instead we can suggest that the Soviet state is rather constrained by the rationality of the socialist economy: production is publicly owned and planned centrally, and distribution, while using market mechanisms, is heavily controlled through centrally-planned prices and supply levels. The problems of central planning are discussed in more detail in chapter 1.

We can see from the application of this logic derived from an analysis of the capitalist state that the nature of the Soviet state, though familiar in some aspects of its form and its resolution of particular interests, is however constrained by different factors than the capitalist state. If we follow this argument further into the field of social policy we can see how these differences are manifested in concrete policies.

In order to understand how the capitalist state intervenes in welfare and hence to explore similarities with the Soviet state we can follow Gough and draw on the ideas of O'Connor. In *The Fiscal Crisis of the State*[8] he argues that capitalist states provide for the interests of capital accumulation and the legitimation of this process through three types of expenditure. The first, social investment, is designed to increase labour productivity such as technical education, industrial health care and so on. The second, social consumption, is designed to ensure the reproduction of labour; for example, support for the family. The third, social expenses, is designed to reduce political conflict or disaffection and hence legitimate the system, such as general education or social work. We can see that the Soviet state must pursue similar activities also in support of economic production and the legitimation of Soviet social relations. However, these three types of state expenditure contain within them conflicting priorities; and since many social policies serve to fulfil more than one function (for example education can both increase productivity and foster political support), the particular nature of state expenditure will reflect the resolution of these conflicting priorities.

For example, public housing in western Europe and America plays a far more residual role than in the Soviet Union. In general, housing policy in the west has merely supported the operations of the private market, both in terms of actually building houses and in terms of regulating general economic activity. Thus concern has centred in O'Connor's categories of social investment and social consumption: to stimulate house building in the interests of productivity and the repro- duction of labour. In the Soviet Union, however, the expansion in house building for low-rented accommodation since the 1950s has been designed to secure in part the political loyalties of workers to Soviet society. It is clear that since house building was a low priority during Stalin's pursuit of industrial growth, it was not considered to be an aid to productivity or the reproduction of labour. In other areas of social policy, however, we can see that the Soviet state has set more familiar priorities; for example, the linking of pension levels to types of work and income differentials.

O'Connor's three types of state expenditure reveal the comparative limitations of social policy under capitalism. But Soviet social policies are in addition determined by a clear ideological commitment to develop a socialist way of life, and ultimately a communist society which has no parallel in the west. This cannot be easily assimilated to O'Connor's framework. We would argue that the structure of the publicly-owned and centrally-planned Soviet economy, and the crucial role of socialist ideology in giving direction to these activities, creates an additional fourth category of state expenditure. We suggest it is one of 'social needs'. This category reflects in particular the more extensive role that socialist social policy plays in Soviet society which we explored in more detail in chapter 6. 'Social needs' refers to the provision of services primarily for the satisfaction of specific needs of individuals or groups of individuals. The fulfilment of this function can be incompat- ible with the fulfilment of other functions. We would argue that though social policy under capitalism fulfils at times the 'social needs' function, there are severe limits to both the extent and the degree to which social policy can pursue this because of the imperatives of private capital. Indeed, 'social needs' are often misleadingly identified by social policy analysis in capitalist societies in expenditures more correctly placed in one of O'Connor's other categories. The public ownership of the means of production and distribution and the socialist/communist nature of the dominant ideology of the Soviet Union make the fulfilment of the 'social needs' function more possible than under capitalism. This is not to deny that there are in the Soviet Union, too, limits to the extent that social policy can pursue the fulfilment of this function but these limits are less severe than they are in the west. These limits stem from the emphasis on rapid industrial growth as well as from some aspects of the dominant ideology.

In conclusion, those aspects of Soviet social policy which appear

similar to the west, for example to stimulate productivity, can be understood in O'Connor's terms. We can argue therefore that some aspects of
capitalist state activity are to be found in the Soviet Union. However,
these limitations of Soviet social policy are more a result of the level of
economic and cultural development than the nature of Soviet society
and the Soviet state.

NOTES

Chapter 1 Economic development and social policy

1   K. Marx, *The Eighteenth Brumaire of Louis Bonaparte*, International
     Publishers, New York, 1969, p. 31.
2   F. Engels, in his letter to Joseph Bloch in Karl Marx, *Selected Works I*,
     pp. 381-3.
3   E.H. Carr, 'Historical Background of the Revolution', in A. Inkeles and
     K. Geiger (eds), *Soviet Society*, Constable, 1961, p. 31.
4   M.H. Dobb, *Soviet Economic Development Since 1917*, Routledge and
     Kegan Paul, 6th ed, 1966, pp. 88-95.
5   *Ibid*, p. 94.
6   *Ibid*, p. 123.
7   A. Nove, *An Economic History of the U.S.S.R.*, Penguin, 1971, p. 111.
8   G. Hyde, *The Soviet Health Service*, Lawrence & Wishart, 1974, p. 88.
9   M.H. Dobb, *op.cit.*, p. 235.
10   R.W. Campbell, *Soviet Economic Power*, 2nd ed, Houghton Mifflin, 1966,
     p. 22.
11   A. Nove, *op.cit.*, p. 267.
12   P. Sorlin, *The Soviet People and their Society*, Praeger, 1968, p. 133.
13   Z. Bauman, *Socialism: the Active Utopia*, Allen & Unwin, 1976, p. 79.
14   G. Hyde, *op.cit.*, p. 98.
15   Stalin's speech on 23 June 1937, in *Leninism*, 1940, p. 368.
16   M.H. Dobb, *op.cit.*, p. 458.
17   Stalin, *Works*, vol. XIII, p. 120, quoted in W. Leonhard, *Three Faces of
     Marxism*, Holt, Rinehart & Winston, 1974, p. 102.
18   R.A. Clarke, *Soviet Economic Facts, 1917-1970*, Macmillan, 1972.
19   *The Times*, 5 August 1963, quoted in M.H. Dobb, *op.cit.*, p. 323.
20   E.G. Liberman, 'The Role of Profits in the Industrial Incentive System
     of the U.S.S.R.', *International Labour Review*, vol. 97, 1968.
21   *Programme of the Communist Party of the Soviet Union*, Novosti Press
     Agency, 1961, p. 143.

22   *Government of the Soviet Union, 1977: Sixty Soviet Years*, Novosti Press Agency, Moscow, 1977, p. 79.
23   R.A. Medvedev, *On Socialist Democracy*, Spokesman Books, 1977, p. 17.
24   M. Lavigne, *The Socialist Economies of the Soviet Union and Eastern Europe*, Martin Robertson, 1974, p. 121.
25   Karl-Eugen Wadekin, 'Income Distribution in Soviet Agriculture', *Soviet Studies*, vol. 27, no. 1, January, 1975.
26   *U.S.S.R., 1977: Sixty Soviet Years, op.cit.*, p. 96.
27   L. Rzhanitsina, 'Public Consumption Funds in the U.S.S.R.', *International Labour Review*, vol. 108, 1973.
28   M. Ryan, *The Organization of Soviet Medical Care*, Blackwell Martin Robertson, 1978, Appendix 3, p.159.
29   N. Bulzyakov, *Welfare, the Basic Task*, Progress, Moscow, 1973, p.115.
30   P. Hollander, *Soviet and American Society*, Oxford University Press, 1973, p.277.
31   R.A. Medvedev, *op.cit.* p.17.
32   Quoted in B. Moore Jr., *Soviet Politics – the Dilemma of Power*, Harper Torchbook edition, 1965, p.69.
33   A.B. Evans, 'Developed Socialism in Soviet Ideology', *Soviet Studies*, vol. 29, no. 3, July 1977.
34   M. Yanowitch, *Social and Economic Inequality in the Soviet Union*, Martin Robertson, 1977, table 2.2, p.30.
35   *Ibid*, table 2.6, p.39.
36   F. Parkin, *Class, Inequality and Political Order*, MacGibbon & Kee, 1971, pp.144-9.
37   D. Lane, *The Socialist Industrial State*, Allen & Unwin, 1976, p.179.
38   F. Engels, *Anti-Dühring*, Moscow, 1954, pp. 305-6.
39   M. Matthews, *Class and Society in Soviet Russia*, Allen Lane, 1972, ch.8.
40   T.H. Friedgut, 'Citizens and Soviets', *Comparative Politics*, vol. 10, no.4, July, 1978.
41   M. McAuley, *Politics and the Soviet Union*, Penguin, 1977, p.313.
42   M. Yanowitch, *op.cit.*, p. 145.
43   K. Marx, Preface to *The Critique of Political Economy, 1859 Selected Works*, Moscow, vol. 1, p.504.
44   K. Marx and F. Engels, *The German Ideology*, International Publishers, New York, 1947, p.24.
45   J. Ellenstein, *The Stalin Phenomenon*, Lawrence & Wishart, 1976, p.60.

Chapter 2 Social security

1   K. Marx and F. Engels, *Selected Work*, Lawrence & Wishart, 1970, p.318.
2   V.I. Lenin, *Collected Works, vol. 17*, Foreign Languages Publishing House, 1963, p.476.
3   B. Madison, 'The Organisation of Welfare Services', in C.E. Black (ed.), *The Transformation of Russian Society*, Harvard University Press, 1960, p.518.
4   D.P. Komarova, *Social Security in the U.S.S.R.*, Progress Publishers, 1971, p.17.
5   B. Madison, *op.cit.*, p.521.
6   V.I. Lenin, *op.cit.*, p.477.
7   M. Dewar, *Labour Policy in the U.S.S.R., 1917-1928*, Oxford University Press, 1956, p.17.

8   B. Madison, *Social Welfare in the Soviet Union,* Stanford University Press, 1968, p.51.
9   E. Levchine, 'The Main Phases in the Development of Social Security Legislation', *The Bulletin of the International Social Security Association,* vol. 17, no. 8-9, August-September, 1964.
10   G.V. Rimlinger, *Welfare Policy and Industrialisation in Europe, America and Russia,* Wiley, 1971, p.265.
11   *Ibid,* p.279.
12   A. Abramson, 'The Reorganization of Social Insurance Institutions in the U.S.S.R.', *International Labour Review,* vol. 31, March, 1935.
13   P.J. Potichnyj, *Soviet Agricultural Trade Unions 1917-1970,* University of Toronto, 1972.
14   B. Madison, 1968, *op.cit.*, p.195.
15   *Ibid.*
16   D.P. Komarova, *op.cit.,* p.60.
17   B. Madison, 1968, *op.cit.*, p. 195.
18   L.P. Yakushev, 'Old People's Rights in the U.S.S.R. and other European Socialist Countries', *International Labour Review,* vol. 113, no. 2, March-April, 1976.
19   W.M. Mandell, *Soviet Women,* Anchor Books, 1975, p.278.
20   V.A. Acharkan, 'State Pensions in the U.S.S.R. Features and Trends', *International Social Security Review,* vol. 29, no. 3, 1976.
21   B. Madison, 'Soviet Income Maintenance Policy for the 1970s', *Journal of Social Policy,* vol. 2, no. 2, April, 1973.
22   *Social Insurance and Allied Services,* HMSO, 1942, Cmd 6404, p.64.
23   M. Ryan, *The Organisation of Soviet Medical Care,* pp.117-25.
24   G.W. Lapidus, *Women in Soviet Society,* University of California Press, 1978, p.305.
25   L.P. Yakushev, *op.cit.*.
26   B. Madison, 'Social Services Administration in the U.S.S.R.', in D. Thurz and J. Vigilante (eds), *Meeting Human Needs: An Overview of Nine Countries,* Russel Sage, 1975, p.254.
27   *The Current Digest of the Soviet Press,* vol. 30, no. 49, 3 January, 1979.
28   D.E. Powell, 'Labor Turnover in the Soviet Union', *Slavic Review,* vol. 36, no. 2, June, 1977.
29   L. Koszegi, 'Labour Turnover and Employment Structure in European Socialist Countries', *International Labour Review,* vol. 117, no. 3, May-June, 1978.
30   J. Minkoff and L. Turgeon, 'Income Maintenance in Eastern Europe', *Social Policy,* March-April, 1976.
31   G.V. Rimlinger, *op.cit.,* p.341.
32   M. Lantsev, 'Progress in Social Security for Agricultural Workers in the U.S.S.R.', *International Labour Review,* vol. 107, no. 2, March, 1973.
33   L. Rzhanitsina, 'Public Consumption Funds in the U.S.S.R.', *International Labour Review,* vol. 108, 1973.
34   M. Lavigne, *The Socialist Economies of the Soviet Union and Eastern Europe*, Martin Robertson, 1974, table 6.13, p. 284.
35   A.N.D. McAuley, 'Soviet Anti-Poverty Policy, 1955-1975', University of Essex Department of Economics, Discussion Paper No. 101, October, 1977, p.10.
36   M. Matthews, *Class and Society in Soviet Russia,* Allen Lane, 1972, p.88.
37   V. George and R. Lawson (eds), *Poverty and Inequality in the Common Market Countries,* Routledge & Kegan Paul, 1979, chapter 7.

38   N. Buzlyakov, *Welfare, the Basic Task,* Progress, 1973, p.57.
39   B. Madison, 1973, *op.cit.*

Chapter 3 Education

1   F. Engels, 'Program of the Blanquist Commune Emigrants', *Selected Works, Vol. II,* Moscow, 1969, p.384.
2   B. Holmes, *Problems in Education,* Routledge & Kegan Paul, 1965, pp.271-2.
3   K. Marx, *Capital, Vol. I* Penguin, 1976, pp.529-30.
4   F. Engels, 'Principles of Communism', *Selected Works, Vol. 1,* Moscow, 1969, p.93.
5   K. Marx, *The General Council of the First International, 1864-1866,* Moscow, Foreign Languages Publishing House, n.d., p.345.
6   K. Marx and F. Engels, *Works* (in Russian), vol. V, p.380, quoted in R.B. Winn, *Soviet Psychology,* Vision Press Limited, 1961, p.50.
7   K. Marx and F. Engels, *Collected Works, Vol. 5,* Lawrence & Wishart, 1976, p.393.
8   N. Hans, *The Russian Tradition in Education,* Routledge & Kegan Paul, 1963, p.189.
9   J. Judge, 'Education in the U.S.S.R., Russian or Soviet?' *Comparative Education,* vol. 11, no. 2, June, 1975.
10   S. and B. Webb, *Soviet Communism: A New Civilisation,* Longmans, 1937, Vol. II, p.889.
11   T.J. Tomiak, *The Soviet Union,* David & Charles, 1972, p.12.
12   *Ibid.,* p.13.
13   Quoted in A.P. Pinkevitch, *The New Education in the Soviet Republic,* John Day Company, 1929, p.375.
14   G.S. Counts, *The Challenge of Soviet Education,* McGraw Hill, 1957, p.22.
15   S. and B. Webb, *op.cit.,* p.897.
16   V. Lenin, *On Youth,* Moscow, Novosti Press Agency, p.253-4.
17   A.A. Kreusler, *Contemporary Education and Moral Upbringing in the Soviet Union,* University of Wisconsin Press, 1976, p.14.
18   M.K. Whyte, 'Educational Reform: China in the 1970s and Russia in the 1920s', *Comparative Education Review,* vol. 18, no. 1, February, 1974.
19   Quoted in G.S. Counts, *op.cit.,* p.70.
20   R. Widmayer, 'The Evolution of Soviet Education Policy', *Harvard Educational Review,* vol. 24, no. 3, Summer, 1954.
21   A.A. Kreusler, *op.cit.,* p.105.
22   Article 121, *Constitution of the Soviet Union,* 1936.
23   R. Widmayer, *op.cit.*
24   G. Bereday, W. Brickman and G. Read (eds), *The Changing Soviet School,* Houghton Mifflin, 1960, p.83.
25   N. Khrushchev's memorandum, 'Strengthening the ties of the schools with life and further developing the system of public education', *Proposals to Reform Soviet Education,* Soviet Booklet, no. 42, 1958, p.5
26   J.J. Schwartz and W.R. Keech, 'Group Influence and the Policy Process in the Soviet Union', in G.K. Bertsch & Th. W. Ganschow (eds), *Comparative Communism: The Soviet, Chinese and Yugoslav Models,* Freeman & Co., 1976, p.230.
27   A. Boiter, 'The Khrushchev School Reform', *Comparative Education Review,* vol. 2, no. 3, February, 1959.

28   D. Pospielovsky, 'Education and Ideology in the U.S.S.R.', *Survey*, vol. 21, no. 4, Autumn, 1975.

29   M. Matthews, 'Soviet Students: Some Sociological Perspectives', *Soviet Studies*, vol. 27, no. 1, January, 1975.

30   J. Tomiak, *op.cit.*, p.84.

31   B. Madison, 'Social Services for Families and Children in the Soviet Union', *Slavic Review*, vol. 31, December, 1972.

32   S. Jacoby, *Inside Soviet Schools*, Hill & Wang, 1974, p.13.

33   N. Kuzin and M. Kondakov (eds), *Education in the U.S.S.R.*, Progress Publishers, 1977, p.32.

34   Ministry of Education of the USSR, *On the Main Trends in the Field of Education in the U.S.S.R. in 1968-70*, Novosti Press Agency, p.21.

35   S. Jacoby, *op.cit.*, p.40.

36   *Ibid*, p.58.

37   'Tying Shoes and Wiping Noses: What Role for the Kindergarten?' *The Current Digest of the Soviet Press*, vol. 31, no. 1, 31 January, 1979.

38   H. Smith, *The Russians*, Quadrangle, 1976, p.149.

39   M. Yanowitch, *Social and Economic Inequality in the Soviet Union*, Martin Robertson, 1977, p.62.

40   M. Matthews, *Class and Society in Soviet Russia*, Allen Lane, 1972, p.299.

41   J. Tomiak, *op.cit.*, and pp.78 and 90.

42   D. Lane, *The End of Inequality?*, Penguin, 1971, p.116.

43   D. Lane, *Politics and Society in the U.S.S.R.*, 2nd edn, Martin Robertson, 1978, p.506.

44   M. Yanowitch, *op.cit.*, p.67.

45   *Ibid*, table 3.3, p.68.

46   *Current Digest of the Soviet Press*, vol. 25, 7 February 1973, pp. 15-16, quoted by S.M. Lipset in M. Yanowitch and W. Fisher, *Social Stratification and Mobility in the U.S.S.R.*, International Arts & Sciences Press, 1978, p.359.

47   M. Matthews, 1975, *op.cit.*, table 4.

48   M. Yanowitch and W. Fisher, *op.cit.*

49   F. Parkin, *Class Inequality and Political Order*, MacGibbon & Kee, 1971, p.110.

50   D. Lane, 1978, *op.cit.*, pp. 457-68.

51   Ch. D. Cary, 'Patterns of Emphasis Upon Marxist-Leninist Ideology', *Comparative Education Review*, vol. 20, no. 1, February, 1976.

52   *Social Science: Guide to Teachers*, Moscow, 1971, p.5, quoted by Ch. D. Cary.

53   *Teachers' Gazette*, December 30, 1961, quoted in S.M. Rosen, *Education and Modernisation in the U.S.S.R.*, Addison-Wesley, 1971, p.132.

54   U. Bronfenbrenner, *Two Worlds of Childhood*, Simon & Schuster, 1972, p.77.

55   *Ibid*, p.80.

56   *Ibid*, p.78.

57   *Ibid*, p.81.

58   M. Matthews, 1975, *op.cit.*

59   A.A. Kreusler, *op.cit.*, p.78.

60   N. DeWitt, 'Recent Trends in Soviet Education', in A. Inkeles and K. Geiger (eds), *Soviet Society*, Constable, 1961, p.439.

61   R.F. Price, *Marx and Education in Russia and China*, Croom Helm, 1977, p.72.

62   N. Kuzin and M. Kondakov (eds), *op.cit.*, p.75.

63   *Ibid*, p.78.

64   A.A. Smirnov, 'The Development of Soviet Psychology', in R.B. Winn (ed.), *Soviet Psychology,* Vision Press Limited, 1961, p.22.
65   *Ibid,* p.25.
66   J. Dunstan, *Paths to Excellence and the Soviet School,* National Foundation for Educational Research Publishing Company, 1978, p.250.
67   H.R. John, 'U.S.A./U.S.S.R. Two Worlds Apart?', *Comparative Education Review*, vol. 19, no. 3 October, 1975.

Chapter 4 Health services in the Soviet Union

1   V.I. Lenin, *Collected Works,* vol. 17, Moscow, 1963, p.476.
2   K. Marx, *Capital,* vol. 1, Penguin, 1976, p.366.
3   *Ibid,* p.521.
4   F. Engels, *The Condition of the Working Class in England,* Panther Books, 1969, p.127.
5   V.I. Lenin, *Collected Works,* vol. 5, p.25, quoted in Y. Lisitsin, *Health Protection in the USSR,* Progress, 1972, p.20.
6   M.G. Field, *Soviet Socialised Medicine,* Free Press, 1967, p.159.
7   V. Navarro, *Social Security and Medicine in the USSR,* Lexington Books, 1977, p.28.
8   A.B. Ulam, *Lenin and the Bolsheviks,* Fontana, 1969, p.677.
9   N.A. Semashko, *The Foundation of Soviet Medicine,* Moscow, 1926, quoted in S. and B. Webb, *Soviet Communism,* vol. II, Longmans, 1937, p.836.
10   Skorokhodov, *A Short Essay on the History of Russian Medicine,* quoted in G. Hyde, *The Soviet Health Service,* Lawrence & Wishart, 1974, p.24.
11   *Ibid,* pp.14-15.
12   M.G. Field, *op.cit.,* p.23.
13   *Ibid,* pp.47-9.
14   E.H. Carr, *The Bolshevik Revolution 1917-1923,* vol. 1, Penguin, 1966, p.82.
15   M.G. Field, *Doctor and Patient in Soviet Russia,* Harvard University Press, 1957, p.13.
16   V. Navarro, *op.cit.,* pp.19-20.
17   N. Grigoryeva, *Medical Workers' Union,* Profizdat, 1975, p.6.
18   M.G. Field, 1957, *op.cit.,* pp.15-20.
19   M.G. Field, 1967, *op.cit.,* p.52.
20   V.I. Lenin, *Collected Works,* vol. 30, Lawrence & Wishart, 1965, p.185.
21   E.H. Carr, *op.cit.,* vol. 2, pp.322-3.
22   M.G. Field, 1957, *op.cit.,* p.100.
23   M.G. Field, 1967, *op.cit.,* p.64.
24   G. Hyde, *op.cit.,* p.99.
25   *Ibid,* p.101.
26   M. Ryan, *The Organisation of Soviet Medical Care,* Blackwell/Martin Robertson, 1978, p.115.
27   M.G. Field, 1957, *op.cit.,* p.163.
28   M. Kaser, *Health Care in the Soviet Union and Eastern Europe,* Croom Helm, 1976, pp. 67-8.
29   V. Navarro, *op.cit.,* p.48.
30   G. Hyde, *op.cit.,* p.121.
31   M. Kaser, *op.cit.,* p.7.

32   Secretary of the Central Committee of the Medical Workers' Union, 'interview', March 1978.

33   M. Kaser, *op.cit.,* pp.44-5, 73.

34   J. Chinn, *Manipulating Soviet Population Resources,* Martin Robertson, 1977, chapter 3.

35   W.W. Eason, 'Demography', in E. Mickiewicz (ed.), *Handbook of Soviet Social Science Data,* Free Press, 1973, p.54.

36   N.T. Dodge, *Women in the Soviet Union*, Johns Hopkins Press, 1966 Chapter 2; M. Matthews, *Class and Society in Soviet Russia,* Allen Lane, 1972, Chapter 1

37   N.T. Dodge, *op.cit.*, p.299.

38   *Ibid*, p.13.

39   M. Kaser, *op.cit.,* pp.48-53.

40   M.G. Field, 'Health', in Mickiewicz, *op.cit.,* p.102; G. Hyde *op.cit.,* p.106.

41   M. Kaser, *op.cit.,* p.48.

42   T.M. Ryan, 'Some Current Trends in the Soviet Health Services', *The Medical Officer,* 13 February 1970, p.83, quoted in M. Kaser, *op.cit.,* p.49.

43   G.A. Popov, *Principles of Health Planning in the USSR,* WHO, 1971, p.42.

44   *Ibid,* chapters 1 and 6; Navarro, *op.cit.,* pp.64, 97-8.

45   Adapted from M. Ryan, 1978, *op.cit.,* pp.36, 96.

46   Adapted from *ibid.,* p.36; M.G. Field, 'Health as a "Public Utility" or the "Maintenance Capacity" in Soviet Society', in M.G. Field, (ed.), *Social Consequences of Modernisation in Communist Societies,* Johns Hopkins University Press, 1976, p.248; DHSS, *Health and Personal Social Services for England,* HMSO, 1977, p.33.

47   M. Ryan, 1978, *op.cit.,* p.38.

48   J. Fry, *Medicine in Three Societies, a Comparison of Medical Care in the USSR, USA and UK,* Medical & Technical Publishing, 1969, pp.221-3.

49   M. Kaser, *op.cit.,* p.52.

50   H. Smith, *The Russians,* Sphere Books, 1976, pp.96-100; R.G. Kaiser, *Russia,* Penguin, 1977, pp.125-30; M. Ryan, 1978, *op.cit.,* pp.95-6; personal observation.

51   V. Navarro, *op.cit.,* pp.46-8.

52   Personal observation.

53   Quoted by M. Ryan, 1978, *op.cit.,* p.48.

54   *Ibid,* p.53.

55   *Ibid,* Appendix 4.

56   Y. Lisitsin, *op.cit.,* p.56.

57   *Ibid,* pp.60, 81.

58   M. Ryan, 1978, *op.cit.,* p.23.

59   Y. Lisitsin, *op.cit.,* p.68.

60   V. Navarro, *op.cit.,* pp.105-8.

61   S. Bloch and P. Reddaway, *Russia's Political Hospitals,* Gollancz, 1977; Malcolm Lader, *Psychiatry on Trial,* Penguin, 1977; Zhores and Roy Medvedev, *A Question of Madness,* Penguin, 1974; Boris M. Segal, 'Involuntary hospitalisation in the USSR', in S.A. and E. O'Leary Corson (eds), *Psychiatry and Psychology in the USSR,* Plenum Press, 1976; US Senate Committee on the Judiciary, *Abuse of Psychiatry for Political Repression in the Soviet Union,* ARNO Press, 1972.

62   M. Ryan, 1978, *op.cit.*, p.67.

63   *Ibid,* p.66.

64   *Ibid,* pp.68, 74.

65   M.G. Field, 'American and Soviet Medical Manpower: Growth and

Evolution, 1910-1970', *International Journal of Health Services,* vol. 5, no.3, 1975.

66   Adapted from V. Navarro, *op.cit.,* p.76; Ryan, 1978, *op.cit.,* p.43.
67   *Ibid,* p.19; N. Buzlyakov, *Welfare the Basic Task,* Progress, 1973, p.78.
68   M. Kaser, *op.cit.,* p.88.
69   M. Matthews, *Privilege in the Soviet Union,* Allen & Unwin, 1978, p.47.
70   M. Kaser, *op.cit.,* p.66; M. Ryan, 1978, *op.cit.,* pp.31-3; M. Matthews, *op.cit.,* p.29; H. Smith, *op.cit.,* p.113.
71   I. Illich, *Medical Nemesis,* Calder & Boyars, 1975.
72   M.H. Cooper, *Rationing Health Care,* Croom Helm, 1975; A.J. Culyer, *Need and the National Health Service,* Martin Robertson, 1976.
73   M. Ryan, 1978, *op.cit.,* p.112.
74   M.G. Field, 'Health and the Polity: Communist China and Soviet Russia', *Studies in Comparative Communism,* vol. 7, no. 4, 1974, pp.420-25.
75   M. Kaser, *op.cit.,* p.66.
76   *Ibid,* p.64.
77   Y. Lisitsin, *op.cit.,* p.66.
78   V. Navarro, *op.cit.,* p.112.
79   M.G. Field, 1974, *op.cit.,* p.424.
80   B. and J. Ehrenreich, *The American Health Empire, Power, Profits and Politics,* Vintage Books, 1971.

Chapter 5 Housing in the Soviet Union

1   F. Engels, *The Condition of the Working Class in England,* Panther Books, 1969, pp.86-7.
2   J.M. Gilison, *The Soviet Image of Utopia,* Johns Hopkins University Press, 1975, pp.36-7; N. Leonhard, *Three Faces of Marxism,* Putnam's, 1974, p.39.
3   F. Engels, *The Housing Question,* Martin Lawrence, 1942, p.54.
4   *Ibid,* pp.77, 96.
5   *Ibid,* p.101.
6   T. Sosnovy, *The Housing Problem in the Soviet Union,* Research Programme on the USSR, 1954, p.13.
7   S. Frederick Starr, *Melnikov – Solo Architect in a Mass Society,* Princeton University Press, 1978, p.63.
8   M. Bliznakov, 'Urban Planning in the USSR: Integrative Theories', in M.F. Hamm (ed.), *The City in Russian History,* University Press of Kentucky, 1976, p.243.
9   A.M. Kollontai, *Communism and the Family,* Pluto Press, 1972.
10   H.K. Geiger, *The Family in the Soviet Union,* Harvard University Press, 1968, p.30.
11   S.F. Starr, *op.cit.,* p.44.
12   M. Bliznakov, *op.cit.,* pp.248-9.
13   Robert J. Osborn, *Soviet Social Policies,* Dorsey, 1970, p.234.
14   M.F. Parkins, *City Planning in Soviet Russia,* University of Chicago Press, 1953, p.24.
15   *Ibid,* p.26.
16   *Ibid,* p.24.
17   *Ibid,* p.26.
18   M. Bliznakov, *op.cit.,* p.246.
19   T. Sosnovy, 'Housing in the Workers' State', *Problems of Communism,* vol. 5, no. 6, 1956, p.35.

20   T. Sosnovy, 1954, *op.cit.,* p.5.
21   A. Block, 'Soviet Housing – The Historical Aspect: Some Notes on Problems of Policy – I', *Soviet Studies,* vol. 3, no. 1, July 1951, p.4.
22   *Ibid,* p.2.
23   T. Sosnovy, 1954, *op.cit.,* p.4.
24   A.J. Dimaio, *Soviet Urban Housing,* Praeger, 1974, p.6.
25   H. Blumenfeld, 'The Soviet Housing Problem', *American Review of the Soviet Union,* vol. 5, no. 1, 1945, p.13.
26   T. Sosnovy, 1954, *op.cit.,* p.9.
27   T.S. Fedor, *Patterns of Urban Growth in the Russian Empire During the Nineteenth Century,* University of Chicago, Department of Geography Research Paper no. 163, 1975, p.174.
28   R.A. Lewis and R.H. Rowland, 'Urbanisation in Russia and the USSR: 1897-1966', *Annals of the Association of American Geographers,* vol. 59, no. 4, December 1969, p.796.
29   R.L. Thiede, 'Industry and Urbanisation in New Russia from 1860 to 1910', in Hamm, *op.cit.,* p.137.
30   W. Hanchett, 'Tsarist Statutory Regulation of Municipal Government in the Nineteenth Century', in Hamm, *op.cit.,* p.98.
31   *Ibid,* p.96.
32   M.F. Hamm, 'The Breakdown of Urban Modernisation: a prelude to the revolutions of 1917', in Hamm, *op.cit.,* pp.195, 182.
33   S.F. Starr, *op.cit.,* pp.38-40.
34   T. Sosnovy, 1954, *op.cit.,* pp.12-14, 228-9.
35   Z.L. Zile, 'Private Rights in a Collectivist Society: A Study of the Non-Socialist Effort in Soviet Urban Housing Construction', Thesis, Harvard Law School, 1967, p.15, quoted in Dimaio, *op.cit.,* p.10.
36   T. Sosnovy, 1954, *op.cit.,* p.39.
37   H. Blumenfeld, *op.cit.,* p.14.
38   A. Block, *op.cit.,* p.12.
39   T. Sosnovy, 1954, *op.cit.,* p.39.
40   A. Block, *op.cit.,* pp.9-10.
41   T. Sosnovy, 1954, *op.cit.,* chapter 5.
42   A. Block, 'Soviet Housing – The Historical Aspect: Some Notes on Problems of Policy – II', *Soviet Studies,* vol. 3, no. 3, January, 1952, pp. 248-9.
43   T. Sosnovy, 1954, *op.cit.,* pp.52-5.
44   S.F. Starr, *op.cit.,* p.48.
45   C.D. Harris, *Cities of the Soviet Union,* Rand McNally, 1970, p.9.
46   S.F. Starr, *op.cit.,* pp.187, 188, 200 and 214.
47   M.F. Parkins, *op.cit.,* p.37.
48   *Ibid,* pp.36-41.
49   *Ibid,* p.44.
50   M. Bliznakov, *op.cit.,* p.253.
51   M.F. Parkins, *op.cit.,* p.48.
52   A.V. Bunin, N.Kh. Poliakov and V. Shkvarikov, (eds), *City Planning,* Moscow, 1945, p.289, quoted in Parkins, *op.cit.,* p.19.
53   T. Sosnovy, 1954, *op.cit.,* pp.57, 66 and 73.
54   A.S. Balinsky, 'Non-Housing Objectives of Soviet Housing Policy', *Problems of Communism,* vol. 10, no. 4, 1961, pp. 17-23.
55   A. Block, 1952, *op.cit.,* pp.251-252.
56   A. Block, 1951, *op.cit.,* p.7.
57   T. Sosnovy, 1954, *op.cit.,* Appendix 1.

58   B. Svetlichnyi, deputy director, Department of Housing, USSR Gosplan, quoted in W. Taubman, *Governing Soviet Cities,* Praeger, 1973, p.25.
59   *Ibid,* p.57.
60   Quoted from I. Prozdov, 'A City without a Master', *Izvestiia,* 20 October 1960, p.3.
61   T. Sosnovy, 1954, *op.cit.,* pp.31-2.
62   *Ibid,* pp.119, 130, and 133.
63   *Ibid,* pp.107-8. H.W. Morton, 'Housing', in E. Mickiewicz (ed.), *Handbook of Soviet Social Science Data,* Collier-Macmillan, 1973, table 4, p.124.
64   D.D. Barry, 'Soviet Housing Law: the Norms and their Application', in D.D. Barry, G. Ginsburgs, and P.B. Maggs (eds), *Soviet Law After Stalin,* Sijthoff-Leyden, 1977, pp.16, 31.
65   M.F. Parkins, *op.cit.,* p.56.
66   T. Sosnovy, 1954, *op.cit.,* p.66.
67   M.F. Parkins, *op.cit.,* p.115.
68   T. Sosnovy, 1954, *op.cit.,* pp.127; T. Sosnovy, 1956, *op.cit.,* p.34.
69   A. Block, 1952, *op.cit.,* p.252.
70   M.F. Parkins, *op.cit.,* p.118.
71   W. Taubman, *op.cit.,* pp.28-9.
72   K. Zhukov and V. Fyodorov, *Housing Construction in the Soviet Union,* Progress, 1974, pp.25-9.
73   E.A. Gutkind, *Urban Development in Eastern Europe: Bulgaria, Rumania and the USSR,* International History of City Development, vol. 8, Free Press, 1972, pp.304-12.
74   D.D. Barry, 'Housing in the USSR, Cities and Towns', *Problems of Communism,* vol. 18, no.3, May-June 1969, p.4.
75   H.W. Morton, 'Low Cost Housing in the USSR', in P.F. Rad et al. (eds), *Proceedings of the I.A.H.S. International Symposium on Housing Problems – 1976,* p.101.
76   A.J. Dimaio, *op.cit.,* p.180.
77   R.J. Osborn, *op.cit.,* p.237.
78   M. Frolic, 'The Soviet City', *Town Planning Review,* vol. 34, no. 4, 1964, pp. 285-7.
79   R.J. Osborn, *op.cit.,* pp.237-49.
80   W. Taubman, *op.cit.,* p.22.
81   D.D. Barry, 1977, *op.cit.,* p.3.
82   A.J. Dimaio, *op.cit.,* p.57.
83   W. Taubman, *op.cit.,* p.32.
84   J.H. Bater, 'Soviet Town Planning: Theory and Practice in the 1970s', *Progress in Human Geography,* vol. 1, no. 1, 1977, p.203.
85   D.T. Cattell, *Leningrad: A Case Study of Soviet Urban Government,* Praeger, 1968, p.264.
86   D.E. Powell, 'The Rural Exodus', *Problems of Communism,* vol. 23, no. 6, 1974, pp.1-13. W.A.D. Jackson, 'Urban Expansion', *Problems of Communism,* vol. 23, no. 6, 1974, pp.14-24.
87   J. Chinn, *Manipulating Soviet Population Resources,* Martin Robertson, 1977, p.46.
88   *Ibid,* pp.56-8 and 102-8.
89   H.W. Morton, 'What Have Soviet Leaders Done about the Housing Crisis?', in H.W. Morton and R.L. Tokes (eds), *Soviet Politics and Society in the 1970s,* Free Press, 1974, pp.171, 173.
90   *Ibid,* p.170.
91   D.D. Barry, 1977, *op.cit.,* p.7.

92   J. Chinn, *op.cit.*, p.122.
93   *Ibid*, pp.103-5. M. Matthews, 'Social Dimensions in Soviet Urban Housing', in R.A. French and F.E.I. Hamilton (eds), *The Socialist City*, John Wiley, 1979, p.114.
94   R.J. Osborn, *op.cit.*, p.225.
95   J. Chinn, *op.cit.*, p.49.
96   From R.A. French, 'The Individuality of the Soviet City', in French and Hamilton, *op.cit.*, p.77.
97   Calculated from Morton, 1974, *op.cit.*, p.171, and Bater, *op.cit.*, p.194.
98   Adapted from Morton, 1974, *op.cit.*, p.171, and Bater, *op.cit.*, p.194.
99   D.D. Barry, 1977, *op.cit.*, p.11.
100 A.J. Dimaio, *op.cit.*, p.125.
101 M. Matthews, *Privilege in the Soviet Union*, Allen & Unwin, 1978, p.46.
102 H.W. Morton, 1976, *op.cit.*, p.109.
103 A.J. Dimaio, *op.cit.*, pp.97-101.
104 *Ibid*, p.120.
105 *Ibid*, p.163.
106 D.T. Cattell, *op.cit.*, p.53.
107 *Ibid*, p.69.
108 A.J. Dimaio, *op.cit.*, p.139.
109 D.D. Barry, 1977, *op.cit.*, p.20.
110 A.J. Dimaio, *op.cit.*, p.143.
111 D.D. Barry, *op.cit.*, p.20.
112 J.H. Bater, *op.cit.*, p.191.
113 *Ibid*, p.201.
114 *Ibid*, pp.199-200.
115 F. Kotov, Y. Ivanov and I. Prostyakov, *The USSR Economy in 1976-1980*, Progress, p.91.
116 Personal observation.
117 M. Matthews, 1979, *op.cit.*, p.110.
118 H.W. Morton, 1974, *op.cit.*, p.168; N. Buzlyakov, *Welfare, The Basic Task*, Progress, 1973, p.26.
119 R.J. Osborn, *op.cit.*, p.226.
120 W. Taubman, *op.cit.*, pp.38-40.
121 D.T. Cattell, *op.cit.*, pp.48-51.
122 L. Gordon and E. Klopov, *Men After Work*, Progress, 1975.
123 H. Stretton, *Urban Planning in Rich and Poor Countries*, Oxford University Press, 1978, p.53.
124 H. Stretton, *Capitalism, Socialism and the Environment*, Cambridge University Press, 1976, p.204.
125 *Ibid*, p.206.
126 D.T. Cattell, *op.cit.*, p.65.
127 D.E. Powell, *op.cit.*, p.7.
128 G. Konrad and I. Szelenyi, 'Social Conflicts of Under-Urbanisation', in A.A. Brown, J.L. Licari and E. Neuberger (eds), *Urban and Social Economics in Market and Planned Economies*, Praeger, 1974.
129 K.J. Kansky, *Urbanisation under Socialism, The Case of Czechoslovakia*, Praeger, 1976, p.253.

Chapter 6 The political economy and social policy of the USSR

1   M.H. Dobb, *Socialist Planning: Some Problems*, Lawrence & Wishart, 1970, pp.21-2.
2   M. Rokouski, 'Marxism and the Analysis of Soviet Societies', *Capital and Class*, no. 1, Spring, 1977.
3   1977 Constitution of the Soviet Union, p.14.
4   A.B. Evans, 'Developed Socialism in Soviet Ideology', *Soviet Studies*, vol. 29, no. 3, July, 1977.
5   M. McAuley, *Politics and the Soviet Union*, Penguin, 1977, p.326.
6   *Ibid*, p.310.
7   M. Matthews, *Privilege in the Soviet Union, a Study of Elite Life Styles under Communism*, Allen & Unwin, 1978, p.31.
8   W. Wesolowski, 'The notions of Strata and class in socialist society', in A. Beteille, *Social Inequality*, Penguin, 1969.
9   F. Parkin, *Class Inequality and Political Order*, McGibbon & Kee, 1971, p.158.
10   M. Yanowitch, *Social and Economic Inequality in the Soviet Union*, Martin Robertson, 1977, chapter 4.
11   G. Skilling, 'Interest Groups in Communist Politics', *World Politics*, vol. 18, no. 3, April, 1966.
12   W. Taubman, *Governing Soviet Cities, Bureaucratic Politics and Urban Development in the U.S.S.R.*, Praeger, 1973, chapter 2.
13   R.L. Heilbroner, 'What is Socialism?', *Dissent*, Summer, 1978.
14   Z. Ferge, 'Societal Policy and the Types of Centralized Redistribution', in T. Huszar, K. Kulczar and S. Szalair (eds), *Hungarian Society and Marxist Sociology in the 1970s*, Corrina Press, 1978, p.55.
15   J.P. Roos, 'Social Policy in Socialism and Capitalism: A Conceptual Analysis', *The Greek Review of Social Research*, no. 29, 1977.
16   *Ibid.*
17   S. Strumilin, 'The Economics of Education in the U.S.S.R.', in UNESCO, *Economic and Social Aspects of Educational Planning*, Paris, 1964, p.69.
18   M. Lantzev, 'The Correlation Between Social Security Measures and Labour Problems in the U.S.S.R.', *International Social Security Review*, vol. XXXI, no. 4, 1978.
19   A. Inkeles and R.A. Bauer, *The Soviet Citizen*, Harvard University Press, 1959, p.236.
20   S. Strumilin, quoted in B. Mieczkowski, *Personal and Social Consumption in Eastern Europe*, Praeger, 1975, p.33.
21   *Ibid*, p.39.
22   Z. Ferge, *op.cit.*, p.69.
23   N. Buzlyakov, *Welfare, the Basic Task*, Progress Publishers, 1973, p.76.
24   I. Szelenyi, 'Social Inequalities in State Socialist Redistributive Economies', *International Journal of Comparative Sociology*, vol. 19, *Nos. 1-2*, March-June, 1978.
25   *Ibid.*
26   V. George and R. Lawson (eds), *Poverty and Inequality in Common Market Countries*, Routledge & Kegan Paul, 1980.

Appendix 2 – The nature of the Soviet state

1   Ray Pahl, 'Collective Consumption', in R. Scase (ed.), *Industrial Society, Class, Cleavage and Control,* Allen & Unwin, 1977, pp.153-5.
2   John Holloway and Sol Picciotto (eds), *State and Capital,* Edward Arnold, 1978, p.25.
3   Ian Gough, *The Political Economy of the Welfare State,* Martin Robertson, 1979.
4   Ibid, pp.39-40.
5   Ibid, pp.41-42.
6   R. Miliband, *The State in Capitalist Society,* Quartet Books, 1973.
7   V. George and P. Wilding, 'Social Values, Social Class and Social Policy', *Social and Economic Administration,* vol. 6, no. 3, September, 1972, p.240.
8   J. O'Connor, *The Fiscal Crisis of the State,* St. James Press, 1973.

Bibliography

Abramson, A. 'The Reorganisation of Social Insurance Institutions in the USSR', *International Labour Review*, vol. 31, March, 1935.

Acharkan, V.A. 'State Pensions in the U.S.S.R. Features and Trends', *International Social Security Review*, vol. 29, no. 3, 1976.

Balinsky, A.S. 'Non-housing Objectives of Soviet Housing Policy', *Problems of Communism*, vol. 10, no. 4, 1961.

Barry, D.D. 'Housing in the USSR, Cities and Towns', *Problems of Communism*, vol. 18, no. 3, May-June, 1969.

Barry, D.D. 'Soviet Housing Law: the norms and their application', in Barry, D.D., Ginsburgs, G. and Maggs, P.B. (eds), *Soviet Law After Stalin*, Sijthoff-Leyden, 1977.

Bater, J.H. 'Soviet Town Planning: Theory and Practice in the 1970s', *Progress in Human Geography*, vol. 1, no. 1, 1977.

Bauman, Z. *Socialism: the Active Utopia*, Allen & Unwin, 1976.

Bereday, G. Brickman, W. and Read, G. (eds), *The Changing Soviet School*, Houghton Mifflin, 1960.

Bliznakov, M. 'Urban Planning in the USSR, Integrative Theories', in Hamm, M.F. (ed.) *The City in Russian History*, University Press of Kentucky, 1976.

Bloch, S. and Reddaway, P. *Russia's Political Hospitals*, Gollancz, 1977.

Block, A. 'Soviet Housing – The Historical Aspect: Some Notes on Problems of Policy – I', *Soviet Studies*, vol. 3, no. 1, July, 1951.

Block, A. 'Soviet Housing – the Historical Aspect: Some Notes on Problems of Policy – II', *Soviet Studies*, vol. 3, no. 3, January, 1952.

Blumenfeld, H. 'The Soviet Housing Problem', *American Review of the Soviet Union*, vol. 5, no. 1, 1945.

Boiter, A. 'The Krushchev School Reform', *Comparative Education Review*, vol. 2, no. 3, February, 1959.

Bronfenbrenner, J. *Two Worlds of Childhood*, Simon & Schuster, 1972.

Bunin, A.V., Poliakov, N.Kh. and Shkvarikov, V. (eds) *City Planning*, Moscow, 1945.

Buzlyakov, N. *Welfare, the Basic Task*, Progress, 1973.

Campbell, R.W. *Soviet Economic Power*, 2nd ed., Houghton Mifflin, 1966.

Carr, E.H. 'Historical Background of the Revolution', in Inkeles, A. and Geiger, K. (eds), *Soviet Society*, Constable, 1961.

Carr, E.H., *The Bolshevik Revolution 1917-1923*, vols 1, 2, Penguin, 1966.

Cary, Ch.D., 'Patterns of Emphasis upon Marxist-Leninist Ideology', *Comparative Education Review*, vol. 20, no. 1, February, 1976.

Cattell, D.T., *Leningrad: a Case Study of Soviet Urban Government*, Praeger, 1968.

Chinn, J. *Manipulating Soviet Population Resources*, Martin Robertson, 1977.

Clarke, R.A. *Soviet Economic Facts, 1917-1970*, Macmillan, 1972.

Constitution of the Soviet Union, 1936.

Constitution of the Soviet Union, 1977.

Cooper, M.H. *Rationing Health Care*, Croom Helm, 1975.

Counts, G.S. *The Challenge of Soviet Education*, McGraw Hill, 1957.

Culyer, A.J. *Need and the National Health Service*, Martin Robertson, 1976.

Current Digest of the Soviet Press, vol. 30, no. 49, 3 January, 1979.

Current Digest of the Soviet Press, 'Tying Shoes and Wiping Noses: What Role for the Kindergarten?' vol. 31, no. 1, 31 January 1979.

Department of Health and Social Security *Health and Personal Social Services for England*, Her Majesty's Stationery Office, 1977.

Dewar, M. *Labour Policy in the U.S.S.R., 1917-1928*, Oxford University Press, 1956.

De Witt, N. 'Recent Trends in Soviet Education', in Inkeles, A. and Geiger, K. (eds), *Soviet Society*, Constable, 1961.

Dimaio, A.J. *Soviet Urban Housing*, Praeger, 1974.

Dobb, M.H. *Soviet Economic Development Since 1917*, 6th edn. Routledge & Kegan Paul, 1966.

Dobb, M.H. *Socialist Planning: Some Problems*, Lawrence & Wishart 1970.

Dodge, N.T. *Women in the Soviet Union*, Johns Hopkins University Press, 1966.

Dunstan, J. *Paths to Excellence and the Soviet School*, National Foundation for Educational Research Publishing Company, 1978.

Eason, W.W. 'Demography', in Mickiewicz, E. (ed.), *Handbook of Soviet Social Science Data*, Free Press, 1973.

Ehrenreich, B. and J. *The American Health Empire, Power, Profits and Politics*, Vintage Books, 1971.

Ellenstein, J. *The Stalin Phenomenon*, Lawrence & Wishart, 1976.

Engels, F. *Anti-Dühring*, Moscow, 1954.

Engels, F. *The Condition of the Working Class in England*, Panther Books, 1969.

Engels, F. 'Program of the Blanquist Commune Emigrants', *Selected Works*, vol. II, Moscow, 1969.

Engels, F. *The Housing Question*, Martin Lawrence, 1942.

Evans, A.B. 'Developed Socialism in Soviet Ideology', *Soviet Studies*, vol. 29, no. 3, July, 1977.

Fedor, T.S. *Patterns of Urban Growth in the Russian Empire During the Nineteenth Century*, University of Chicago, Department of Geography Research Paper no. 163, 1975.

Ferge, Z. 'Societal Policy and the Types of Centralized Redistribution', in Huszar, T., Kulczar, K. and Szalair, S. (eds), *Hungarian Society and Marxist Sociology in the 1970s*, Corrina Press, 1978.

Field, M.G. *Doctor and Patient in Soviet Russia*, Harvard University Press, 1957.

Field, M.G. *Soviet Socialised Medicine*, Free Press, 1967.

Field, M.G. 'Health', in Mickiewicz, E. (ed.), *Handbook of Soviet Social Science Data*, Free Press, 1973.

Field, M.G. 'Health and the Polity: Communist China and Soviet Russia', *Studies in Comparative Communism*, vol. 7, no. 4, 1974.

Field, M.G. 'American and Soviet Medical Manpower: Growth and Evolution, 1910-1970', *International Journal of Health Services,* vol. 5, no. 3, 1975.

Field, M.G. 'Health as a "Public Utility" or the "Maintenance Capacity" in Soviet Society', in Field, M.G. (ed.) *Social Consequences of Modernisation in Communist Societies,* Johns Hopkins University Press, 1976.

French, R.A. 'The Individuality of the Soviet City', in French, R.A. and Hamilton, F.E.I. (eds) *The Socialist City*, John Wiley, 1979.

Friedgut, T. 'Citizens and Soviets', *Comparative Politics,* vol. 10, no. 4, July, 1978.

Frolic, M. 'The Soviet City', *Town Planning Review,* vol. 34, no. 4, 1964.

Fry, J. *Medicine in Three Societies: a Comparison of Medical Care in the USSR, USA, and UK,* Medical & Technical Publishing, 1969.

Geiger, H.K. *The Family in the Soviet Union,* Harvard University Press, 1968.

George, V. and Lawson, R. (eds) *Poverty and Inequality in Common Market Countries,* Routledge & Kegan Paul, 1980.

George, V. and Wilding, P. 'Social Values, Social Class and Social Policy', *Social and Economic Administration,* vol. 6, no. 3, September, 1972.

Gilison, J.M. *The Soviet Image of Utopia,* Johns Hopkins University Press, 1975.

Gordon, L. and Klopov, E. *Men After Work,* Progress, 1975.

Gough, I. *The Political Economy of the Welfare State,* Martin Robertson, 1979.

Grigoryeva, N. *Medical Workers' Union,* Profizdat, 1975.

Gutkind, E.A. *Urban Development in Eastern Europe: Bulgaria, Rumania and the USSR,* International History of City Development, vol. 8, Free Press, 1972.

Hamm, M.F. 'The Breakdown of Urban Modernisation: a prelude to the revolutions of 1917', in Hamm, M.F. (ed.) *The City in Russian History*, University Press of Kentucky, 1976.

Hanchett, W. 'Tsarist Statutory Regulation of Municipal Government in the Nineteenth Century', in Hamm, M.F. (ed.) *The City in Russian History*, University Press of Kentucky, 1976.

Hans, N. *The Russian Tradition in Education,* Routledge & Kegan Paul, 1963.

Harris, C.D. *Cities of the Soviet Union,* Rand McNally, 1970.

Heilbroner, R.L. 'What is Socialism?', *Dissent,* Summer, 1978.

Hollander, P. *Soviet and American Society,* Oxford University Press, 1973.

Holloway, J. and Picciotto, S. (eds) *State and Capital*, Edward Arnold, 1978.

Holmes, B. *Problems in Education,* Routledge & Kegan Paul, 1965.

Hyde, G. *The Soviet Health Service,* Lawrence & Wishart, 1974.

Illich, I. *Medical Nemesis,* Calder & Boyars, 1975.

Inkeles, A. and Bauer, R.A. *The Soviet Citizen,* Harvard University Press, 1959.

Inkeles, A. and Geiger, K. (eds) *Soviet Society,* Constable, 1961.

Jackson, W.A.D. 'Urban Expansion', *Problems of Communism,* vol. 23, no. 6, 1974.

Jacoby, S. *Inside Soviet Schools,* Hill & Wang, 1974.

Jahn, H.R. 'USA/USSR, Two Worlds Apart?', *Comparative Education Review,* vol. 19, no. 3, 1975.

Judge, J. 'Education in the U.S.S.R., Russian or Soviet?', *Comparative Education,* vol. 11, no. 2, June, 1975.

Kaiser, R.G. *Russia,* Penguin, 1977.

Kansky, K.J. *Urbanisation under Socialism: The Case of Czechoslovakia,* Praeger, 1976.

Kaser, M. *Health Care in the Soviet Union and Eastern Europe,* Croom Helm, 1976.

Khrushchev, N. 'Strengthening the ties of the schools with life and further developing the system of public education', *Proposals to Reform Soviet Education,* Soviet Booklet no. 42, 1958.

Kollontai, A.M. *Communism and the Family*, Pluto Press, 1971.

Komarova, D.P. *Social Security in the U.S.S.R.*, Progress Publishers, 1971.

Konrad, G. and Szelenyi, I. 'Social Conflicts of Under-Urbanisation', in Brown, A.A., Licari, J.L. and Neuberger, E. (eds) *Urban and Social Economics in Market and Planned Economies*, Praeger, 1974.

Koszegi, L. 'Labour Turnover and Employment Structure in European Socialist Countries', *International Labour Review*, vol. 117, no. 3, May-June, 1978.

Kotov, F., Ivanov, Y. and Prostyakov, I. *The USSR Economy in 1976-1980*, Progress, n.d.

Kreusler, A.A. *Contemporary Education and Moral Upbringing in the Soviet Union*, University of Wisconsin Press, 1976.

Kuzin, N. and Kondakov, M. (eds), *Education in the U.S.S.R.*, Progress Publishers, 1977.

Lader, Malcolm *Psychiatry on Trial*, Penguin, 1977.

Lane, D. *The End of Inequality?* Penguin, 1971.

Lane, D. *The Socialist Industrial State*, Allen & Unwin, 1976.

Lane, D. *Politics and Society in the U.S.S.R.*, 2nd edn. Martin Robertson, 1978.

Lantzev, M. 'Progress in Social Security for Agricultural Workers in the U.S.S.R.', *International Labour Review*, vol. 107, no. 2, March, 1973.

Lapidus, G.W. *Women in Soviet Society*, University of California Press, 1978.

Lavigne, M. *The Socialist Economies of the Soviet Union and Eastern Europe*, Martin Robertson, 1974.

Lenin, V.I. *Collected Works*, vol. 17, Foreign Languages Publishing House, 1963.

Lenin, V.I. *Collected Works*, vol. 30, Lawrence & Wishart, 1965.

Lenin, V.I. *On Youth*, Moscow, Novosti Press Agency.

Leonhard, W. *Three Faces of Marxism*, Putnam's, 1974.

Levchine, E. 'The Main Phases in the Development of Social Security Legislation', *Bulletin of the International Social Security Association*, vol. 17, nos. 8-9, August-September, 1964.

Lewis, R.A. and Rowland, R.H. 'Urbanisation in Russia and the USSR: 1897-1966', *Annals of the Association of American Geographers*, vol. 59, no. 4, December 1969.

Liberman, E.G. 'The Role of Profits in the Industrial Incentive System of the U.S.S.R.', *International Labour Review*, vol. 97, 1968.

Lisitsin, Y. *Health Protection in the USSR*, Progress, 1972.

McAuley, A.N.D. 'Soviet Anti-Poverty Policy, 1955-1975', *University of Essex Department of Economics, Discussion Paper No. 101*, October, 1977.

McAuley, M. *Politics and the Soviet Union*, Penguin, 1977.

Madison, B. 'The Organisation of Welfare Services', in Black, C.E. (ed.), *The Transformation of Russian Society*, Harvard University Press, 1960.

Madison, B. *Social Welfare in the Soviet Union*, Stanford University Press, 1968.

Madison, B. 'Social Services for Families and Children in the Soviet Union', *Slavic Review*, vol. 31, December, 1972.

Madison, B. 'Soviet Income Maintenance Policy for the 1970s', *Journal of Social Policy*, vol. 2, no. 2, April, 1973.

Madison, B. 'Social Services Administration in the U.S.S.R.', in Thurz, D. and Vigilante, J. (eds) *Meeting Human Needs: an Overview of Nine Countries*, Russel Sage, 1975.

Mandell, W.M. *Soviet Women*, Anchor Books, 1975.

Marx, K. Preface to *The Critique of Political Economy*, 1859, *Selected Works*, Moscow.

Marx, K. *Capital*, vol. 1, Penguin, 1976.

Marx, K. *The Eighteenth Brumaire of Louis Bonaparte,* International Publishers, 1969.

Marx, K. *The General Council of the First International, 1864-1866,* Foreign Languages Publishing House.

Marx, K. and Engels, F. *The German Ideology,* International Publishers, 1947.

Marx, K. and Engels, F. *Selected Work,* Lawrence & Wishart, 1970.

Marx, K. and Engels, F. *Collected Works,* vol. 5, Lawrence & Wishart, 1976.

Matthews, M. *Class and Society in Soviet Russia,* Allen Lane, 1972.

Matthews, M. 'Soviet Students: Some Sociological Perspectives', *Soviet Studies,* vol. 27, no. 1, January, 1975.

Matthews, M. *Privilege in the Soviet Union: a Study of Elite Life Styles under Communism,* Allen & Unwin, 1978.

Matthews, M. 'Social Dimensions in Soviet Urban Housing', in French, R.A. and Hamilton, F.E.I. (eds), *The Socialist City,* John Wiley, 1979.

Medvedev, R.A. *On Socialist Democracy,* Spokesman Books, 1977.

Medvedev, Zhores and Roy *A Question of Madness,* Penguin, 1974.

Mieczkowski, B. *Personal and Social Consumption in Eastern Europe,* Praeger, 1975.

Miliband, R. *The State in Capitalist Society,* Quartet Books, 1973.

Ministry of Education of the USSR *On the Main Trends in the Field of Education in the U.S.S.R. in 1968-1970.*

Minkoff, J. and Turgeon, L. 'Income Maintenance in Eastern Europe', *Social Policy,* March-April, 1976.

Moore, B., Jr. *Soviet Politics – the Dilemma of Power,* Harper, Torchbook Edition, 1965.

Morton, H.W. 'Housing', in Mickiewicz, E. (ed.), *Handbook of Soviet Social Science Data,* Collier-Macmillan, 1973.

Morton, H.W. 'What Have Soviet Leaders Done about the Housing Crisis?', in Morton, H.W. and Tokes, R.L. (eds), *Soviet Politics and Society in the 1970s,* Free Press, 1974.

Morton, H.W. 'Low Cost Housing in the USSR', in Rad, P.F., et al. (eds), *Proceedings of the I.A.H.S. International Symposium on Housing Problems – 1976.*

Muller, W. and Neususs, C. 'The "Welfare State Illusion" and the Contradictions Between Wage Labour and Capital', in Holloway, John and Picciotto, Sol, *State and Capital,* Edward Arnold, 1978.

Navarro, V. *Social Security and Medicine in the U.S.S.R.,* Lexington Books, 1977.

Nove, A. *An Economic History of the U.S.S.R.,* Penguin, 1972.

O'Connor, J. *The Fiscal Crisis of the State,* St. James Press, 1973.

Osborn, Robert, J. *Soviet Social Policies,* Dorsey, 1970.

Pahl, Ray 'Collective Consumption', in Scase, R. (ed.), *Industrial Society, Class, Cleavage and Control,* Allen & Unwin, 1977.

Parkin, F. *Class, Inequality and Political Order,* MacGibbon & Kee, 1971.

Parkins, M.F. *City Planning in Soviet Russia,* University of Chicago Press, 1953.

Pinkevitch, A.P. *The New Education in the Soviet Republic,* John Day Company, 1929.

Popov, G.A. *Principles of Health Planning in the USSR,* World Health Organisation, 1971.

Porket, J.L. 'Old Age Pension Schemes in the Soviet Union and Eastern Europe', *Social Policy and Administration,* vol. 13, no. 1, Spring, 1979.

Pospielovsky, D. 'Education and Ideology in the U.S.S.R.', *Survey,* vol. 21, no.4, Autumn, 1975.

Potichnyj, P.J. *Soviet Agricultural Trade Unions, 1917-1970,* University of Toronto, 1972.

Powell, D.E. 'The Rural Exodus', *Problems of Communism,* vol. 23, no. 6, 1974.

Powell, D.E. 'Labor Turnover in the Soviet Union', *Slavic Review,* vol. 36, no. 2, June, 1977.

Price, R.F. *Marx and Education in Russia and China,* Croom Helm, 1977.

Programme of the Communist Party of the Soviet Union, 1961.

Rimlinger, G.V. *Welfare Policy and Industrialisation in Europe, America and Russia,* Wiley, 1971.

Rokouski, M. 'Marxism and the Analysis of Soviet Societies', *Capital and Class,* no. 1, Spring, 1977.

Roos, J.P. 'Social Policy in Socialism and Capitalism: A Conceptual Analysis', *The Greek Review of Social Research,* no. 29, 1977.

Rosen, S.M. *Education and Modernisation in the U.S.S.R.,* Addison-Wesley, 1971.

Ryan, T.M. 'Some Current Trends in the Soviet Health Services', *The Medical Officer,* 13 February 1970.

Ryan, T.M. *The Organisation of Soviet Medical Care,* Blackwell/Martin Robertson, 1978.

Rzhanitsina, L. 'Public Consumption Funds in the U.S.S.R.', *International Labour Review,* vol. 108, 1973.

Schwartz, J.J. and Keech, W.R. 'Group, Influence and the Policy Process in the Soviet Union', in Bertsch, G.K. and Ganschow, Th.W. (eds), *Comparative Communism, the Soviet, Chinese and Yugoslav Models,* Freeman & Co., 1976.

Segal, Boris, M. 'Involuntary Hospitalisation in the U.S.S.R.', in Corson, S.A. and E., O'Leary, *Psychiatry and Psychology in the U.S.S.R.,* Plenum Press, 1976.

Skilling, G. 'Interest Groups in Communist Politics', *World Politics,* vol. 18, no. 3, April, 1966.

Smirnov, A.A. 'The Development of Soviet Psychology', in Winn, R.B. (ed.), *Soviet Psychology,* Vision Press Limited, 1961.

Smith, H. *The Russians,* Sphere Books, 1976.

Social Insurance and Allied Services, Cmd. 6404, HMSO, 1942.

Sorlin, P. *The Soviet People and their Society,* Praeger, 1968.

Sosnovy, T. *The Housing Problem in the Soviet Union,* Research Programme on the USSR, 1954.

Sosnovy, T. 'Housing in the Workers' State', *Problems of Communism,* vol. 5, no. 6, 1956.

Starr, S. Frederick *Melnikov — Solo Architect in a Mass Society,* Princeton University Press, 1978.

Stretton, H. *Capitalism, Socialism and the Environment,* Cambridge University Press, 1976.

Stretton, H. *Urban Planning in Rich and Poor Countries,* Oxford University Press, 1978.

Strumilin, S. 'The Economics of Education in the U.S.S.R.', in UNESCO, *Economic and Social Aspects of Educational Planning,* Paris, 1964.

Szelenyi, I. 'Social Inequalities in State Socialist Redistributive Economies', *International Journal of Comparative Sociology,* vol. 19, nos. 1-2, March-June, 1978.

Taubman, W. *Governing Soviet Cities, Bureaucratic Politics and Urban Development in the USSR,* Praeger, 1973.

Thiede, R.L. 'Industry and Urbanisation in New Russia from 1860 to 1910', in Hamm, M.F. (ed.), *The City in Russian History,* University Press of Kentucky, 1976.

Tomiak, T.J. *The Soviet Union,* David & Charles, 1972.

Ulam, A.B. *Lenin and the Bolsheviks,* Fontana, 1969.

U.S.S.R., 1977: Sixty Soviet Years, Novosti Press Agency, 1977.

US Senate Committee on the Judiciary *Abuse of Psychiatry for Political Repression in the Soviet Union,* Arno Press, 1972.

Wadekin, K.E. 'Income Distribution in Soviet Agriculture', *Soviet Studies,* vol. 27, no. 1, January, 1975.

Webb, S. and B. *Soviet Communism: A New Civilisation,* Longmans, 1937.

Wesolowski, W. 'The notions of strata and class in socialist society', in Beteille, A., *Social Inequality,* Penguin, 1969.

Whyte, M.K. 'Educational Reform: China in the 1970s and Russia in the 1920s', *Comparative Education Review,* vol. 18, no. 1, February, 1974.

Widmayer, R. 'The Evolution of Soviet Education Policy', *Harvard Educational Review,* vol. 24, no. 3, Summer, 1954.

Winn, R.B. *Soviet Psychology,* Vision Press Limited, 1961.

Yakushev, L.P. 'Old People's Rights in the U.S.S.R. and other European Socialist Countries', *International Labour Review,* vol. 113, no. 2, March-April, 1976.

Yanowitch, M. *Social and Economic Inequality in the Soviet Union,* Martin Robertson, 1977.

Yanowitch, M. and Fisher, W. *Social Stratification and Mobility in the U.S.S.R.,* International Arts & Sciences Press, 1978.

Zhukov, K. and Fyodorov, V. *Housing Construction in the Soviet Union,* Progress, 1974.

Zile, Z.L. 'Private Rights in a Collectivist Society: A Study of the Non-Socialist Effort in Soviet Urban Housing Construction', Thesis, Harvard Law School, 1967.

Index

Index

Index

Hans, N., 68
Health, Ministry of, 111, 115, 117-18, 121
Health and Accidents Act 1912, 35-6, 107
health and health services:
administration, 177; assessment, 122-8; finance, 121-2; labour and, 110, 118, 127; Marx and Lenin on, 104-6; needs, 112-15; occupational, 14; services, 115-21; under Czarism, 106-7; Bolshevik reforms in, 6, 107-8; under New Economic Policy, 11, 109; in industrialisation period, 109-11; in post-War period, 23, 111 see also doctors, hospitals, screening
Heilbroner, R.L., 165
Higher and Secondary Specialised Education, Ministry of, 87
higher education, 87-9, 93-5, 97
Holloway, John, 180
Holmes, B., 66
hospitals, 115, 116-18
house committees, 152
housing: administration, 178-9; assessment, 155-9; demand, 146-9; finance, 153-5; Marxism and, 129-34; supply, 149-53; in UK, 150, 172; history: under Czarism, 134-5, Bolshevik reforms in, 6, 135-6, in war communism period, 136-7; New Economic Policy and, 137-9, 141, in industrialisation period, 139-42, in post-War period, 18, 142-3, under Krushchev, 20, 143-5, 148, 152, 157, under Brezhnev, 23, 152
Howard, Ebenezer, 131
Hyde, G., 11, 14

ideology, political: education and 71-2, 74, 96-9; effect on policy, 1; see also capitalism; communism; socialism
incentives, economic and ideological, 3, 20-1
income, see wages
Industrial Accidents Act 1903, 35
Industrialisation: health and, 109-10, 118, 126-7; under New Economic Policy, 10; social policy and, 173; under Stalin (industrialisation

period), 12-15, see also under education; health; housing; social security
industry: conflict with soviets over housing, 147-8; decentralisation, 24; participation in, 4-5, 27-8; profits, 20-1; rate of growth, 24-5; relation to agriculture, 10; history: under early Bolshevik rule, 4-6, under New Economic Policy, 9, in post-War period, 17
inequality, see egalitarianism
Inkeles, A., quoted, 170
institutions, for aged and disabled, 55

Jacoby, S., 82, 83
Judge, J., 68

Kansky, K.J., 158
Keech, W.R., 78
Keynes, J.M., 165
Kollontai, A.M., 131-2
Komsomol, 97-8
Kondakov, M., quoted, 82, 101-2
Kosygin, A.N., 21
Koszegi, L., 57
Kreusler, A.A., 71, 75, 100
Krushchev, N.: communism, view of, 161; downfall, 21; education under, 19-20, 77-9, 80, 93; housing under, 20, 143-5, 148, 152, 157; influence on policy, 1; interpretation of Lenin, 3; reforms of, 18-20, 111; social security under, 19, 42; wages under, 25
Kucherenko, 144
Kuzin, N., quoted, 82, 101-2

labour: discipline, 7, 14, 17, 40; health services and, 110, 118, 127; social security and, 39-40; see also industry; unemployment
land reform, 5
Lane, D., 26, 91
Lantzer, M., 168
Lapidus, G.W., quoted, 54
Lavigne, M., 22
Le Corbusier [C.E. Jeanneret], 132
Lenin, V.I.: authority of, 29; democratic centralism of, 23; on education, 71; on health, 104-6; on housing, 129, 131, 136, 155; influence on policy, 1; on literacy,

209

Index

Index

participation under, 27-8; rise to leadership, 16, 29-30; wages under, 14-15, 25
Stalinism: Krushchev's rejection of, 18; nature of, 30
Starr, S.F., quoted, 136
State Committee for Labour and Wages, 61
State Pension Law 1956, 42
Stretton, H., 156
Strumilin, S., 127, 144, 168, 170
Szeleny, I., 171-2

taxation, 26
Teachers' Gazette, quoted, 97
technicums, 86-7, 92
Tomiak, T.J., 69, 80-1
town *see* city
trade unions, social security administration and, 61-2
Turgeon, L., 57-8

Ulam, A.B., 105
unemployment, social security and, 55-8
United Kingdom: health services in, 117, 119, 121, 122-3, 126-7; housing in, 150, 172; pensions in, 47; poverty in, 62; public schools in, 181; social services in, 32; widows in, 50
United States of America: health services in, 117, 121, 123, 127;

poverty in, 62; social services in, 32
universalism, in education, 65, 69-70, 73-4, 90
universities, *see* higher education
'Urals-Siberian method', 12
urbanisation, housing and, 134-5, 139, 146
utopianism, 7-8, 139

wages: agricultural, 22, 26; in Civil War, 6-7; differentials, 3, 14-15, 19, 25-6, 174; social security and, 59
war communism, 6-8; housing and, 136-7
Webb, Beatrice, 69, 71
Webb, Sidney, 69, 71
Wesolowski, W., 162
Whyte, M.K., quoted, 72
Widmayer, R., 77; quoted, 75
widows' benefits, 50-1
Winiewski, M., 170
women: in health services, 110, 120-1; wages, 26; *see also* maternity benefits; widows' benefits
workers, participation of, in industry, 4-5, 27-8
World War, Second, 16-17

Yakushev, L.P., quoted, 46, 55
Yanowitch, M., 26, 28, 87, 91-2
youth movement, 72, 97-8